The
ESSEX
Village Book

Compiled by the Federation
of Essex Women's Institutes from notes
sent by Institutes in the County

with illustrations by Joan Bill

Published jointly by
Countryside Books, Newbury
and the FEWI, Chelmsford

First published 1988
This new expanded edition 2001
© Federation of Essex Women's Institutes 1988, 2001

COUNTRYSIDE BOOKS
3 Catherine Road
Newbury, Berkshire

To view our complete range of books, please visit us at
www.countrysidebooks.co.uk

ISBN 1 85306 685 0

Front cover photo of Wendens Ambo and
back cover photo of Tillingham taken by Robert Hallmann

Produced through MRM Associates Ltd., Reading
Typeset by Techniset Typesetters, Newton-le-Willows
Printed by J.W. Arrowsmith Ltd., Bristol

FOREWORD

Welcome to the second edition of *The Essex Village Book*. This is one of the largest counties in England, and is a county of infinite variety. With small towns and villages to the north, coastal areas to the east, the Thames estuary to the south, and the busy M11 motorway bordering the western fringes, the history, people and events make each place in this county unique. There is so much to explore, so many delightful places to visit, many of which you will read about in this fascinating book. I am sure you will find much to interest, educate and delight you in the following pages, and I hope you will visit many of the places mentioned, and enjoy all they have to offer.

Anne O'Riordan
Federation Chairman, 2000

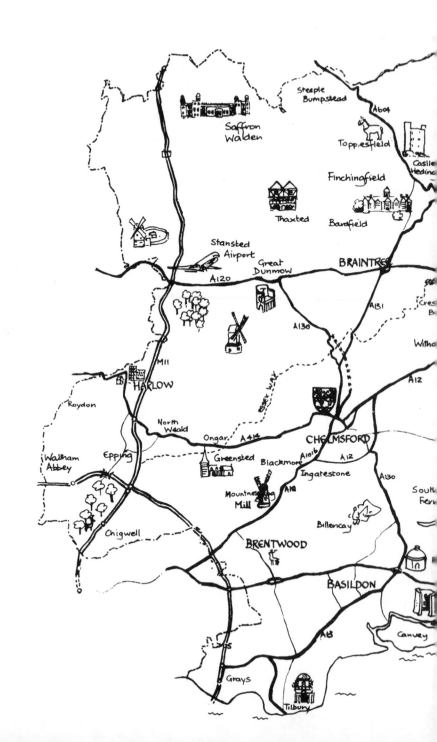

ESSEX

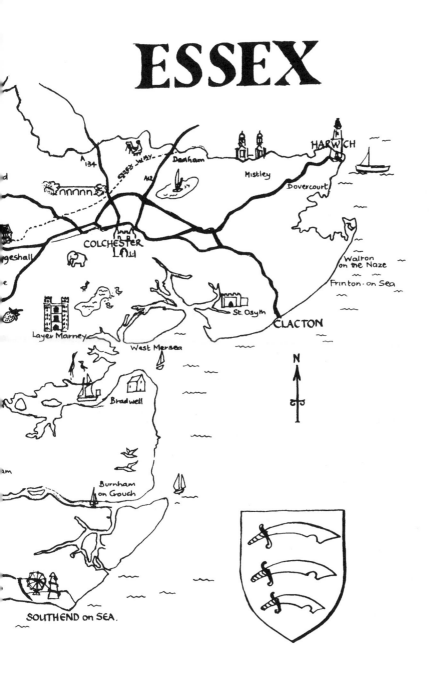

🍁 ACKNOWLEDGEMENTS

The Federation of Essex Women's Institutes is very grateful to all the WIs whose members have contributed to this new edition, either by updating their original entries, or by providing new material, and to Brenda Scraggs, who has co-ordinated this latest project. Our thanks also go to Joan Bill, whose delightful illustrations enhance our publication.

We would like to acknowledge the work of the late Jocelyn Need, who co-ordinated the first edition of *The Essex Village Book*, published in 1988, in which she wrote – 'there is a delightful cameo of village life past and present' – and that is very true of this new edition too.

Some of the charming cottages to be seen in Essex

❧ ABBESS RODING

The village of Abbess Roding lies to the south of the main A414 road. It is an attractive village with some interesting buildings, including the medieval church of St Edmund. One building with a fascinating history is Anchor House.

Anchor House was once a public house of special character, being established by the chapel trustees as a respectable inn for refreshments for the congregation between services. The first publican was Isaac Reed who was keeping the inn in 1851 at the age of 75. In 1855 he was succeeded by Jacob Pavitt, in 1870 by William Westwood and in 1866 by John Parmenter.

During the time services were on in the chapel, no beer or other refreshments were consumed on the premises. The services were from 11 am–12.30 pm and 2 pm–3 pm. In between services lunch was served. The working class folk had theirs in the tap room. The lunch consisted of two pints of beer and a pennyworth of rolls and cheese. The rolls were made in the baker's shop which was run in conjunction with the inn. The gentry used a separate entrance, now the front door of the house. They took their lunch in a large upstairs room which reached across almost the whole of the inn. There were stables for a considerable number of horses and carriages and there were sometimes as many as 50 carriages.

The licence having ceased in 1910, Messrs Ridley sold the premises to Mr F. Parmenter. The inn sign, an iron anchor, was at one time removed but later presented to Mr Parmenter by Messrs Ridley. It still hangs over the front door.

The remains of the chapel were used by Mr Parmenter as piggeries and are still there today. The current owner of Anchor House is Mr R. Parmenter, great grandson of John Parmenter.

❧ ABRIDGE

Abridge is situated 20 miles from central London, between Epping and Romford, a small village before the Second World War which has spread and grown quite rapidly since.

Some think that a lot of progress has occurred, and undoubtedly it has. But in the days of the 1920s and 1930s at least we had a swimming pool! Situated on the marsh behind the White Hart, it was fed by a wind pump from the river, fenced in by a close-boarded fence, and sported hutted changing rooms. It was accessible by a small bridge over the river, and was very popular with many folk in the surrounding area; it had a grand opening by the then Lord Lambourne and his lady.

In the Market Place there was a Whitbread Brewery store, and every day horse-drawn wagons took beer to Whitbread Brewery in Chiswell Street, London. The horses for this purpose were stabled adjacent to the Blue Boar, in a building which is still standing, and which was in fact used as an air raid shelter during the Second World War.

In the Market Place there was a drapery and general store, a baker's shop and bakehouse, with a daily delivery by horse and cart of bread and pastries. There was a sweet shop and tea rooms, a blacksmith and saddlery, and a butcher's shop. The post office was also called 'The Retreat', and served teas etc in the tea room at the rear, catering for many cyclists, cycle clubs and others. The shop next to the Maltsters, now used as a gun shop, sold fruit and vegetables.

St Mary's and All Saints' church, which is the parish church, is in a beautiful country setting. It dates back to 1100. The chapel of ease in the village was built in 1833.

Roding House is a listed building and was once used as a private school, owned and run by two old Scottish ladies, the Misses Brown. The house opposite named The Sycamores dates back to the mid 1500s, and was once a coffee shop. The school, now over 100 years old, has not altered a great deal. It has been extended and improved, but the main building still stands.

Lord and Lady Lambourne owned and lived at Bishops Hall. He owned most of the land for miles around, and certainly almost all the farms and several houses. Quite a few people from the village were employed on the estate as house staff, dairy maids, gardeners, gamekeepers and so on.

Abridge remains a village, though few people are now employed within its borders.

🍁 ALDHAM

Travellers on the A1124, Cambridge to Colchester road, are probably too busy negotiating the hill, the bend, the bridge, the parked cars and avoiding juggernauts, to realise that they are passing through one of the prettiest village streets in North Essex.

Aldham is still an agricultural area, although not an agricultural community; farming is arable, with one fruit farm. The farmland of Aldham is criss-crossed with footpaths, including the Essex Way, and walking them is becoming an increasingly popular occupation. These paths were made for a more utilitarian purpose though, and are hundreds of years old. They led to and from neighbouring villages, to the church, to the school and to people's places of work.

Aldham Hall is the oldest house in the village, a medieval hall house steeped in history. The screens passage is still intact, the courtroom still exists and a priests' hole was found during renovation work. It is surrounded by lawns and box-edged gardens, probably laid down in the reign of Queen Elizabeth I. There is a reference to a party being held on the lawns when oysters were eaten, so large that each one served several people!

In Ford Street there are splendid timber-framed houses, including The Old House. Both the Queen's Head and the Cooper's Arms are ancient inns, timbered and dark inside. Earlier landlords were not just victuallers, but also coopers, wheelwrights, butchers and even an undertaker who put people further down than just under the table! In 1848 there were 20 artisans working in the Street. Today only the blacksmith remains, working in the age old way, spending his days making exquisite wrought iron work.

Ford Street Hill leads east to the village green, known as Gallows Green. Aldham was one of the few villages to have a gallows, which was probably taken down after 1868 when public hangings were abolished. Records in the old parchment register show that plague victims in Elizabeth I's reign were buried in an orchard nearby. The tiny weatherboard cottage on the corner of the green was the tollgate keeper's home with the village pound beside it. A horse was tethered on the green and used, when necessary, to help pull heavy loads up the hill. The village pond on the green has been cleared out and is now refilled with water.

Aldham church, standing at the crossroads at the top of the hill, its white spire topped by a golden weathercock, can be seen as a landmark for miles around. There is a great feeling of permanence about it, cool on a summer's day, the sunshine filling the chancel with light and colour. The church was built early in the 13th century and the porch, carved and beautifully moulded, added in 1330. There does not seem to be anything unusual in that; the point that people find hard to believe is that the church was originally built a mile and a half away, right on the edge of the present village. In 1854, after much discussion, deliberation and, no doubt, argument, the original church was pulled down, to be rebuilt in a more central position.

The Rev Charles Bannantyne, a determined and far-seeing man, was instrumental in rebuilding the church. He was a benefactor to the village, encouraging the school to be built, starting the library and also building four almshouses for the poor. The school closed in 1956, and now children leave the village every morning to attend school in the neighbouring villages.

A school and a road in Colchester pay tribute to another illustrious rector of Aldham – the Rev Philip Morant – a great historian, most famous for his *History of Essex* published in 1768. Two great volumes are filled with the material that he gathered from 'The Best and Most Ancient Historians from Domesday Book Onwards'.

On the green outside the village hall is the village sign, which was designed and crafted by local residents to commemorate the centenary of Parish Councils and the silver jubilee of Aldham Women's Institute. Moving into the new millennium a village map has been designed by local residents, but the most impressive millennium feature will be the new playing field, for the use and pleasure of future generations of Aldham children.

🍁 ALRESFORD

Alresford lies approximately six miles to the east of Colchester and has a population of around 2,300. The first reliable written information about the village is to be found in the Domesday Book, when there were 18 households and the manor. However, its history goes back to Roman times; Roman villas can be found marked on the OS map and it is suggested the Emperor Claudius sailed down the river Colne from Colchester into Alresford creek to visit one of the villas.

The creek, which is just over a mile from the village, used to be a busy thoroughfare for sailing barges going up to Thorrington Mill. Slates and lime were brought to Alresford and straw was shipped out to London. In more recent times sand and ballast were transported by motorised barges from quarries still to be seen along the creek. This form of transport no longer exists and the only signs of this trade remaining are the derelict quay and three gantries which supported overhead buckets employed to fill the barges. The ford which provided a shortcut to Brightlingsea is still in existence, but is not to be recommended as it is now rather muddy. Today, the creek is a popular spot for sailing, bird-watching and picnicking. It is a pleasant walk along the riverside to the head of the creek at Thorrington Mill or in the other direction to the mouth of the creek. Here can be seen remains of saltpans from which the Romans obtained salt through evaporating sea water. The waterside footpath continues along the remains of the old railway track through to Wivenhoe, about three miles distant.

The railway arrived at Alresford in 1866. This was a single track linking Colchester and Walton. The station building on the up-track dates from this time. A branch line went from Wivenhoe to Brightlingsea via a swing bridge across Alresford creek. This bridge was demolished as a result of the closure of the branch line in the 1960s during the era of railway rationalisation.

In Alresford there are two churches. The elder, dating from 1320, is alas now just a shell, having been mysteriously destroyed by fire in 1971. The new church, dedicated in 1976, is a pleasant multi-purpose building sited half a mile nearer the main part of the village. The ruins of the old church can be visited and plaques are in place to assist visitors to note items of interest, including the nave and chancel from the early Norman or Anglo Saxon period.

At the time of Domesday, Alresford possessed primarily rough grazing land. By the 18th and 19th centuries it had become mostly an area of arable farming; by this time there were eleven farms. Most of the farmhouses can still be found in the village, now as private homes and often surrounded by post Second World War houses. The building boom started in Alresford in the mid 1950s and has continued until quite recently.

🍁 ALTHORNE

The typically long village of Althorne lies between the banks of Bridgemarsh creek and the river Crouch to the south and Green Lane, a pleasant straight road, to the north. The parish is bordered east and west by Mayland and Latchingdon. It is on the B1010 from Maldon and about four miles north-west of Burnham-on-Crouch.

Bridgemarsh Island with its low red brick farmhouse was flooded irrecoverably in the high spring tides of 1928 and the extent of the once rich acres can now be seen only at low tide. Tides run very strongly in the narrow creek, a danger to the unwary. A brass tablet on the north wall of the church recalls the two Teasdale brothers and Leslie Macdonald, all between 15 and 18 years of age, who drowned in these treacherous currents on Easter Monday, April 1919. Bridgemarsh is no longer the quiet area it was, since a marina has sprung up there with many moorings and extra traffic.

There are still eight or nine working farms, mostly arable but with some cattle, sheep, pigs, poultry, horses, and a small game farm. The Crouch valley is designated an area of outstanding natural beauty and the panoramic views are enjoyed by, amongst others, the residents of Althorne Hall Farm, which has been in the hands of branches of the same family for over 100 years. Barns Farm with wide views over the rivers Blackwater and Crouch, is a pleasant four-square farmhouse. The Mansion House was extended and modernised and is now a residential home for elderly people. Summerhill Farmhouse, so well placed on the hill and with its lovely long south window, was demolished in 1970 to make way for the development of Highfield Rise and Austral Way.

The ancient parish church of St Andrew stands high on the ridge, looking over to the massive tower of St Nicholas, Canewdon. A church was endowed in Althorne in the 13th century and though much restored, a building in something like the present form has stood here since the late 1400s.

'Ford's of Althorne's' is the sign on the red and cream luxury coaches carrying touring parties in this country and abroad, local works buses, school buses and the regular town and country bus service. The family firm was established on the site now known as Ford's Corner in the early 1920s.

It is very clear in this home owning community that most houses built before about 1970 have been 'improved' in some way and usually enlarged. There are a few easily recognised exceptions. The Essex-style houses designed by Peter Cooper ARIBA, who lived in Althorne for about 30 years from 1935, often have part mansard roofs and seem intended to defy alteration. The two weatherboarded late Victorian houses with low verandahs, built for Gilder Drake on Summerhill and Fambridge Road are still remarkably unchanged. The same Henry Gilder Drake endowed eight attractive one-storey cottages on Summerhill in 1930 for older folk from the parishes of Althorne, Mayland, Latchingdon and Southminster. The row of listed Dutch-style cottages adjoin the Black Lion in a pleasant group; the Old Forge is nicely restored and all the cottages from the late 1700s appear to be in good order. Many similar cottages have of course been demolished over the years. The Old Post Cottage near the Black Lion has recently been very carefully restored.

You will not see otters and oyster beds in the creek, toads do not creep in Garden Close and the patches of purple cuckoo orchids have long since disappeared. But the lark still sings and Althorne really is a very nice place to live.

🍁 ARDLEIGH

Ardleigh, on the main route from Colchester to Harwich, claims to be the largest Essex parish when the tide is in! (St Osyth being the other claimant.) One interpretation of Ardleigh is 'high pasture'.

Archaeological digs have proved that the village has been settled since Bronze Age times. One of the oldest houses in the centre of the village dates back to the 14th century. It is now called The Ancient House but was the Kings Head public house. The four manors of the village – Bovills, Martells, Piggotts (Ardleigh Hall, burnt down in 1979) and Moze – were used until recently by the local school as names for their teams.

A famous and influential inhabitant was Rev John Kelly, vicar of Ardleigh, who, in 1796, was afraid that the French might invade and the village be overrun. He visited all the farms and houses and made a list of all his parishioners. No other successful census was issued until 1841. Kelly is also noted for translating the Bible into Manx and it is said that when he was shipwrecked on his way to England from the Isle of Man he, like Caesar, held his manuscript in one hand high above his head so that it should not get wet.

Cannibal Jack – The true autobiography of a white man in the South Seas tells of the adventures and travellings of William Diapea, born at Ardleigh in the early 1800s. He traded amongst all the islands in the Pacific Ocean dealing with anything from muskets to pigs.

Ardleigh was affected by the great English earthquake on the morning of 22nd April 1884. Mr D. E. Cardinall, living at Bovill's Hall, reported that '. . . the walls of the room undulated, all the household were shaken rapidly from side to side as in a poor railway carriage on a badly laid line'. Two large chimneys at Crockleford Mills fell and local people who were indoors felt their houses were coming down.

The annual Ardleigh Garden Show, which used to be held in Newth Meadow, was always a big event and was famous for miles around. The Royal Eastern Counties Railway used to run special trains here. Farmworkers were given the day off to enjoy the fun of the fair, the marching displays, bands, athletics and the horticultural competition.

A more recent famous character in the village was Shedrach Sparling, the 'midnight baker'. He always began his round about 11 pm and when greeted with 'You're late!', replied 'No, I'm early. I should be here tomorrow morning.' The bakery, one of the last coal-fired bakeries using traditional tools and methods, was closed in 1986.

🍁 ARKESDEN

Arkesden has been called 'the gem of the Essex Highlands'. People have lived here for thousands of years, bronze implements found here are now in the local museum. Saxons were settled here and after the Norman Conquest lands previously owned by Saxons were catalogued in the Domesday Book.

The village, surrounded at one time by dense woodland, was always a centre of agriculture. In medieval times it was mainly pastoral, but today there are no sheep, pigs and cattle, and farming now consists of arable crops. Several of the old farm names, such as Becketts, Chandwell and Hob's Acre, still survive.

Interesting buildings are The Green Man, formerly an inn and the oldest house in the village, which boasts a priest's hole; Sexton's, formerly a farm called 'Saxons'; Wood Hall (the manor house) which in Norman times was called 'Archesdana'; Jeffreys, the oldest freehold in the parish; and Becketts, a Tudor house. A private house called The Ancient Shepherd used to be an alehouse. The church of St Mary the Virgin has a Norman font. An impressive memorial to the Cutte family dated 1592 bears traces of iconoclasm by Cromwell's men who were quartered in the district.

Local names which have survived for more than a hundred years are Bailey, Wombwell, Reed, Patmore, Dyer, Kemp and Pluck. The population of Arkesden has varied, in 1862 it was 506 and today it is 298. Many small cottages which housed a large family have been combined into larger ones, and there has been some new building, though there is some restriction of building as Arkesden is in a conservation area. Few farmworkers remain, many of the breadwinners commuting to London or neighbouring towns.

❧ ASHDON

The present day heart of Ashdon lies just two miles from the northern border of Essex with Cambridgeshire. It is an attractive and lively village, with a great sense of community. Many books have been written about the village over the last century, both factual and some with a touch of writer's licence about them, which delight new residents and sometimes annoy older families with several generations of Ashdon history behind them.

The village has a long agricultural past, but like so many villages today, many of its occupants work in either the larger towns nearby or in Cambridge or commute to London.

Despite the change in society, Ashdon has a thriving village life. There is a County primary school, which also takes the children from nearby Hadstock, a shop and post office, and the Rose and Crown public house, which has a long history and a room with murals dating back to the Cromwellian era.

In the village centre there is also the village hall, once the Conservative Club. The other hall in the village, which used to belong to the Labour Party, was bought by public subscription by the people of the village to house the Village Museum. The museum started as a private collection over years, by Mr Glenn Miller, whose ancestry goes back for generations in the village. He gave the collection to Ashdon and after a lot of hard work the museum, now a registered charity, opened in its new home in June 2000.

The Baptist church is also in the centre of the village, it has a good choir and the congregation of both the Baptist church and the Church of England, All Saints, at the top of the hill on the way to Saffron Walden, and site of the original village, work together for the whole community. There is a combined Churches Holiday School every year during the school summer holidays.

Ashdon has over 100 public footpaths which are clearly marked and it is possible to walk for a couple of hours without crossing roads or going through built up areas, in complete peace and tranquillity. The houses in the village are now of many periods but conversions and new buildings have been sympathetically done so that the charm of the village has not been lost.

The one remaining windmill, now minus its sails, will be restored in due course. A Trust has been formed and money is being raised, administration is in hand to formalise legal ownership, and it will eventually be open to the public.

🍁 ASHELDHAM

Asheldham is situated between Southminster and Tillingham on the B1021 and can be approached via Latchingdon, Mayland to Asheldham.

It is a hamlet full of interest, with a nature reserve made out of a water-filled gravel pit, which can be reached off the B1021 on the left hand side of a row of wooden and brick houses, the best entrance being past the official entrance and over a stile which leads to a well-planned walk through a small wood, by the side of the lake.

Carrying on past the row of houses on the B1021, turn right on the road to the Dengie and Amenity site and you come to the Dengie crop driers. Their chimney emitting white smoke is a landmark for miles around. Past the crop drier on the left is Asheldham church, which has now been converted into the Asheldham youth centre, used by young people from all over the British Isles and abroad.

Carry on due east and you come to Dengie with its manor on the left and just around the corner, the church of St James made of stonework. The road will take you on to Keelings and Landwycke Farm and around the marshes to Tillingham, but access to the sea wall is not possible.

🍁 ASHINGDON

Nine hundred years ago, when Canute decided to bring his fight for the kingdom with Edmund Ironside to an all out battle, he found the countryside of Essex on the Crouch river very flat. He must have wondered if he could gain any sort of advantage in a water meadow landscape. The battle commenced and quickly a foothold was established on a hill about a mile from the river. The date was 1016.

History tells that Canute defeated Edmund and the *Anglo Saxon Chronicle* reports that in 1020 the victor returned to consecrate a stone church and dedicate it to the souls of the slain. A silver coin of Canute has been found in the churchyard. Ashingdon church overlooks the village and the river Crouch, a guardian of long ago, but still the centre of village life. St Andrew's Minster, as it is called, has a model Viking ship over the centre aisle and this brings many visitors and historians to enjoy the peace of a truly country church.

An hour's train ride from London, the village has attracted many commuters and new houses have sprung up to swell the community. The village school is a busy part of life, with an active PTA and youngsters from all parts of the county. The village also has a thriving hall where many clubs meet and enjoy social life.

🍁 AVELEY

Since the Second World War, the character of Aveley has changed completely, but when reading any books about Aveley, and particularly the manor house of Belhus, it can be seen there is much to learn of its past history.

Belhus mansion, now demolished, stood in its own grounds close to Aveley village. It was originally a deer park and in the year 1327 Nicholas Bellhouse – hence the name – built the first house, believed to be of timber. In 1458, it changed hands and the Barrett family became the owners. In 1520 John Barrett changed the appearance of the house to the Tudor style, altering windows etc to the look many villagers still remember. An ice house in the grounds has recently been restored.

A Barrett descendant, Lord Dacre, commissioned Capability Brown to landscape the grounds in 1740 and to this day his pond still remains. Small farms owned locally, paid rent which was a source of income, together with the breeding of horses. Thomas Barrett, another descendant died in 1919 and consequently the contents of the house were sold in an eight day sale in 1923. Many older Aveley residents still remember the animal cemetery in the park surrounding the house. There were graves for mice, cats, dogs, horses, etc. Sir Thomas Barrett-Lennard was a great animal lover and it was he who ensured the animals had a serene resting place.

In the 16th century, Aveley had a market held in the High Street opposite the church gate. Also in much the same situation was an inn called Sign of the Harrow and there several men met to form a 'Lunatick Club' in 1763. This club provided a meeting place where members could chat and listen to information which rumour provided. Rules were drawn up, including fines for bickering, swearing and being drunk.

The church itself dates back to 1120 when work was begun on the building. Inside there are brasses of Radulphus de Knevynton who it is thought may have lived in a house on the site of the present Sir Henry Gurnett along Romford Road. Another brass commemorates Nathaniel and Elizabeth Bacon who died in 1588, being infant children of Edward Bacon. These brasses are well known and people travel from all over the country to see them. The Barrett-Lennard family are also laid to rest in the churchyard.

Barling & Little Wakering

Barling and Little Wakering are adjoining villages on the edge of the Essex creeks and marshes east of Southend. On the surface they may appear to a visitor as rather desolate, and sand and gravel pit workings being used as a landfill do not add to the attractions, but under the surface is much history, and walking by the creeks you can find birds, beauty and peace.

The creek from Barling runs into the river Roach, which in turn runs into the Crouch, this running into the North Sea. Following the creek eastwards it enters the Thames estuary.

Records in Elizabethan times show Barling as having a large fishing fleet and in the 19th century Thames barges were plentiful in the creeks, carrying hay and bricks up to London and rubbish back and building up the sea walls with it.

All Saints', Barling stands where it has solidly stood for centuries, with its medieval tower and shingle spire being a landmark in the flat surrounding countryside and no doubt to the boats coming home.

In the church is an excellent model of the windmill made by Henry Manning, the last miller around the turn of the 20th century. Barling windmill, a smock mill, was built in 1760 and ceased working in 1903 when it became unsafe. It was demolished early in the Second World War. The first reference to a mill was dated 1181.

Near the church, Scarfe Cottage is an interesting old house, recently renovated, with dates of 1480 and 1627; this was formerly an alehouse. Down an unmade road to the side of the church, standing close to the river, is Barling Hall which was rebuilt in 1822 after the earlier house was burnt down.

After Mill House, Church Road becomes Mucking Hall Road and further along stands Bannister House with its tales of tunnels and smugglers. Records of 1792–95 show F. B. Bannister paying the Hair Powder Tax. Further along still stands a typical Essex clapboard farmhouse, Bolts, with its beautiful garden, and round the corner across a field is Mucking Hall with signs of the moat which once surrounded it. Where Mucking Hall joins Barling Road is an ordinary field with an extraordinary past. Known as Gallows Field, this is reputedly where men were hanged as Barling held the right of 'furca and fossa' – to hang the men and dip the witches.

Blewhouse, overlooking the field, is a clapboard cottage. It and its adjoining house were once one, and are thought to be the oldest houses in Barling since a stone house near Jail Farm Cottage was knocked down. Near here was the Bishop's prison. Mrs Watson's father was the last village constable and she remembers him taking men there handcuffed. More recently the prisoners from Chelmsford gaol were taken nearby to work the land where Ropers and Trumpions once stood backing on to the river.

Barling post office is now in Little Wakering and the Castle Inn has long been there. The exact date of the building of St Mary's church is not known but there is proof it was in being before 1150. On the vicars' name board in the church is recorded that of Rev Downing, an 18th century vicar and friend of Captain Cook, the circumnavigator and explorer. He officiated at the marriage ceremony of Captain Cook to Elizabeth Batts of Shadwell, which was near the village of Mile End, at St Margaret's, Barking in 1762.

Barling and Little Wakering are linked now but it was not always so. Nearly 60 years ago the vicarage at Barling was sold and St Mary's vicarage became home for the vicar of the united benefice. One hundred and fifty years ago the residents of Barling were alarmed by a light in the night. The vicar, a herbalist, was discovered sowing herbs by the light of a lantern!

🍁 BARNSTON

The village of Barnston is situated in rural mid-Essex on the A130 road, two miles south of the small Roman town of Great Dunmow. It is surrounded by intensively farmed arable land within attractive countryside which includes, on the boundary, Garnetts Wood, home of a small herd of fallow deer and preserved as a woodland walk and picnic area.

One of the most attractive parts of the village, especially in springtime, is Parsonage Lane where the parish church and other old houses are situated. The small church is thought to have originated from Saxon times with a timber building, rebuilt with flint walls, plastered inside and out, by the Normans, at which time the beautiful moulded main doorway was added.

Situated near to the church on the west side is Barnston Hall, a large house probably built in about 1540 on the site of an earlier building. The house is still in good repair and other adjacent buildings include picturesque stables and a dovecote, as well as a large farm barn. Barnston Hall was the home of Mr H. B. Turner JP who from the late 19th century until 1945 farmed most of the land in Barnston and employed many of its residents. He was much involved in village affairs, a keen hunting and shooting man and the Hall was often the meeting place for these events. His gardener/groom planted a mass of daffodils in the green expanse in front of the house to read 'God is Love' and this can still be seen in springtime today.

An old bridlepath crosses the A130 to follow the brook to its junction with the river Chelmer on the northern boundary of the village. Southwards this path passes by an area near to the road which was originally allotments for the local people. It then continues through to the High Easter road where stands Albans, another original house thought to date from the 15th century. In earlier times this was a favourite place for the Hunt to meet and a special 'Hounds' room was built which can still be seen. The pathway is thought to have been used by monks and other travellers on their way from London to the priory at Little Dunmow.

Barnston includes within its boundaries an area known as Hounslow Green, where there are several attractive old houses and farms. It was here, on the site of the Taverners, that until its closure in the early 1970s stood the only public house in Barnston, known as the Onslow Tavern and owned by the local brewery.

Just 150 inhabitants were recorded for Barnston in 1914, mostly employed in local agriculture, today the population is nearly 1,000. It retains its country character, however, and with easy access to London, Barnston is an attractive place for commuters. Along with the provision of new housing, the village also has benefited from the building of a new public house, the Bushel and Sack.

With the support of a local farmer, Mr John Salmon, who also provided the land, villagers worked hard to raise the necessary funds and to build their own village hall, which is now in constant use. Barnston now also has a small industrial site developed from the factory originally built by Mr Salmon to manufacture mechanical sugar beet harvesters, which he invented.

BELCHAMP ST PAUL

The name Belchamp is derived from the old English word 'Bylcham', which means a house with a beamed roof. St Paul comes from the fact that in AD 930 the King granted the manor to St Paul's Cathedral. It is a beautiful chestnut tree-lined village, surrounded by fields. Knowl Green which is at the south end of the village is named from knoll, meaning 'high point'. The green that end is enclosed by a hawthorn hedge which dates back to the Enclosure Act. There is a population of just over 300 people, made up largely of newcomers seeking peace and quiet from town life.

One famous inhabitant during the history of this old village was Arthur Golding, who in Henry VIII's reign resided in Pauls Hall, behind the church. He was a classical scholar and translated plays from the Latin, which Shakespeare made use of. In fact, there are people who believe that he and his brother-in-law, the Earl of Oxford were the real authors of Shakespeare's plays. His descendants living in the USA presented a stained glass window in the parish church, dedicated in 1935. Unfortunately, this was badly damaged in the 1987 October gale.

It is not known when the first church was built – the first mention being in 1181. St Andrew's church was rebuilt during the latter part of the 15th century being completed in 1490. It is large for a small village, and today stands about a mile from the village centre. The chancel has two choir stalls of 15th or early 16th century with grotesque and foliated misericords (only two churches in Essex have misericords). In 1999 a new oak and glass tower screen, which won the highest award in its category in the Chelmsford Diocesan Advisory Committee Design Awards, was erected, and dedicated by the Bishop of Colchester.

Until the Second World War the majority of the men worked on local farms. There are sheep and cows but it is mainly arable farming in this area. Originally there was a forge, a shoemaker with three men working for him, a coffin maker and three bakers, namely Amos, Mantle and Crisps. The latter lived and worked at the mill (now demolished). A descendant of the Crisps – 'Annie at the Mill', lived to be 100 years old and died on 7th February 1963. There were two grocers' shops, a separate post office, a wheelwright and four public houses. Now all that is left are two public houses – the Half Moon and the Cherry Tree. The Plough has partly retained its character, providing desirable Bed and Breakfast accommodation, and the owners regularly host money raising events for local organisations.

There was a reading room on the village green, but this was pulled down at the end of the Second World War and replaced with the Pemberton Room, named after former inhabitants and benefactors. Money was left for a charity to be paid to the poor of Belchamp St Paul and this continues to be done to the present day.

After the Pemberton Room, the village was presented with the present beautiful village hall called the Community House, by the Bryce family of Birdbrook, who were friends of the then vicar. This was opened in 1951 and endowed for its upkeep. It is a reed thatched house, looking very much like a stately home.

🍁 BERDEN

Three miles north of Manuden is Berden, with its small, pebble and flint cruciform church dedicated to a favourite Norman saint, St Nicholas, in 1200. However, the village is much older as the Roman tiles embedded in the exterior church wall prove. These were reclaimed from a Roman villa in Dewes Green. The church tower with its four bells is 15th century, other parts being 13th and 14th century.

Berden Priory was founded in 1200 by the Rochford family and dedicated to St John the Evangelist. Of the St Augustine order, it survived until 1536 when it was dissolved. It remains as a private house. Another important village house, Berden Hall, built about 1580 on an older site, is a lovely red brick building retaining many original features. For many years it has been used for an important annual event – the village fete, which was previously held in the adjoining hamlet of Little London. There used to be two pubs, now both closed; the Raven in The

Street, which boasted 300 years continuous service and sported a skittle alley, and the King's Head (now a private house) on the Dewes Green Road.

In 1901 Rev H. K. Hudson, Berden's vicar, revived the ceremony of the Boy Bishop to celebrate St Nicholas's Day on 6th December. The play performed is based on the life of the saint with the central character being taken by a child dressed in bishop's clothing. This child then holds the office of 'Bishop' for a year. The practice ended in 1937 with the departure of Rev Hudson from the village, but the staff and cross used in the ceremony are preserved in the church.

As final proof of the antiquity of this area, in 1907 workmen digging footings for the village hall, on the site of the old Wesleyan chapel, unearthed a human skeleton, armlet and beaker which archaeologists believe to have been placed in a Bronze Age burial mound. The remains of these bones and the beaker can be seen in the local museum, tangible proof that man was here 4,000 years ago.

🍁 BICKNACRE

Bicknacre is situated some seven miles east of Chelmsford and five miles west of Maldon, in the parish of Woodham Ferrers. The name is derived from Bicca, a Saxon chief, and acre, a Saxon word for a clearing in a wood.

Walking around a small village it is often possible to gain a sense of the history of the place by noting the road names: Priory Road, Priory Lane, Monks Mead, Augustine Way, Canons Close can surely only mean one thing – a very strong connection with a religious house. And there behind the hedge at Priory Farm is the one remaining tower arch of an Augustinian priory founded around 1156.

Overshot Hill on the boundary between Bicknacre and Danbury was the site of a water mill (possibly the one mentioned in the Domesday Book for Woodham Ferrers). It was an overshot mill, in other words the water drove the wheel from the top with the weight of the water pushing the wheel around. The mill has long since gone but the name remains.

White Elm Road leading to White Elm Corner is a more modern name which became popular with the story of a notorious highwayman being executed and buried at the crossroads with an elm stake through his body.

Mill Lane has an obvious meaning, being the lane leading on to

Bicknacre Common or Hooe, on which stood a windmill. It is believed it was a postmill and can be traced back to at least 1686 using documents as points of reference. The last mill was destroyed by fire in 1911 after a decline in popularity for this type of small working mill.

The Old Salt Road runs behind Thriftwood (an ancient woodland) and was part of the route for the salt on its way from Saltcoats on Woodham Ferrers marshes (now South Woodham Ferrers) to markets around the country.

 BLACKMORE

Blackmore is a very old parish steeped in history, principally because of its priory of Augustinian canons and its association with Henry VIII. It is generally accepted that its name derives from the original dark soil which has now largely disappeared, though the swampy nature of its soil is evident after heavy rain.

During the 12th century an Augustinian priory was founded by the de Sanford family and dedicated to St Laurence, who is reputed to have been martyred in Rome by being roasted on a gridiron. A detailed and interesting history of this priory exists, showing that it was dissolved in 1525 by John Alen, an agent of Cardinal Wolsey, and passed into the hands of Henry VIII in 1532. Later it was granted to John Smyth and his heirs and finally demolished in 1844.

In the spring of 1349 the terrible epidemic known as the Black Death gripped England. It is supposed that 300 out of a population of 450 died. It was probably at this time that the plague roads, Service Lane and Red Rose Lane, came into being as a means of bypassing the village. Rumour has it that Nine Ashes was so named after the cremation there of those who died of the plague.

Perhaps Blackmore's greatest claim to fame is its association with Henry VIII who was presumed to have 'Gone to Jericho' when in fact he was visiting his mistress Elizabeth Blount at the priory, where she gave birth to a son, Henry Fitzroy in 1519. Henry Fitzroy was Henry's pride and joy and he was created Earl of Nottingham at the age of six and later Duke of Richmond and Somerset and elected Knight of the Garter. Sadly he died at the age of 17 and was buried in Norfolk.

Blackmore's church, the priory church of St Laurence has been largely unaltered for the past 400 years. The timber tower, erected in 1475, is a

Blackmore Church

masterpiece of joinery and has been described as the most impressive of its type in England. It contains of carillon of five bells, three of which were cast by Miles Gray, famous for his tenor bells.

Until the 20th century the population of Blackmore had remained static at about 600. It was a rural community, its inhabitants mainly concerned with the cultivation of cereal crops. Hay was sent twice weekly to London's Haymarket and charcoal burning was carried out in High Woods until 1900.

Modern development has included the building of three estates but now all expansion has stopped and the centre of the village has been made a conservation area. Blackmore today is an extremely pleasant village boasting three village greens, a modern primary school, a large village hall and a sports and social club, as well as a library (part-time), a garage, post office, village store and craft shop. It is also proud of its many flourishing societies.

🍁 BLACK NOTLEY

Situated on the fringes of Braintree, Black Notley is a village proud of its identity. This is a name, along with its neighbour, White Notley, which arouses curiosity. It appears that after the Norman conquest the manor of 'Nutlea' came into the possession of Geoffrey de Mandeville, Earl of Essex and Roger Bigod, Earl of Norfolk. They founded the two churches, glebe lands and manor houses upon their own lands. Thus Black Notley and White Notley came into being.

The green lane which runs between the Witham and Chelmsford roads is the remnant of a Saxon road forgotten and unseen by the general public. There is evidence from old maps that a farmhouse and cottages once stood alongside this old highway. These have long since disappeared, the only living evidence of their existence is a luxuriant growth of bullace trees and oddments of bricks and tiles in the ground.

Today Black Notley is a busy place. The Braintree bypass cuts across its northern boundary. The large additional residential area of White Court has added to its population. The White Court estate itself has an interesting history, being once the manor of Oaklands which, along with the manor of Great and Little Slamseys, formed part of the endowment of Lees Priory and came within the ecclesiastical boundary of White Notley. This area was declared part of Black Notley after the Divided Parishes Act of 1889. In the early 1960s old cottages were demolished in the centre of the village and farmland purchased to make way for the Bedalls and Brain Valley estates.

The church dedicated to St Peter and St Paul is of Norman origin and has undergone many repairs and alterations over the centuries. Bombing in 1943 caused much damage and restoration was not complete until 1953. As a result the ancient stairs leading to the rood loft are exposed in the north wall. Today the church still stands in a peaceful oasis enhanced by the barn roofs and buildings of the 16th century manor house of Black Notley Hall.

The naturalist, John Ray, who is buried here, is Black Notley's most famous son. Born in 1627 at the village smithy, he went to school in Braintree and then on to Trinity College, Cambridge. His first book, a collection of proverbs, was built up from conversations during his early years. He discovered plants previously unrecorded in the lanes and hedgerows of Black Notley. The 300th anniversary of his most famous work *Historia Plantarum* was celebrated by a John Ray supper held in the village hall in 1986.

🍁 BOBBINGWORTH

Bobbingworth (commonly called Bovinger) was mentioned in the Domesday Book 1086. Situated approximately two miles from Ongar and five miles from Epping, the village with two names is unique in that it has never had a public house or a village street. The village consists of small groups of houses scattered amid arable farmland.

St Germaine's church derives its name from the French missionary turned soldier whose battle cry was 'Alleluia', some 1,500 years ago. Now 'Alleluia' is the name given to the church magazine. The present building dates back to the 13th century and the list of rectors starts before 1276. The last resident rector left in 1981 and since then there has been a priest-in-charge residing at Fyfield.

Originally there was a wooden spire, this was replaced by the present stone tower in 1840, and six bells were installed at the expense of the Reverend William Oliver, who was the incumbent from 1838 to 1899. Because the tower is not high enough to accommodate the bells, they are rung from the porch, the congregation having to walk carefully through the ringers to enter the church door. There is seating for about 120 people in the high box pews which were installed at the expense of the Rev William Oliver in 1857.

Bovinger mill was shown on old maps as early as 1678. A three storied wooden post windmill with a brick roundhouse below ceased to work between 1912–14. Bread was baked in the ovens on the premises and sold in the mill shop as well as delivered to many local households by horse and cart until 1942. The Essex huffer, a three cornered roll, was a speciality. Sadly, Bovinger windmill was blown down during a heavy storm in 1923, and the roundhouse was subsequently demolished. The mill shop is now Bovinger post office.

Records show that there was a manor of Blake Hall in the 12th century.

The estate was purchased by Capel Cure in 1789 and since that time Blake Hall has remained in the same family. In 1940 the RAF requisitioned the whole house. The south wing rooms have not been restored and now house items of RAF memorabilia.

 BOCKING

The earliest events of which there are records are in connection with the church. The present church on the original Saxon site was probably begun about the reign of Edward III, when the main aisle with its graceful pillars and arches, in the Decorated style, was built. A large part was added and the whole embellished in Tudor times, when the wool trade was flourishing and money was plentiful. The church is built mainly of flint and is a fine example of its kind. The small turret on the tower which gives a special character to it, is a later addition of the 18th century.

The oast house at Bocking

The famous Bocking bells are eight in number. The tenor bell is reputed to the most musical note in Essex and weighs just under a ton, one of the heaviest in the country.

Messrs Courtaulds' silk factory was the chief feature of Bocking, employing hundreds of hands and famous for its output throughout the world. The first enterprise of this firm in Bocking was the purchase of the old Baize watermill in 1819. They already had mills at Pebmarsh, a mill north of Halstead, where they had started 20 or 30 years earlier, and at Braintree where an old flour mill on the river had been purchased in 1809. The silk industry took the place of the old wool industry, and went from strength to strength. The large factory at Bocking dates from various periods since the 19th century.

In the 19th century the factory was chiefly concerned with the manufacture of black crepe, some secret process of crimping being an important feature. With the disuse of crepe for mourning, business was not so good, but the increased use of silk fabrics of all kinds and the discovery of artificial silk more than restored the fortunes of Bocking.

The rivalry of Braintree and Bocking is of long standing shown by an old rhyme, which John Ray in 1660 (as he walked up Hoppit Hill) heard the boys of Braintree singing to the disparagement of Bocking.

> Braintree boys, brave boys,
> Bocking boys – rats!
> Church Street – puppy dogs!!
> High Garrett – cats!!!

After many years of disagreement and controversy, the twin communities are now united in one Urban District of Braintree and Bocking, but Bocking still holds onto its individuality.

🍁 BOREHAM

There is evidence of Roman occupation in Boreham and the old A12 was once a Roman road leading from London to Colchester.

Boreham is mentioned in the Domesday Book and its importance at that time is indicated by the fact that its annual value to the king's revenue was equal to that of Chelmsford. The parish was divided into six manors: Old Hall, New Hall, Calwaltes (Culverts), Walkfares, Brent Hall and the manor of Porters.

The church is of Saxon origin and some Saxon work still remains. It has a Norman tower which was added later. It is unique in Essex in that it is the only one remaining with a central tower. The tower is Norman but after the first 15 feet there is an arch made of Roman brick.

The Sussex Chapel was built in the late 16th century as a tomb for the Earls of Sussex, who were given the manor of New Hall by Elizabeth I. The Tyrell family of Boreham House also have their own vault at the back of the church.

New Hall is mentioned in the Chelmsford Hundreds as having one of the finest avenues of lime trees in the kingdom. It originally belonged to Waltham Abbey, being given to them in 1062. Then in 1350 the canons exchanged it for manors nearer Waltham Abbey.

Under Henry VI and Margaret of Anjou, it became Crown property and was to know, in the years that followed, Lancastrian and Yorkist ownership according to the fortunes of the rival houses. Finally, when a victory on Bosworth Field in 1485 brought Henry VII to the throne he granted New Hall to Thomas Boteler, Earl of Ormond. Then through the marriage of Ormond's daughter it was inherited by the Boleyn family. From Sir Thomas, Ann Boleyn's father, Henry VIII acquired New Hall in 1517. He enlarged and beautified the palace. Delighted with it he called it Beaulieu.

Boreham House was built in 1728 for Benjamin Hoare, on land which was once part of the New Hall estate. He had sold New Hall to build for himself this smaller house. It changed hands several times, until it was bought by Sir John Tyrell who owned and lived in Boreham House around 1810.

Bowers Gifford

The parish of North Benfleet adjoins the parish of Bowers Gifford. There have always been close and friendly associations between these two parishes and during the last few years the churches have been joined by Royal Assent, so that the title is now 'Bowers Gifford with North Benfleet'.

In the reign of Edward II, 1307–1327, the population of Bowers Gifford lived down on the marshlands and worked for the owners of the farms, of which there were seven in all. They were occupied with the keeping of sheep, which in those days numbered about 18,000 and with the making of cheese from the sheep's milk for which there was a good demand. The cheese was strong in flavour and had good keeping qualities, and so was used to help stock ships with food when setting out on voyages.

The largest farm was Earl's Fee. It was situated towards the Benfleet creek on the marshland. The creek was deep, for from Morant's History we read that 'vessels of good burthen may come up'. Sir John Gifford held the farm and in addition rented 500 acres from Sir John de Vere, the seventh Earl of Oxford, for which he had to pay sixpence per year and also to provide 'Silver Spurs for a Knight's Horse'.

Another large farm was Jarvis Hall, which was situated on the Benfleet side of the creek. This farm was held by Sir Roger de Mortimer who also had the custody of Hadleigh castle, which had been built in 1230.

Sir John Gifford, who gave his name to the parish, was in France with Edward III's army and fought at the great and victorious battle of Crecy in 1346. His brass, in his coat of armour, is still preserved in the church of St Margaret.

🍁 BOXTED

Boxted (population 1,600) is on the Essex/Suffolk border north of Colchester. Most of the properties were built near the farms or on small parcels of land owned by artisans, such as weavers. This type of development is responsible for the sprawling nature of the village, with single houses and clusters spread over much of it. Recent years have seen major developments both in council and private housing.

The parish church of St Peter was started before the Norman conquest. There is a magnificent Norman arch leading into the chancel – recently refurbished and its ceiling decorated. Alterations made over the centuries are several. St Peter's however, remains small and compact, largely made of rubble and Roman brick – with puddingstone, reputedly from the Roman river, in the tower. The parish of Boxted was linked with that of Langham in 1978 to form a United Benefice. The two parishes became a single parish in 1999.

Church Street is separated from The Cross by a small valley and it is easy to suppose that the original village grew up round the church, but this is not so. Various manor houses were built; Boxted Hall (mentioned in the Domesday Book) and Pond House are near the church, as is

Cheshunts. To the east on the parish boundary is River's Hall whose lands take in The Cross. The survey of this estate in 1586 by John Walker of Hanningfield shows its fields and dwellings in minute detail. Songers on Cage Lane, dating from the year 1250, was on this survey and has the distinction of being the oldest thatched A-frame cottage in Essex.

A 'Labour Colony' to put 'Landless people on peopleless land' was set up by the Salvation Army in 1906. Some 67 smallholdings were created in Boxted of which at least 50 were occupied when visited by General Booth four years later. A story of this visit relates that when being driven in an open carriage from North Station to Boxted, they passed Severalls Mental Hospital. On hearing the usage of Severalls, the General halted the procession, and much to the embarrassment of his retinue, rose to his feet and discharged himself of a homily on the evils of Demon Drink, Opium and the Devil. The visit seems to have done little for the 'Colony', for already there was discontent with the administration and tenants were being evicted. The whole scheme was wound up and sold by 1916, with the County Council buying many of the smallholdings on which to resettle ex-servicemen from the First World War. Later in 1952, all these were sold off to the sitting tenants. More recently, since the holdings were so small (six acres), making a living from them was difficult. Many retained just the house and sold or let off the land.

What the General thought of the other parts of the village is not recorded, a pity perhaps, since the village possessed at least six public houses or houses licensed to sell liquor. During alterations to the Cross Inn (now 'Seven Gables', a private house) they found a priest-hole in the roof. With the persecutions and bigotry of the time, this was well placed for an escape by the back roads to Harwich. The Cross Inn was also in Walker's 1586 survey and evidence was found of an earlier 15th century building on the site. Now the Wig and Fidget is Boxted's only pub. It grew, probably, from a kitchen-alehouse at the crossing of the cart-tracks over the heath and the Straight Road.

In true East Anglian non-conformist style, Boxted's Methodist church has flourished since Charles Wesley's day. Until the Education Act of 1944, the small 'hall' next to the church served as the Boxted junior school. From here, the children went on to finish their education at the Church of England school – opened in 1837 – at the other end of the village. Such ecumenism as this demonstrated was then, and is still, a much valued asset. The Boxted Methodist Silver Band – one of few that still remain – is well known and much loved, and has numerous engagements at events well beyond the parish. During Christmastide, the band playing carols by lantern light at points all through the village will be remembered by very many.

The demise of agriculture and horticulture over the past decades has brought change to Boxted. Gone now are the one-time major employers. The farms are mainly run by outside contractors, so far as cultivation and harvesting are concerned. Gone, too, is the fruit farm that once employed many, both as full-time and casual labour, to deal with all the pruning, picking and packing. Of all this but two things remain: firstly, the walnuts. Boxted has the only walnut orchard in the country. Secondly, all the temperature controlled storage and packing sheds for the fruit, have now become a mini-enterprise zone, housing many small businesses each doing their own highly skilled 'thing'. Compounding all this change is the recent loss of the village shop, and with it the post office.

🍁 BRADFIELD

Wander along by the old main road through Ardleigh and Mistley, where it becomes the B1352, and keeping close to the river Stour go towards Harwich. After leaving the last houses in Mistley you will cross a brickbuilt bridge, erected to carry the road over a railway line that was never completed. As the road turns right, you can have a panoramic view of the estuary of the Stour and standing high up on your right is the old part of the village of Bradfield clustered about its 13th century parish church. You can see the church tower, not built until the 16th century, showing quite a lot of red bricks and standing up in a most commanding position; the top of the tower would have been a good place from which to have looked out for sailing vessels coming up the river or distinguished visitors approaching by horse-drawn coach or even the approach of the press-gang!

Not far from the church is an inn, the Stranger's Home. The inn was rebuilt some years ago and is not on its original site, but why the Stranger's Home? It is said that like the French word *étranger* it means foreigner, and refers to the Huguenot weavers. On the same corner is a shop, formerly a typical village general store although now an antiques shop. Near to the shop is a fine specimen of magnolia grandiflora, grown as it should be with the protection of a wall and producing its lovely large cream coloured blooms at least from July until September and, if the autumn is mild, even until November. Almost adjacent is a cast-iron mile-post. Pause on your walk to admire the Village Sign located on the well-maintained playing field. It was commissioned and erected as part of the millennium celebrations. It stands proud as a reminder to all of Bradfield's heritage.

Continue your walk through Bradfield, you will see behind the inn called the Village Maid a well preserved cottage which was originally two cottages built in the local style. Further on, on your right, is the Methodist church; the present building is 140 years old and is on the site of an earlier building erected more than 200 years ago.

Barrack Street contains typical modern bungalows but also has some of the old traditional cottages. The name arises because it contained a building in which soldiers were once housed ready to defend this part of the country from Napoleon. The road to the right at the crossroads is called Windmill Road and photographs still exist showing a windmill in full sails in that road. The village post office and stores is adjacent to the corner and is a good example of a well run village store that makes a tremendous contribution to the community; in a sense it is the hub of the village and central to its life.

Bradfield had two windmills but it also had a steam driven mill and the next stretch of the road is called Steam Mill Road. At the next road junction and on the left is the large farm belonging to Bradfield Hall.

Within living memory the old manorial house, a moated farmhouse, Bradfield Hall, still existed, but age took its toll and it has been replaced by a modern house. Its most famous occupant was Sir Harbottle Grimston, born in the house in 1603. He was a distinguished judge, Member of Parliament and Speaker of the House of Commons. He managed to continue to serve the country both under the monarchy and under Cromwell. John Evelyn, the 17th century diarist, records that Sir Harbottle had a small acorn nursery at Bradfield and that having raised little oak trees, he planted them out in his fields in uniform rows about 100 feet from the hedges and so '... did wonderfully improve both the beauty and the value of his Demeasnes'. It could be that some of the oaks still on the estate are derived from Sir Harbottle's planting.

🍁 BRADWELL-ON-SEA

Bradwell-on-Sea is probably best known for its 7th century Saxon chapel of St Peter but there are a remarkable number of items of interest to be found here. The chapel was built right at the edge of the marshes by St Cedd, a missionary who had converted the East Saxons. He chose this remote site for his principal church, which he constructed from the masonry of the Roman coastal fort of Othona in whose gateway it now stands.

The strange yellow and red pyramids on the saltings are not bird hides, but direction markers. These were used with the nearby watch tower to guide planes using the bombing range, out to their targets on the mud flats.

Opposite to the school is Cage Row, an attractive terrace of timber framed cottages. The name is derived from the square, brick built cage or lock up, that stands at the corner of the churchyard. This parish prison would have housed the drunks or felons, before they were brought up before the magistrate. Its last occupant is said to have been a suspicious looking foreigner who foolishly had wandered into Bradwell during the First World War. Another little gem can be found at the churchyard gate. A mounting block, or 'jossing' block to assist riders to mount or dismount from their horses.

The church, dedicated to St Thomas, dates from the 14th century but it has been much altered through the centuries. The chancel is of the earliest date, the nave having been rebuilt in 1706 and the tower in 1743. The fine 14th century timber porch is oddly enough, a modern addition. It was placed here in 1957 when its original home, Shopland church near Southend, was demolished.

In the village centre many of the houses, despite their Georgian brick facades date back much earlier. White Lyons hides a fine timber framed home behind its elegant frontage. The same is true of neighbouring New Hall. Look out for the cast iron advertising plaques that are displayed on the old smithy. The village hall was designed by the architect of London's Savoy Hotel, Arthur Heygate Macmurdo, a leading member of the Art Nouveau movement.

Bradwell is really a collection of villages. The Waterside has grown around the safe anchorage in Bradwell Creek with the adjacent marina providing further facilities for boat owners. The stately fleet of Thames sailing barges, that once sailed from here, have been replaced by a wide variety of yachts and motor craft. The Bradwell Outdoor Education Centre provides a variety of sailing and outdoor pursuit courses.

Overlooking the estuary and the Waterside is Bradwell Power Station, one of the first commercial nuclear generating stations to be built in Britain. Construction began in 1957 and power was first raised in 1961. It is due to shut down in 2002 but it will be some years before decommissioning is completed. There is a visitors centre and conducted tours are available.

🍁 BROOMFIELD

Broomfield hospital serves a huge area of Essex around Chelmsford. In the grounds of the hospital was found a Roman coin dating back to AD 287. In a curious way, the coin and the hospital represent the two ends of Broomfield's known history.

In a field not far from the hospital are traces of Broomfield's prosperous 4th century Roman villa. It once commanded an extensive area of arable land near to a prehistoric trackway which runs through this part of Essex but, when the Roman army left Britain in AD 410, the villa farm gradually fell into decay.

Once the Roman garrisons had gone, eastern Britain was open to invasion by the Saxons. First came the raiders and then came the settlers. One settler, following the ancient trackway, found the overgrown and abandoned Roman fields. He called the place 'Scrub lands', or 'Brom Feld' in his own tongue. Another Saxon settler called Paecc set up his wooden hall about one mile to the south where the track forded a small stream. Today the area is still called Patching Hall. Yet another Saxon settlement was on the other side of the river at a place we now call Belstead Hall.

To begin with, these East Saxon settlers were independent farmers who only temporarily banded together for defence but in due course they would elect one of their number to be a perment king of Essex. One of these kings was buried beside the old track about halfway between Brom Feld and Paecc's Hall. The grave goods of this pagan burial and their layout are reminiscent of those at Sutton Hoo although not quite on such a lavish scale. Like Sutton Hoo there is no sign of a body. Was it cremated at Belstead which according to some linguists means 'the place of fire'? The pagan regalia was found by Victorian gravel diggers and is now in the British Museum.

After 1066 the manor farms were shared out among William's followers. The de Mandeville family had many manor farms in Essex including Broomfield and one of the Patching manors. About this time, Broomfield church was built next to the manor house. It consisted of a nave and a short chancel with corners built almost entirely from Roman building tiles. The walls contain pieces of hypocaust and tiles, some with the Roman mortar still attached. A local legend tells of a dragon moving the stones there at night. The field where the Roman villa stood is still called Dragon's Foot Field!

Walter de Mandeville, younger brother of the infamous Geoffrey, first Earl of Essex, held Bromfield at the time when all the Barons were building themselves stone castles. Not to be outdone, Walter had a strong tower built onto his church. It is one of only six round towers in Essex.

Many of the great timber-framed houses for which Essex is so renowned were built in the 14th and 15th centuries. Broomfield's two pubs, the Kings Arms and the Angel were built about 1450, although the first was a private house for many years. At this time also, the church had a tall timber spire built on top of its circular flint tower. The huge timber beams forming the frame are still there. Two timber-framed houses near the church, Vineries and Well House, were built soon afterwards.

Philip Morant, the famous Essex historian, was vicar of Broomfield from 1734 to 1738 and we depend on his work for much of the early history of the parish. His neat writing appears in the church records of that time.

By 1851 there were 180 dwellings in Broomfield, housing a population of 851. A school had been provided by one of the local landowners but many villagers wanted a National school. The whole village voted on it and a National school was built in 1873. The boys school is now the church hall and the girls school is tucked away behind the Old Bakehouse.

Broomfield Court and grounds, constructed in 1904 by Mr Christy the owner of Brooklands for his daughter Mrs Nash, was bought in the 1930s in order to build a hospital for the treatment of tuberculosis. Later it became a general hospital.

🍁 BUCKHURST HILL

In 1852 the sale of King's Place Farm estate of 157 acres took place to the British Land Corporation for £10,546, and this sale marked the turning point for Buckhurst Hill from rural to suburban.

The major event of this period was the coming of the railway in 1856. The Eastern Counties Railway from Bishopsgate (now Liverpool Street) to Stratford was then extending its line to Loughton and named its new station 'Buckhurst Hill'. Planning of the railway speeded up the growth of the population considerably.

The clay was ideal for making bricks to build homes 'above the line' and Ephraim Butler (the landlord of the Bald Faced Stag) who owned this patch of land, developed brick production on site, bringing the limestone and coal via the new railway to the railway yard adjacent to the Railway Tavern in Queen's Road. Brick production, which had depended on Chigwell for many years, was now firmly established in Buckhurst Hill (and was to continue through to the late 1940s).

The lane running down from the Bald Faced Stag, 'Back Lane', was extended beyond King's Place over a new railway bridge down to Alfred Road, from which the footpath still ran across the field to the White Bridge and to Chigwell. At the top of the hill, the High Road was realigned in 1858 taking it close to the church and giving Buckhurst Hill a straight road from Woodford through to the cricket field before the steep descent to Loughton. The winding section by Lord's Bushes became first 'Hospital Lane' and then later 'Knighton Lane', from which Monkhams Lane ran through the Forest to Monkhams Farm and on to Woodford Bridge.

Buckhurst Hill continued to grow apace. The 1881 census shows a population of 3,421 – having practically doubled over the previous decade. By 1891 it had grown to 4,130 living in some 755 dwellings. The pressure of numbers raised the need for more school places and in 1872 St John's School ceased to take boys in the junior department. All boys were then educated in the new board school in Princes Road, St John's School being reserved entirely for girls and infants.

However, the biggest change in local life that took place in this period was the sudden expansion of the 'Sunday Population'. Railway records show that Buckhurst Hill station saw in excess of 20,000 visitors each Sunday, carried by the railway from London to enjoy the delights of the Forest. These day-trippers were poor Eastenders and their needs were catered for by the local inns and tea-gardens and by three 'retreats' – Guys near to the present Roebuck, Riggs in Brook Road, and one in Queen's Road. The old Roebuck Inn had been demolished in 1875 and the name taken over by John Green, who opened a 'tea garden' in Epping

New Road which used the name and had a hall in which 500 persons could dine and over 20 acres of pleasure ground. These establishments served thousands of teas every Sunday and gave entertainment with swing boats and donkey rides. In 1896 there was on Connaught Waters a coal-fired clinker-built paddle steamer 90 ft long capable of carrying 250 passengers! Buckhurst Hill and the Forest was the Victorian equivalent of the more modern Southend 'Kiss me quick' hats and candy floss!

🍁 BULPHAN

Sitting like a top hat on Thurrock, Bulphan has borders with Basildon, Brentwood and Havering and is easily missed altogether as you travel from The Halfway House to the Orsett Cock. Ye Old Plough House Motel places it on the map for some, but most residents of Bulphan (past and present) have been happy to be off the beaten track.

At the time of the Domesday Book, Bulgenen as it was then (meaning marshland by a fortified place) had a large number of sheep, from whose milk cheese was made. Pinkerton's farm standing on the A128 is still called Wick Place to denote this.

The main village at the turn of the 20th century stretched from the church of St Mary the Virgin, past the school and rectory, centring on the post office, coal merchant and Went's bakery at China Lane and continuing to the Harrow pub, where Bill Thomas was the stonemason.

The Fen was enclosed by three Fengates. Villagers had grazing licences and Fred Jiggens still has his licence entitling him to keep 2½ sheep there! As the Fen was marshy and wet, it was the custom to run any geese through a puddle of tar, and then sand, to 'waterproof' their feet. The local sport was quoits and as the quoit-ground in front of the forge was often a quagmire, the men from the Harrow would sometimes take off their heavy workboots in order to keep their footing. These two facts combined led to surrounding villages considering Bulphan folk queer as they shod their geese and went barefoot themselves!

Farmworkers' children who lived near the Fengates would listen out for horses whilst they were carrying out their daily chores and run to open the gate, saving the driver from climbing down and usually earning a penny which would be spent on a 1d bar of Sharp's toffee at Mrs Thomas' tuckshop at the Harrow.

With the railway to East Horndon arrived the weekend and holiday

Londoners. They bought plots and put up huts. With the Second World War, many of these families built more substantial homes and moved into the village permanently. There is a parallel today with the self-build plots that are a prominent feature of Bulphan now.

The Fen has always been a damp, misty and mysterious place. During the First World War, Mr Walford the gravedigger and his family failed to turn into their gateway at Stone Hall, and ended up – pony, trap and all – in the Mardyke by the Harrow Bridge. Even today, many drivers misjudge that same bend in the fog and end up nose-down in the Mardyke!

🍁 Buttsbury

Sometimes one thinks that the various local authorities in Essex – to say nothing of the map-makers – combine deliberately to try and mislead any innocent traveller who may be searching for Buttsbury. Should such a traveller be coming northwards from the direction of Billericay, going towards Chelmsford, he will come first to the village of Stock. Right in the centre of the village is a signpost directing him to keep straight on for Chelmsford, or to turn right for Wickford or left for Margaretting. This, as I say, is right in the middle of Stock village, but should he glance up to the stop of the signpost he will see a circular plate telling him he is not in Stock but in the parish of Buttsbury!

Now, if he should retrace his steps and go southwards again, he will see a turning on the right directing him to Ingatestone – nowhere else. Let him proceed along this road, with the charming name of Honeypot Lane, and about midway between Stock and Ingatestone, right in open farm country with only a few cottages in close proximity, he will find the ancient and charming little church of St Mary, Buttsbury! But where is the village?

Historians have put forward various theories as to the disappearance of a village around the church. One theory is that the village may have been decimated by the Black Death in about 1348, and another is that there never were any houses, but that the church was built near the junction of two or three roads or tracks to make it more easily accessible from all quarters. If that were so, one might expect the church to be dedicated to St Giles, patron saint of travellers, but the church is dedicated to St Mary. The whole area might well repay archaeological investigation to establish the truth.

Undaunted, the traveller may retrace his steps, or turn his car, and proceed again towards Billericay. Some half a mile along the B1007 road he will see a turning on the right named Orchard Avenue, which will lead him into Perry Street, a well built up area now with many pleasing modern houses. Here he will come across a modern church, Christ Church, the full title of which is 'Christ Church, Buttsbury'.

A little further along the road is another new church, describing itself as Billericay Baptist church, and of course the postal addresses for all the residents in and around Perry Street, is 'Billericay' – though historically they are in Buttsbury. If he continues on towards Billericay station he will come eventually to the only signpost telling him he has just left Buttsbury! So where *is* this elusive place?

To give the true answer one must go back into ecclesiastical and manorial history, when Buttsbury, by reason of its many manors, was a very important place – in fact some of its manorial lands covered nearly all of what is now the village of Stock, and extended southwards to join the ancient parish of Burstead – now modern Billericay. Since the early 16th century much of the land has formed part of the vast estates of the Petre family, and even today Lord Petre is lord of the manor of much of Stock and parts of Buttsbury.

The countryside is pleasantly undulating, with wide views, especially around St Mary's church. Queens Park is now a place of 'most desirable' modern residences, always described as 'sought after' by estate agents. If anyone was brave (or foolhardy!) enough to beat the bounds of this ancient parish, he would 'touch the fringe' of every period of local history, from the Iron Age, through Roman, Saxon, Norman and medieval to modern.

🍁 CANEWDON

Canewdon is bounded on the north by the river Crouch, which takes its rise from two springs at Little Bursted and Laindon. The river meanders through fields and meadows and joins the sea just below Burnham on Crouch. To the south, but at a distance of two or three miles, the river Roach is navigable to Stambridge Mills.

It is said that from Canewdon church tower you can see seven hundred churches; a bit misleading this, as the areas around here have always been known as 'Hundreds' – Rochford Hundred, Dengie Hundred and so on. Even so, the view from the unusual church tower is well worth the climb, with the rivers below like silver ribbons, the green meadows, and in season, the fields ablaze with the brilliant yellow of rape flowers.

Some reminders of the long history of the village are to be found near the church. The famous lock-up and stocks, originally erected in the early 1800s near to the village pond, were moved to this site during November 1938.

The village community hall, erected in 1979, is the hub of village life, and is in constant use for all village events. A village fete is held in and around the hall every year and is well attended.

The start of the Second World War saw Canewdon as the base of one of the first of the new RADAR installations around the coast. Radar was then a closely guarded secret and the rumours abounded as to exactly what the 'pylons' were to be used for. Young airmen were billeted around the area bringing the glamour of their uniform, to the delight of the local girls. The radar installations stood until September 1973 when they were demolished, but instead of taking a few hours work it took nearly two days to dismantle the structures. Some folks said it was the six witches, who are a part of Canewdon folklore. Having accepted the pylons, they would not have them destroyed. Legend has it that as long as Canewdon church tower stands, there will be six witches in Canewdon, three in satin and three in rags.

Let us now take a walk through the village, starting at the church, which is on the western boundary. On the right hand side is the 'new' model village, with its large village green, bordered by houses, and on the left hand side pleasant bungalows. Passing the Congregational chapel on the left and the Chequers, one of the two village inns, on the right, we are now in the part of the street with some of the oldest dwellings in the village, mostly renovated, but retaining much of their original cottagey charm.

At the end of the street is the other inn, the Anchor. Both of these hostelries now serve excellent meals and are well favoured by folks from near and far.

At the village pond, if you are lucky you may be able to count some 17 ducks swimming around hopefully waiting for tit-bits from anyone passing. These ducks alternate their time between this pond and another further down the road, and can often be seen winging their way between their two homes. Another few yards on are more delightful old cottages on the right and on the left the village hall.

The parish boundaries of Canewdon stretch roughly a mile in each direction from the village, encompassing several farms and smallholdings, and many dwelling places. The natural hub of the village, as in most villages, is the church and chapel, the community hall, the village stores and post office and the inns.

CASTLE HEDINGHAM

The village of Castle Hedingham is a picturesque assortment of old cottages, large houses and inns, with narrow lanes connecting its ancient streets, and surrounded by centuries-old farms and woods. It is divided from its neighbouring village of Sible Hedingham by the river Colne, and nestles in the sheltered Colne valley. It dates back to Saxon days, when it was owned by a wealthy Saxon thane named Ulwin but was granted to Aubrey De Vere in the Norman Conquest of 1066 by William the Conqueror.

The 12th-century castle

Since then it has seen many changes and the variety of architecture to be seen as a result of the differing styles from each century only adds to its charm. Small medieval cottages stand alongside imposing Queen Anne, Georgian and Victorian houses (although the elegant facades of these often conceal Tudor or Elizabethan interiors).

It is fortunate to have several shops and businesses, and historically it was always referred to as a town as it was granted the right to hold a weekly market in its wide main street in the time of King John, Monday being market day. The Moot House (now a restaurant) is a lovely old timbered building which stands at the widest end of St James's Street (called the High Street in a map of 1592). Another equally picturesque building is The Falcon in Falcon Square, the very heart of the village. This was once an inn, the valuable hawks and falcons used for falconry at the castle being kept at the back.

The parish church of St Nicholas is situated in the centre of the village, surrounded by a beautifully kept churchyard. This is reputedly one of the finest Norman churches in Essex, being built by the De Veres in about 1180, replacing an earlier, smaller Saxon church dedicated to St James.

At the end of the street alongside the church, behind the row of houses facing it, once existed some small ponds, in which the water collected from the higher slopes. This locality is still known as Church Ponds, although the water is now drained away to the river, and the sites of the ponds are now gardens. On the side of Falcon Square, opposite the church gate stands the Youth Hostel, with its magnificent old chimney, and from the entrance to the little lane beside it (Castle Lane) can be seen a wonderful view of the building from which the village derives its name, and for which it is most renowned – Hedingham Castle.

It was built and owned by the De Veres (later to become the Earls of Oxford) in 1140, and is one of the most important ancient monuments in Essex. Its high position overlooking the village and surrounding countryside commands wide views from the top floor windows, and it contains the widest Norman arch in Western Europe in the Banqueting Hall. It is still privately owned by a descendant of the De Veres.

In the 19th century the village was one of many in North Essex where straw plaiting took place. Wages were poor so women and children took up this skill as a means of bringing extra money into the home. Women could be seen leaning against their garden gates chatting, with their nimble fingers busy plaiting away. The industry died out by the turn of the century, then young girls would walk or take wagons to the local mill in Halstead, the silk mill owned by Sam Courtauld.

The Castle Hedingham sign erected to commemorate the Silver Jubilee was a complete village venture, beneath the castle. Bingham's pottery is depicted, also the De Vere star. The girl is Poll Miles, who today would have been considered a keen bird and animal expert but in the 1800s was thought to be a witch and after drowning in the castle lake was buried outside the village at a crossroads. Even to this day a fresh bunch of flowers is seen every Christmas on the spot, laid by whom nobody seems to know.

✤ CHAPPEL & WAKES COLNE

The combined villages of Chappel & Wakes Colne ramble in all directions and even the oldest inhabitants are not quite sure where one ends and the other begins. Even so, it is one of the prettiest villages in Essex, with lovely views of the surrounding countryside and woods.

Prominent features of the village are its viaducts, the subject of many an artist's drawing and a local landmark. Several pill-boxes were built during the Second World War under these viaducts and are a source of forbidden joy to many a youngster, and the cause of many a broken leg or ankle through jumping off the top. This is not the only place for children to play, however, as they have a well-equipped playground on the land which used to be called the common, where an annual fair known as Chappel Fair used to call but long since has been discontinued.

Many people are also attracted to the village because of the Railway Preservation Society, which has part of the railway line which serves passengers travelling between Sudbury and London. The society run steam trains in the summer and at Christmas, when Father Christmas comes!

The village sign is situated at the crossroads and has Chapel on one side and Wakes Colne on the other. This sign was dedicated to the memory of a local landowner and the dedication service was attended by a descendant of Hereward the Wake. Chappel was formerly called Pontisbright but its name was changed when a chapel was built halfway between Colchester and Great Tey. There are still some cottages called Pontisbright. The mill in Wakes Colne is very old and was the subject of an Albert Campian story by Margery Allingham. It was set in and outside the mill and fields around and the old name of Pontisbright was used.

Also in the village is a monetary fund called The Loves Gift. This was left in trust by an old man named Arthur Love who used to tramp the villages. When he died he left a sum of money to be given out at New Year to the widows, poor and needy etc in the villages he had travelled in.

There are no vicarages left in the village as both were old and are now private houses; the vicar lives in Great Tey. There have been many vicars over the years but perhaps the most memorable was the Rev Jackson Hodgins who revived the age old custom of Rogationtide, when the fields, crops and animals were blessed together with the river water. Two choir boys were bounced on the river bank as a reminder to them never to forget where the boundaries were.

🍁 THE CHIGNALS

There were formerly three Chignal parishes; Chignal St James, Chignal St Mary and Chignal Smealey, the medieval versions of the names being Chigehale Sancti Jacobi (1255), Chigenhale St Mary (1339) and Chygewell Smetheley (1291) respectively.

The church of St James was originally built in the late 13th or early 14th century, but the church of St Mary, a much older structure, had disappeared by 1360 and the parish of St Mary was shared between St James and Smealey. The church of St Nicholas in Chignal Smealey is a Tudor gem, built entirely of brick (even to the font), dating from about 1530 and built on the site of an earlier church as there is a slab in the nave with the indent of a missing brass that predates the present church by at least a century. Chignal Smealey was often known as 'Brick Chignal' after the church was built, or Little Chignal to distinguish it from St James or 'Great Chignal'. The church of St James was deconsecrated in the late 1980s and internally rebuilt as a house.

In addition to agriculture and the usual country craft occupations, there was a small brick making industry in Chignal Smealey, down what was known as the 'Shore Road'. There was a considerable seam of clay suitable for making bricks, which were baked in a small kiln by the side of the road. A number of the older houses in the Chignals are made from bricks made locally.

Chignal Smealey boasted a post office and general store, closed now for 30 years, and the village school closed in the mid 1960s. The local cricket club is thriving, though, and the cricket field won a Gifford Award for the

Best Kept Playing Field. For many years in the 19th century both Chignals boasted a blacksmith, and the country occupations of wheelwright, boot-maker and carpenter were also well represented. There was no windmill in our villages, the nearest being at nearby Mashbury, but there was a medieval water mill at Pengy in Chignal St James.

In the very dry summer of 1974 it was discovered that Chignal St James possessed a Roman villa. First observed from the air as cropmarks, the site proved to be considerably older than the Roman period, excavations of the farm area yielding remains dating to the Iron Age. Many artefacts were rescued from the site before it was subject to gravel extraction, but the actual villa site is safely preserved by a protection order. Gravel extraction is a curse for many rural communities.

There are several fine old houses in the present civil parish of Chignal (created from the old parishes of St James and Smealey in 1888). Pengymill House is of the mid 17th century, Grays Farmhouse is of the late 15th or early 16th century, a classic 'hall house' and Chignal Hall dates from the year 1552, as an inscription on an internal beam announces. There are two ancient pubs in the villages, the Pig and Whistle in Smealey and the Three Elms in St James, both of which have been extended and modernised, and they provide excellent meals as well as good ale!

🍁 CHIGWELL ROW

Chigwell Row lies on the border of Hainault Forest, a survival of the once extensive Royal Forest of Essex, where kings hunted as far back as Norman times. The village is mentioned in the Domesday Book as Cingheuuella or King's Well. There were many water springs in the area; the last known use of the mineral waters was in 1800.

The height of the village above sea level is 280 feet, which gave fine views of the Thames Valley before the area became so built up.

Many would come in the past in charabancs from London for a country outing. Their refreshment was provided by the many front room tea shops in the cottages. Those requiring alcoholic beverages would frequent one of the public houses, the most well known of which was the Maypole.

All Saints church, a fine stone-dressed building, was consecrated in 1867. The western porch, much appreciated in wet weather, made an impressive building for what was then a small village community. Before this villagers used the chapel, which is now the United Reformed church. In 1831 a day school was started (2d per pupil per day). In 1839 a more permanent school was built near Millers Lane, but after a fire in 1885 it was rebuilt in red brick. In the 1830s a dame school and Sunday school existed opposite the recreation ground. The two bungalows there now have the original doors from the Sunday school.

There are a few wooden cottages left in the village. The timber for these was re-used from barns which had been storehouses for grain etc during the Napoleonic wars. Other timber from the Forest was used for ship-building in the 17th and 18th centuries and in 1775 2,000 trees were ordered to be converted into charcoal for the powder mills at Barking and Enfield. One of the earliest trades mentioned in the baptismal records of All Saints church is 'charcoal burner'.

One local story has it that John Roger Arnold of Manchings, Gravel Lane, helped to win the Battle of Trafalgar. In fact he was a watchmaker who improved the action of the chronometer used in navigation at that time. His foreman, Thomas Prest, also started a business in Chigwell Row in 1821 and patented the 'attached winding movement' of watches as opposed to the detached key.

In a press report of 1828, an illegal fight was recorded between Tom Sweeney and Ned Savage in a secluded spot in the Forest, near the Maypole for £5 a side. In the *28th* round Savage fell and could not rise again. His seconds had to give in for him.

🍁 CHILDERDITCH & LITTLE WARLEY

To the south of Brentwood lie the villages of Childerditch and Little Warley, where the traveller comes to the ridge overlooking a wild and lovely common. Gorse covered and an area popular for picnic parties during warm weather, remote, secretive and desolate during the winter, this is the common of Little Warley and Childerditch.

Looking across the common to the hollow below the visitor would scarcely realise that these were villages he was seeing as there are no shops and no village street, and although the old village school still stands, with the school bell on top, this is now the village hall. In fact this is really a typical example of a Saxon village.

Mentioned in the Domesday survey of 1086, Little Warley (then known as Warley Parva to distinguish it from its neighbouring village of Great

Warley) and Childerditch (possibly named after the stream which runs through the village) are so closely integrated that it is hard to say where either village begins and ends.

There are a few whitewashed cottages of lath and plaster, red brick or black and white Essex weatherboard, and clusters of brick farmhouses and buildings, the names of which have been handed down over the years. Whitehouse Farm, as an instance, is a protected building, known to be over 300 years old and having two Norman chimneys; during building work there in 1987 a William III coin was found. These old buildings are intermingled with some modern properties.

On the site of the old school house have been erected three bungalows. These have been funded by the 17th century Hugh Chappington Charity.

The little church of All Saints and St Faith at Childerditch was rebuilt in 1869, the original church having been destroyed by fire. This older church is described as 'having a steeple of brick at the bottom and timber above that, with a spire shingled'. The 14th century font escaped the fire and there is also an ancient lectern of uncertain age.

The parish church of St Peter in Little Warley is a patchwork building showing work of many centuries. It seems that the roof was thatched until about the 19th century as there is still much debris of such a roof under the present tiles. The chancel dates back to the 16th century and the tower two centuries later. Somewhere about 1600 the whole of the nave and chancel appears to have been filled with box pews, in fact they still form the only seating accommodation, designed with care and still in excellent condition.

Beside the church stands Little Warley Hall, an early 16th century brick house, originally moated, with delightful grounds (now much smaller than the original house). In 1642 the Hall was acquired by the Royalist, Sir Denner Strutt, who, with the first of his four wives is commemorated by monuments on either side of the altar of the church.

In 1742 the Seven Years War brought a military camp to Warley. Eventually a barracks was built which was, for many years, the headquarters of the Essex Regiment. From about 1840 to 1860 Warley Barracks was owned by the East India Company and many of their old soldiers lie buried in the churchyard of St Peter's church. Indeed, the church was regarded for a long time as the parish church for the barracks, the soldiers marching down to the church for services.

🍁 CLAVERING

The drainage of the Fens, and the taming of the Lee valley by locks and weirs, have diminished the river Stort and Wicken Water to tiny streams which are today little more than flood ditches: but even now the occasional wet period serves to remind us that they can quickly revert to the much more formidable barriers to communication that they must have been for much of the year in Saxon times. It was here at Clavering that one Robert Fitz Wymarc established one of the first 'Norman' castles in the kingdom – actually before the invasion of 1066. Some authorities believe that it was one of the places of safety to which the Normans and other foreigners retired during the times of trouble between the death of the Confessor and the Norman Conquest.

All that remains of the castle is an extensive system of earthworks surrounding the square moated compound where the keep once stood. It is noticeable that the older parts of the village are sited round the rim of the original castle bailey, which remains as an undeveloped green central core to the village, some 8 acres in extent. The castle which gave birth to the village still dictates its layout.

Clavering is really a cluster of hamlets, or 'Greens', some 11 of them, covering an area of about 4,000 acres in all. The transition from a mainly agricultural community to a well mixed cross section of businesses, trades and occupations has seemed relatively smooth.

Clavering church was built about the end of the 14th century, replacing an earlier foundation which may have been the castle chapel. The church itself is very fine and large. There are some very interesting monuments, and the windows contain some of the finest medieval stained glass in Essex. Associated with the parish is an unusual charitable bequest – 'A barrel of whit herrings, and a cade of red, in Lent, issuing out of a farm called Valence'. This has long been converted into a sum of money, but Herring Charities are rare, and only few villages were once so endowed.

Church End, with its ancient Guildhall, is one of the most photographed and painted scenes in Essex. The Old House between the Guildhall and the road contains some fine murals and some interesting panelling. It was once the home of the Barlee family, whose monuments are prominent in the church. Another sight that will be familiar to many is Middle Street, with its ford, its row of picturesque cottages and the distinctive roofline of The Old Posthouse at the top end.

Between these two, and secluded in its grounds is the oldest house in the village, The Bury. Pleasant but unremarkable from the outside, recent investigations have shown it to be an aisled hall manor dating from the 13th century. It, like the newly reconverted Guildhall and the Old House, is now a private residence.

🍁 COLD NORTON

At first sight, Cold Norton is a very ordinary village, no picturesque village green, no charming cottages clustered around an ancient church. You can drive through it and hardly notice it. And yet, this undistinguished place has a long history. It was mentioned in the Domesday Book under the name of Nortuna, but remained a very small village and had only 173 inhabitants even at the beginning of the 20th century. It grew considerably with the arrival of the railway, but the bulk of its development dates from the early 1960s.

Saint Stephen's church stands on the hill beside Norton Hall. The present building replaces the 12th century church which fell into disrepair, and was built at his own expense in 1855 by the rector, William Holland. (He was fortunate in having a wealthy wife!) Portraits of William and Mathilda Holland can be seen in the church. That of Mathilda shows Cold Norton church in the background. The rebuilding must have taken place with some urgency as the last service in the old church was at Easter 1855 while the new church was dedicated in time for Christmas the same year.

Another notable landmark in Cold Norton is the great white water tower, built in 1967 and visible for many miles around. It was a boon to the villages, as, before its construction, in dry summers the water in the taps was reduced to a feeble trickle. Old people who remember the days before piped water recall having to trudge four miles for a cup of water in dry periods.

Cold Norton lost its railway in 1953 and the site of the station is now occupied by Greentrees Avenue, though the commuters who trek to North Fambridge each morning sorely regret the severing of the rail link.

In recent years Cold Norton has become more and more a quiet residential village, and yet it has mysterious qualities. Many people speak of an inexplicable urge to live here and a surprising number have moved away, only to return after a few years, unable to settle anywhere else.

Another mystery is the unusual fertility of this place. A stranger to the village cannot fail to notice the number of babies and small children, the ever-expanding school and thriving playgroup and mother and toddler club. Census figures reveal that Cold Norton has a higher birthrate than any of the surrounding villages.

Various theories have been put forward to explain these mysteries, but the most convincing one is the ancient belief that ley lines (the lines of magnetic force in the earth's crust) affect fertility. Several leys pass through Cold Norton. In prehistoric times fertility rites were conducted at standing stones or stone circles which marked the places where ley lines crossed.

It is intriguing to think that the earth's powers may go on working in our modern scientific age and goes to prove that a village should not be judged by its nondescript modern appearance. It may have links with an ancient, magical past!

🍁 COLNE ENGAINE

Colne Engaine is the second largest of the four Colnes with over 1,200 inhabitants. Up until about 1790 it was called Gains Colne, being named after one of the sons of the then owner, the Earl of Oxford.

It is set round a village green on which there is a sign donated by the WI and designed by Nick Pudney, who was born in the village. It was made by the blacksmith from Wakes Colne, so named from another son of the De Vere family. It is a pleasant village to live in with an active church, the rector being shared with Earls Colne, the biggest village and White Colne, the smallest; Witta was the wife of the Earl of Oxford.

There is a church school with over 100 pupils, and a pub, the Five Bells, which provides food as well as the usual refreshment. There is also a football team, The Engines and a team of bell ringers. The village hall, a gift from the Courtauld family in 1921, is well used, warm and attractive. There is still a small shop and post office, a recreation ground with play equipment and, until very recently, a garage.

Like other villages, small estates have been built here, bringing welcome new people into the community.

🍁 COPFORD

Copford is situated just off the A12 in north-east Essex approximately four miles from Colchester and a mile from Marks Tey. Copford used to be a far larger village than it is now (in 1815 there were eleven miles of road in the village) with parts of the original Copford now incorporated into the surrounding areas of Stanway, Lexden, Aldham and Eight Ash Green. The village is roughly T-shaped, with London Road (the old A12) representing the 'cross-bar' of the T and the stem or vertical branch of the T leading southwards away from the main road to the more rural area of the village. Because of its former usage as the main road from London to the East Anglian coast and beyond, the present London Road consists of a mixture of both commercial and residential properties. A considerable number of new houses have been built in the northern part of Copford on land between this and the new A12.

Immediately beyond the school is the area of Copford known as Copford Green. The entrance to the green is a most attractive one, being marked by two listed buildings, both of them barns. The village green itself is triangular in shape and in the centre of this there stands a beautiful oak tree which was planted by the village residents to commemorate the Coronation of Edward VII in 1902. Some houses built in Copford in the 15th century of local sand and clay were very strongly built and one of these, Pink Cottage on the green, still stands today.

Alongside the green there is the Alma public house which, although originally having been named both the Lion and the George, was renamed following the battle of Alma in 1854, during the Crimean War. Around this time the building itself also encompassed a brewery, but the only part of this remaining today is the current cellar. Today the Alma is a popular rendezvous with both local residents and visitors alike.

Leading away from the village green there are three roads – one of which leads to the small village of Easthorpe, which combines with our village to form Copford with Easthorpe Parish Council. Another road leads to another neighbouring village, Birch, passing on the way both the chocolate factory, where delicious home made chocolates are produced and also the road to Hill Farm. Church Road leads around to the south-eastern corner of Copford.

Copford Hall, which remains in the ownership of descendants of the Harrison family even today, is surrounded by beautiful grounds, covered with magnificent oaks, cedars and other trees amidst attractively landscaped grounds. This old red-brick mansion which, during the First World War was used as a military school of divisional instruction, is currently being leased for private commercial purposes.

Copford church, now called St Michael and All Angels, was formerly dedicated to Our Lady the Mother of Jesus. This church was built soon after 1125 and the earliest murals were painted as soon as the church was completed, but it is thought that there was an earlier place of worship on the site. The present roof dates from the 14th century and the bell turret was added a short time after that. In all medieval ironwork placed on timber it was usual to insert leather or cloth between, to prevent sweating timber from rusting metal and, in the case of the ironwork on this door the leather was found, centuries later, to be human skin, popularly but improbably thought to that of a Dane.

Copford Cricket Club ground adjoins both the Hall and the church. A notable feature of the club ground is the presence in its midst of a beautiful oak tree which, under certain circumstances, is considered to be a 'fielder', and about which special local playing rules have been written.

Immediately behind the playground is the area known as Pits Wood. This wood was bought by the Parish Council several years ago both in order to prevent it from falling into the hands of property developers and also to preserve it as an area of nature conservation and relaxation for village residents to enjoy for posterity. The wood has now been extended and this area was formally opened in the year 2000.

🍁 CRANHAM

Looking at modern 'Cranham Broadway', it is, perhaps, difficult not to regret the passing of a true village atmosphere. However, walk a little way to the south of the railway, and you will find green fields and a hill crowned by All Saints church.

The first reference to a church in Cranham occurs in 1254, and the building raised in the 13th century lasted until 1873 when the present church was built, at a time when the living was in the gift of St John's College, Oxford. Former fellows of that college were appointed rector.

Cranham Hall has certainly stood near the church since 1600, and perhaps before that. The best known person to reside there was General James Oglethorpe who, in 1743, married Elizabeth Wright, heiress to Cranham Hall. He had returned from two expeditions during which he founded the colony of Georgia, and then defended it against attack from Spain. After his marriage he became a Member of Parliament in 1754 and then retired to farm his wife's estate and to entertain friends like Oliver Goldsmith and Dr Samuel Johnson. He died in 1785, at the great age, for those days, of 89, and is buried in the family vault in All Saints church. Americans still visit the church to lay wreaths on the grave of the founder of Georgia, and they are entertained by local people.

From 1818 to 1854, Cranham's children were taught, at the parish's expense, in the schoolmistress' cottage. A wooden building was then erected for them, and was also used for a Sunday school and for evening classes. The first purpose-built school was erected in 1870 as a memorial to Sarah Boyd, a schoolmistress who had done much for education in the village. She remained in control of the hundred or so children until she retired in 1889, aged 88! 'The Old Boyd School' and the teacher's house still stand, though they have not been used for education since 1950. Cranham has now two primary schools and a large comprehensive school.

Between the 11th and 18th centuries the population of this village stayed at around 200. By 1931 it had passed 1,200, and in the next 20 years rose to just under 5,000. By 1961 that figure had increased three-fold! Now it becomes important that the Green Belt is not breached further, and that what remains of village life can survive.

🍁 CRAYS HILL

Crays Hill is in the parish of Ramsden Crays and is situated two miles east of Billericay. Ancient records date the village from the 13th century.

The parish church of St Mary stands near the middle of the parish. In 1870 the church was entirely rebuilt at a cost of £1,120, but incorporates some old work; the nave has a 15th century roof. The church is nestled in countryside and in a popular area for walkers and horse-riders.

Like many other villages, Crays Hill is a mixture of old and modern properties. A new development stands at the top of the hill, but at the foot of the hill by the village store is a pair of cottages which are known to be well over 300 years old. Whilst renovating his cottage a few years ago, the present owner of one of the cottages found coins dated 1663 and 1691.

Pump Cottage at the foot of Crays Hill was built around 1860, about ten years after the village well was built. Villagers who had not contributed towards the cost paid one shilling a quarter for use of the well. The well still exists in the garden of Pump Cottage and is believed to run under the road near the bus stop. A blacksmith's shop stood between Pump Cottage and Manor Cottage but this was demolished in 1933.

Crays Hill National school built in 1863 for 100 pupils stood in the church hall grounds, but was demolished 50 years later and another school was built on land which was part of Great Barns Farm.

The Shepherd and Dog public house which stands at the top of the hill was originally built about 300 years ago and, although it has been rebuilt and modernised over the years, retains some original charm inside.

There is a story of a phantom boy dressed in white (of course!) who haunts the spot at Crays Hill where, according to rumour, the gallows used to stand.

 CREEKSEA

Creeksea is a small village, about three miles from Burnham-on-Crouch. The few houses are reached by one country lane.

At the top of the lane is Creeksea church, originally built in Roman times. It has been rebuilt on the original foundations three times over the years but still retains some of the Roman stone and brickwork. Next to it is Creeksea Hall, the oldest building in Creeksea dating back to the 13th century. Part of the building was demolished and added to, but part of the original building is still standing.

Further down the lane is Creeksea Place, an Elizabethan mansion house built in 1563. Two of the three original wings were demolished in 1741 and a new east wing built on. Adjoining the main house is a bailiff's cottage and a lodge at the main entrance. It stands in extensive grounds. Entrance to the house from Creeksea Lane is through wrought iron gates and over a bridge spanning three ornamental lakes. The house has always been haunted. Various occupants have all experienced strange happenings, including the ghost of a spirited white stallion. This horse has been seen thundering about the grounds with tail and mane flying. It is said, that a once owner of Creeksea Place was thrown by this horse breaking his neck and the horse was subsequently destroyed, but his ghost lingers on. The house remained unoccupied after the end of the Second World War, after which time it was bought by the present owner in 1950 as a caravan park.

'The Old Tudor Cottage' stands facing the Crouch. A picturesque half timbered black and white building, it was built in 1490 and then known as the Ferry House. The owners had the ferry rights for conveying passengers and cattle across the river to Wallasea Island.

In 1865 the house became the Greyhound Inn. The licensee was a man named Woolf who was renowned for selling the finest brandy in the district. In 1929 extensive restoration work was carried out and a smuggler's den was found. The only access to it was by iron rungs up the old Tudor chimney. Old folks living nearby and who remember it as an inn, immediately said 'That must be where old Woolf hid his brandy'.

Brandy Hole higher up the river is so named as it was a well known spot for the smugglers to dump their brandy, to be recovered later when the coast was clear.

❧ DANBURY

Many villages can boast a great house, hall or castle, but Danbury has a palace set in a wooded park, where three peaceful lakes, created in the 13th century, now give pleasure to thousands of visitors from a wide area.

No royal connections gave the house its status of palace, but great Essex families, St Cleres and D'Arcys, rode and hunted through the deer park from the time that Danbury and its manors were given to Geoffrey de Mandeville, the first Earl of Essex, by William the Conqueror.

Sir Walter Mildmay, founder of Emmanuel College, Cambridge, built a house in the deer park between 1560 and 1589, and called it Danbury Place. The grounds were 'well grown with timber of oaks'. The family lived there until the death of John, the last of the Mildmays, when the estate passed to his widow and her descendants. Eventually the house fell into decay and in the 1830s John Round pulled down the Mildmay mansion and built the present house in the Elizabethan style.

It was sold to the Ecclesiastical Commissioners for £24,700 and became in 1845, Danbury Palace, the residence of George Murray, 96th Bishop of Rochester. The palace now looked outward to the village. The school children enjoyed annual treats in the park and were rowed round the largest lake by young Mr Murray, the Bishop's son, 'the one who sang the best having the longest ride.' Thus began an association between palace and local people which has continued and increased till the present day. The 98th Bishop, Dr Claughton, entertained the parish to a 'capital supper' for Queen Victoria's Golden Jubilee in 1887, but when he became the 1st Bishop of St Albans the palace ceased to be the official residence of the Bishops. General and Mrs Wigan who came to the palace in 1919 were the last private owners and were interested in the life of the village.

During the Second World War it was used as a maternity home and many local people were proud to claim that they had been born in a palace.

In 1947 the park was bought by the Essex County Council and a new era began. The palace is now part of the Anglia Polytechnic University, a conference centre and an attractive venue for weddings. The park is home to Danbury Park School, in its own corner. Opened in 1974 it is a thriving part of village life. The rest is divided between the Country Park which attracts many visitors in all seasons, and the County Youth Camp where young people from all parts of the county enjoy a wide variety of outdoor activities.

DEBDEN & DEBDEN GREEN

Approaching Debden from the local market town of Saffron Walden, the major landmark on entering the village is the massive radar tower used to guide aeroplanes to the new airport of Stansted. Behind the tower is the old Second World War Debden airfield.

The road from Walden drops down to a crossroads. To the left in its own parkland is Debden Manor. An imposing building of white brick with a stone extension, it was built in 1796 as the rectory. Proving too large for the rector as long ago as 1908, it was subsequently known as Harleyfield House and used as the quarters for the commanding officer of the adjacent Debden airfield during the war. Charles Bland acquired the house and the manorial rights between the wars and was responsible for planting many of the trees around the house. He also planted the avenue of horse chestnuts on either side of the main road into the village.

On the opposite side of the crossroads is a fine thatched cottage. Formerly the Fox public house, it was one of five refreshment houses in the village.

The fine red-brick school, with headmaster's house attached, was built in 1852 with funds provided by the then rector Henry Hodgson. When the airfield was converted into a barracks in 1979, the doubling of the school population with children from the army families meant the old building was too small. An extension was built in sympathy with the old building, but a portable classroom is still needed to meet present demand.

A wooded road to the right of the school leads down to the church. Built in the 13th century, the building today looks much as it must have done following an extensive restoration in the late 18th century. At the same time the Chiswells, lords of the manor, built themselves a private chapel of white brick. Almost octagonal in shape, the chapel forms the east end of the church and the Coade stone coat of arms on the exterior still looks new today.

The Chiswell family and their descendants lived in Debden for 150 years. Richard Chiswell, a London merchant purchased the Debden Hall estate in 1715. Although there had been a house on the site of Debden Hall since the 14th century, major improvements were made to the house in 1750. Towards the end of the 18th century the park with a substantial lake was laid out. Debden Hall was demolished in 1935. Today's visitor, who follows the footpath downhill past the church, can still view the boating lakes, now somewhat overgrown. In the field adjacent to the church are some red-brick buildings and a high brick wall. Now three private houses, these are the old Debden Hall gardens.

The large number of modern houses in the centre of the village replace the wooden cottages destroyed in the great fire of Debden in 1907. A Mrs Buntin poured paraffin on her boiler fire and set her chimney alight. Although Mrs Bunting's cottage was unharmed, 20 buildings were affected by the fire and twelve completely destroyed.

About a mile along the road to Thaxted from the centre of the village is Debden Green, the second major centre of population in the parish. Until the 1950s Debden Green consisted of several small farms, each independently run, and a row of cottages. Today most of the farmhouses are separated from their surrounding land, which is farmed by two or three larger farmers. Some modern bungalows have increased the population. Debden Green merges into Hamperden End, where old cottages and farmhouses mix with more modern dwellings. The Three Horseshoes thatched cottage was once the fifth pub in the village.

🍁 DEDHAM

Dedham lies in 'Constable country' on the border of Essex and Suffolk between Colchester and Ipswich. It is bordered on the north side by the river Stour which forms the boundary between the two counties. John Constable, the famous landscape painter, lived at Flatford, two and a half miles down river from Dedham, but he was educated at the old grammar school in Dedham, and found inspiration for many of his paintings from the local countryside. The grammar school was founded in 1571 and four years later was granted a charter by Queen Elizabeth I. It is a handsome building which has been added to over the years.

During the 13th and 14th centuries the village became prosperous through the weaving industry, and the magnificent church, which dominates the village, was built at this time, largely through the generosity of two leading wool merchants. It is well known in the area for

Dedham Vale

its wonderful flower arrangements, particularly at Harvest Festival time. Since 1965 most of the old pews have been replaced by new ones, individually carved in memory of parishioners or some historical event such as man's first landing on the moon.

Dedham is rich in architecture, from the medieval Flemish cottages to the elegant houses of the High Street with their Tudor framework and Georgian facades. One of these, built originally as a clothier's house, was owned by the Sherman family, ancestors of General Sherman of the American Civil War. It is now owned by the National Trust. The Flemish cottages are Tudor cottages built to form a quadrangle round the master weaver's house, and were homes for the Flemish weavers brought in to teach the locals the art of weaving.

The river has played a large part in the history of Dedham, and until recently there was a large working corn mill, painted by Constable, and now converted into luxury flats. There is still a thriving boat hire business, and the water meadows make a popular picnic place in the summer. In earlier days the river provided facilities for washing the cloth woven in the district as well as providing water for both humans and animals. It also served as a highway for the transport of goods to and from the market towns along its banks. Le Talbooth, now a well-known restaurant, was originally the toll station for boats using the river, but it fell into ruin and at one time was used as a lime kiln.

Farming has always been an important side of Dedham life, and although the dairy farms are now gone, sheep have returned in large numbers. At one time the village had eight smithies of which Forge Street is now the only reminder. Footpaths are a legacy of the old farming days, and are kept in good condition by the parish council in conjunction with a local footpath society. One of these paths carries the curious name of Pennypots. At one time it led to the site of a pest house on the outer edge of the village and its name derives from the custom of leaving money in a jar at the village boundary in exchange for provisions brought by outsiders in times of plague. Near this footpath lies a small plot of land known as The Cage. This marks the site of the old village lock-up.

Tourism brings its own problems, and the parish council and local preservation society work hard to keep the village unspoilt and yet a viable place in which to live. Great care has been taken to preserve the beauty and dignity of the High Street, and yet at the same time there are excellent shopping facilities, which include a butcher, a chemist, a Co-op store and an excellent delicatessen.

🍁 DODDINGHURST

Doddinghurst lies about four miles between Brentwood and Ongar.

In 1876 it had a recorded population of 426, consisting of a few cottages and some outlying farms, no pub but a Georgian three storey mansion for the priest and a large gabled brick house known as Doddinghurst Hall with farm buildings surrounding it. The old rectory was pulled down and sold for housing at Bakers Meadow. It has been replaced by a modern rectory. Doddinghurst Hall has also disappeared and the Moat House pub built on the site.

Mr Wooltorton who owned the Hall in 1934 sold off small plots of land to London Eastenders for weekend cottages which proved a boon to owners for a respite from the intensive bombing of the East End during the Second World War. Some of these still remain in Doddinghurst Road and Wyatts Green.

Main gas was piped to the village before the Second World War, electricity immediately afterwards. The early 1960s saw the laying of a main sewerage system. Now with all 'mod-cons' available, an explosion of very desirable houses were built situated in cul-de-sacs with such delightful names as Apple Tree Crescent, Beehive Chase, Bakers Meadow and Plovers Mead.

During the 1880s the then rector carried out extensive rebuilding of the chancel of All Saints church. Out of his own pocket he also built a school next to the church. A few years ago this was converted to a modern house – the school population having outgrown the little building. Children were having to be 'bussed' to Blackmore (the next village along) to school before the county council bought glebe land and built a modern infants and junior school next to the village hall. M. Wainwright of Emblems House was responsible for bringing a second hand entertainments hut to use as a village hall. The beautiful building of All Saints church, typical of a small Essex church spans history from the 13th century door to the recently refurbished spire covered in cedar wood shingles.

On the left of the path up to the church is the grave of an Indian princess who it is said married an Englishman and died of a broken heart and lack of sun. One notable parson Nehemiah Rogers buried here in 1660 is remembered for his writings on the parables. West of the church stands Priest House, an Essex boarded cottage dating from Elizabethan times and lived in until very recently. Now it makes a welcome meeting place for coffee after morning Sunday services.

🍁 DOWNHAM

Downham is a small village situated on rising ground to the north of the river Crouch, north-west of Wickford and adjacent to Ramsden Heath. It is a pleasing mixture of period cottages, farmhouses and newer properties mostly built in keeping with the rural atmosphere.

Clustered together are the village pond, the small roadside garden created to commemorate Queen Elizabeth II's Silver Jubilee, the old school now converted into a house and the village hall.

Approaching the village from Wickford, St Margaret's church dominates the skyline. The first mention of the church was in 1086 in Domesday Book when it was noted under the name Ramesdana. Various restorations and rebuildings have occurred over the centuries, the last being as recently as 1977 when a 16 year old boy deliberately set fire to the church by pouring oil on the altar and lighting it. Fortunately the Tudor tower and the outer stone walls were saved. The villagers refused to let their church die and restoration was completed by Pentecost 2000.

Below the church lies Downham Hall, now smaller than the original 17th century mansion, at one time the home of the De Beauvoir family, descendants of Osmund De Beauvoir who was rector of Downham for 61 years and whose name was, until recently, immortalised in the 'De Beauvoir Arms', the village public house. This is now a restaurant.

An original 17th century dovecote used to stand in the vicinity of Downham Hall. As it was becoming increasingly derelict it was decided to move it adjacent to the entrance to the churchyard. During this project it was discovered that in the churchyard there is the largest pollarded field maple in the British Isles, some 5 metres in girth.

Two other interesting older houses in the village are Downham House, originally the home of a branch of the well known Gascoyne-Cecil family and the Grange which up until the late 1960s was owned by the Keddie family who tragically lost all three of their sons in the Second World War. Two of the bells in the church were recast at their expense and dedicated to the memory of their sons.

The old pump which once supplied the whole village with water still stands on the hill, below the inn, restored and maintained by the Parish Council.

The northern boundary takes in part of the attractive South Hanningfield reservoir, a favourite haunt of bird watchers hoping for a glimpse of rare waterfowl: but the deep dark waters have their own secret, for beneath them lies the once grand manor house of Fremnells. The reservoir supports one of the country's best still-water trout fisheries and there are many other recreational facilities.

🍁 DUDDENHOE END

The picturesque little hamlet of Duddenhoe End with its share of old world thatched cottages sits in the north-west corner of Essex, on the top of the 'Champion', a hill of the East Anglian Heights about 410 feet above sea level with an ancient history.

Local clay was used for making the black dye used by the Anglo-Flemish wool trade. One merchant was William Cade (died 1166) of East Anglia who probably used the old Roman road once called Cades Lane before becoming Beards Lane. Another use of this clay was in the manufacturing of clay pipes.

Duddas Hall was held by the Saxon Dudda, Earl of Wessex in 1066, after which the first Norman name appears and the name changed to Duddenhoe Grange and was placed into the hands of Abbots of Tilty Abbey. After Henry VIII demolished the monasteries it became the property of the Earls of Suffolk, then Lord Audley de Walden as part of the Audley End estates.

The green was known as Bridge Green and is still recognised on Ordnance Survey maps today, taking its name from 'the Champion' Thomas le Bruges 1273 and held by John le Bruggere in 1294. This Norman family named the hill, Champion.

During the 17th century 'the green' became Duddenhoe End with thatch cottages dotting both sides of the road. This took in most of 'the green' leaving a small part of the west end and this became the recreation place for the village where fêtes, teas and fairs were held. The most frequent visitor was the Langley Brass Band, playing most Sunday mornings. These people were dissidents from the Anglican church and a little cottage was converted into a Methodist chapel with about 80 members, but closed down in 1935.

Timber was a big industry for the estate, having approximately 450 acres of woodland in 1808. These woods were familiar to the hunt back to when the countryside was open fields. Since 1725 the Puckridge Hunt hunted over these lands and Rockells Wood was known as 'the joy of fox hunters'.

The Wilkes family of Lofts Hall, Wenden Lofts had purchased most of the area by 1866. The Rev Robert Fiske (Wilkes) acting as squire controlled the life of the community, from the 10th century church dedicated to St Dunstan with which Duddenhoe End was associated until its closure in 1928. In 1859 the barn of its glebe farm 'The Parsonage' was converted into 'Hamlet Church'. This beautiful little church is reputed to be the only thatched church in Essex and is well worth a visit.

🍁 EARLS COLNE

Earls Colne is situated on the A604 between Colchester and the small market town of Halstead. It is the largest of the four villages receiving their name from the river Colne. At the time of King Edward the Confessor it belonged to a Saxon named Ulwin. Ulwin's whole estate was given by William the Conqueror to Alberic De Vere, who later became the Earl of Oxford, thus the name Earls Colne.

A priory was founded in 1100 on the bank of the river by Alberic De Vere; it was surrendered to Henry VIII on 3rd July 1534 by Robert Abel, the prior. A large house now stands near the site and is still known as the 'Priory'.

There is a very fine church dedicated to St Andrew, in a prominent position looking over the Colne valley. The tower has ornamental stone carvings depicting the coat of arms of John De Vere, the 16th Earl of Oxford, dated 1532. A notable vicar of the parish from 1641 until 1683 was the Rev Ralph Josselin MA who kept a unique diary, an edition of which has been published. The village architecture is most interesting and has been featured in a BBC documentary. Standing in the High Street are a number of 16th century houses still with their Tudor interiors, but alas they now have Georgian or Victorian facades.

R. Hunt & Co Ltd, makers of agricultural machinery, has been of importance to the village during its short but prosperous history. It provided jobs for the villagers, and many amenities were given by the Hunt family. The factory closed down in June 1988. When William Hunt of Colne Place died, he left a trust fund to Earls Colne to be used for the benefit of the residents.

In recent times two golf courses have been designed, one near the river in the picturesque Colne valley, and the other on the Earls Colne airfield. This airfield was home to the 455 Bomber Squadron of the American Air

Force in 1943. The roof of the public house in Coggleshall Road had to be removed to accommodate the bombers taking off.

A school with instruction in grammar as the chief subject was founded in Earls Colne in 1520 by Christopher Swallow, vicar of Messing. In 1673 the last Earl of Oxford sold the school estates to the Cressener family, who became patrons of the school. By the mid 18th century the school had achieved a high reputation, but it was closed in 1837. It reopened in 1843 under a new scheme as a Free grammar school. However in the reorganisation on comprehensive lines the grammar school closed in July 1975.

The village Church school was started on the 18th August 1813 and in 1843 Vicar Watkinson built a school in Park Lane, enlarged in 1875. In 1938 a new wooden building was put up in Park Lane opposite the church. The Earls Colne primary school is now a new building on the site of the old wooden one.

In addition to the Anglican parish church there are two other denominations in the village. The Baptist church was founded in 1786 in two converted cottages on the village green. The Quakers set up a meeting house in 1674. It is the oldest meeting house still in use in Essex.

🍁 EAST HANNINGFIELD

The main road of the village is largely unchanged in outline since John Walker made maps of the area in the 17th century.

The church of All Saints, which was very ancient, was destroyed by fire as the result of a faulty flue pipe, in December 1883. A medieval painting was removed from the old church and is now housed in the Victoria and Albert Museum. This building dated from about 1381 and until the plague, was the centre of the village. A stream, called the Pan, runs nearby, also 'Frogs Island' the watery site of osier beds which provided a village basket making industry. The new church consecrated in 1885, stands in the present village, on the Tye.

The old rectory, now a block of luxury flats, was set in spacious grounds, with many beautiful trees and an attractive stable block. Near the kitchen door was a well sunk in 1790. It was 347 feet deep and was built of 39,500 bricks, without the aid of cement. This well was one of the deepest in the country, providing water free for villagers who came before 10 am. A pump for public use stood on the green. This was fenced around with white railings, and until the mains water supply, frequently used.

In 1863 a Church school was opened, but prior to this a bungalow was used as a dame school. This Church school is now a private house. The village now has a new primary school and community centre.

Several local characters lie buried in the churchyard in unmarked graves. 'Friday' Lord the chimney sweep was to be seen riding a bike, with his brushes and rods tied to the crossbar. He and his clothes were so covered with soot that only the whites of his eyes gleamed. 'Poddy' Reeve the blacksmith toiled in his forge, wrapped in a leather apron. The gnarled old men who had retired gathered in his 'shop' for a gossip daily. Mr Wood the cobbler lived in a small room surrounded by brads and fat tabby cats. Mr and Mrs Wood were very short and stout, ideally matched in fact. Mr Wood managed to hold a conversation with a mouth full of small nails.

THE EASTONS & TILTY

Little Easton was also known as 'Estaines Parva', meaning small, or 'Easton by the Manor' as the residence of the lord was here from the 12th century.

There is no lord now but many 'Bakers' and 'Barkers' still living in the village, descended from the men who barked the trees, as charcoal burning was a local occupation. 'Butcher' is a local name coming from 'Bouchier', the name of the old lords of Estaines in 1420. An interesting thing to note is the letter 'M' on several old houses in the village which came from the name Maynard, a man who was granted the manor of Easton and all its entitlements by Queen Elizabeth I.

Frances Evelyn Maynard inherited the estate of Easton Lodge in 1865 at the age of three. She became the Countess of Warwick in 1893, when her husband succeeded to the title.

H. G. Wells was a writing friend of the Countess of Warwick and came to live at The Glebe, the old parsonage in 1911. While at The Glebe, H. G. Wells wrote *Mr Britling Sees It Through* a semi-autobiographical novel based on Little Easton during the First World War.

Amateur theatricals were a constant diversion for the Wells family and their guests, and these could often be performed at the Barn Theatre, the great tithe barn beside the church, which the Countess of Warwick turned into a theatre at the turn of the century. The Countess's dear friend Ellen Terry performed many times at the Barn. Shaw produced *The Taming of the Shrew* and Ellen Terry coached the cast. There is a plaque in memory of Ellen Terry in Little Easton church.

The 'Fighting Parson of Great Easton', the Reverend Horatio Bladen Capel, was born at Easton Lodge, which was his home until he came to Great Easton in 1877. Having been a champion boxer in the Navy in the days of sail, he was to enounter much opposition, as he was a dictator practising high church worship, and Great Easton was very low church. His chief opponent was the village blacksmith. Much discussion and argument took place between them and finally the rector said to the blacksmith 'Let's fight it out and the best man will be the winner'. So into the churchyard they both went, the rector won and from then on they were the best of friends.

Tilty was well established in the 12th century, with its abbey of St Mary the Virgin, arable and grazing land, fish ponds and vineyards. However, much of the abbey and buildings were destroyed by the soldiers of King John through a dispute with the Prior over extortionate taxes in the early 1200s. There remains of this extensive abbey only the chapel at the gate, now the parish church for Tilty and Duton Hill, with its beautifully restored east window and a section of the old flint wall on an adjoining meadow.

It was the Reverend Hugh Cuthbertson, vicar of Tilty, who, having had experience of curing tobacco in Chile, started the tobacco plant club in the late 1940s. This arose out of a modest money-raising scheme to pay for repairs to Tilty Abbey tower and was so successful that not only was the tower repaired, but the three windows in the West wall were replaced; an inscription on one of them records this. Mrs Cecily Down, Reverend Cuthbertson's daughter, of 'Abbey Gates', the former vicarage, is involved in the tobacco club, supplying plants to members nationwide in the spring and giving them advice on home-curing the product.

🍁 EIGHT ASH GREEN

As parishes go in Essex, Eight Ash Green is a virtual newcomer, having been created as a new civil parish in the rural district of Lexden and Winstree in January 1947. Land was acquired from the neighbouring parishes of Aldham (four acres), Stanway (125 acres), Copford (641 acres) and Fordham (844 acres). Lying five miles to the west of Colchester, the parish straddles the main A1124 road to Cambridge.

In 1949 the total population was 660, most of whom were involved in agriculture or local trades. Today the population has grown enormously to over 2,000, reflecting the increasing popularity of this part of Essex as improved road and rail links attract both new industries and commuters. As a result, where 40 years ago there was prime agricultural land, there are now modern housing estates.

Because of the manner of its creation, Eight Ash Green, unlike most Essex villages, has no ancient centre. There are some scattered timber-framed houses of considerable interest, dating mainly from the late 16th century, while Gatehouse Farm on Fordham Heath is actually mentioned in a document of 1291. Fordham Heath itself may well have been the site of an early manufacturing industry; in 1968 a particularly fine example of a Neolithic polished flint axe was found in a field behind the Cricketers, where there were many other flints of a similar honey colour.

The church of All Saints was built of locally made brick beside the main road in 1898 to serve this northern outpost of the parish of Copford, whilst the nearby Methodist chapel was opened in 1936 to replace a little one which stood in Huxtables Lane at the edge of the heath. Here, it is said, in fine weather services were often conducted from a farm wagon open to all the winds blowing across a treeless heath where cattle grazed and birds sang.

In one respect Eight Ash Green is blessed above almost all other Essex villages. It is a village of greens. The original green which gave its name in 1777 to the little hamlet of cottages clustered at the end of Blind Lane, has been gradually eaten away until only a pathetic remnant remains, looking for all the world like a rather wide roadside verge. Even the old village pond has been filled in. But there are others.

Daisy Green and Seven Star Green, lying south of the main road, together account for almost nine acres of open land. Both had small clusters of cottages on their edges. Daisy Green has one 18th century farmhouse and a series of modernised cottages which were originally built in the mid 19th century to accommodate workers on the new railway line. The name given to one of them perpetuates the old country name for an animal no longer seen hereabouts – the sally is a hare, and a hare-catcher once lived there.

Seven Star Green also has one 18th century house, the Maltings, whose name reflects one of the most important rural industries of an agricultural area. A few old cottages remain, but the inter-war years saw the beginning of development along the edges of the green as the need for grazing decreased. Today, these two small greens are being returned to their original state of ancient grazing common land. Both these greens were given to Eight Ash Green Parish Council in 1974, by deed of gift, by the lord of the manor of Copford, Mr Brian Harrison.

Fordham Heath is another matter entirely. An ancient heathland with rights of common grazing, and reputed to be the second largest village green (of some 36 acres) in Essex, it was granted by Act of Parliament to the parish of Eight Ash Green in 1965, the rights of common grazing being confirmed in 1980. Older villagers remember a very different heath from that which exists today. Apart from the military lands at Berechurch and Donyland, it is the last surviving remnant of the seven great heathlands which surrounded Colchester in the past, but which have succumbed to the sprawl of housing or to the extraction of the gravel which gave them their being.

Today the upper heath is a valuable recreational amenity for the village, and is the home of the cricket and football clubs originating in the immediate post-war period.

In addition to the greens and common land, the village is fortunate to possess a nature reserve owned by the Essex Wildlife Trust. The Iron Latch Reserve contains a wildflower-rich meadow and a coppiced woodland, both managed to enhance their wildlife potential.

🍁 ELMSTEAD MARKET

The village of Elmstead Market is situated four miles to the east of Colchester, bounded by a brook. In the centre of the village is a green which, years ago, was used for a market and fair, started in 1253 in the reign of Henry III when Richard De Tany obtained a licence to keep a market and fair at Elmstead – hence the current name Elmstead Market. The market gradually died out but the fair was held annually every May until 1914. Modern revivals have taken place from time to time.

Elmstead Market is situated one mile south of Elmstead Church and Hall on the main A133 Colchester to Clacton on Sea road. Many houses date back to the 17th century, including Momples Hall Hunting Lodge, which was used as a workhouse for the poor. Later it became the village bakery and has now reverted to a private dwelling.

The parish church has evidence of a former Saxon building on the site, though much of what we see today is 13th century. The North door (uncovered in 1931) is Norman. Over the door is an arch of Roman bricks above which is a Saxon arch uncovered in 1988. The original door preserved in the church was replaced by a replica made by Mabbett's Wood Carvers, Colchester.

The Wesleyan Methodist chapel, built in 1816–1817 and restored in 1863, was demolished in 1999 to make way for a modern building and is now called the Trinity Christian Centre. It was completed in the year 2000.

The Church of England school built in 1846 was enlarged several times and vacated in 1973, finally being converted into a thriving Community Centre in May 1976. The original village school, a thatched and boarded building built circa 1830, is still standing in Old School Lane as a private dwelling.

The Bowling Green public house situated on the north side of the main road finally ceased trading in 1999 and has now reverted to a private dwelling. The surrounding car park and garden has been redeveloped and now contains three new houses. The last remaining public house in the village is still flourishing.

James Noah Paxman, famous founder of the world-wide engineering works known as Davey Paxman & Co of Colchester 1865, was the son of James Paxman, 'wheelwright and machine maker'. He was born at Elmstead where his father had a forge and engineering works in the village, where he made traction engines.

Beth Chatto's gardens at Elmstead Market are now nationally famous. Beth and her late husband used their vast knowledge to turn swamp, scrub and wasteland into acres of beautiful lakes and gardens. A treasure visited by many as the gardens and nursery are open to the public.

🍁 ELSENHAM

Elsenham is a typical country village, situated between Stansted Mountfitchet and Thaxted and adjacent to the 'Third London Airport'. It has an ancient background, being mentioned in the Domesday Book.

The last lord of the manor was Sir Walter Gilbey, 1875–1914. Sir Walter is well remembered because in 1900, in memory of his wife, he had a pump erected in the village street. It has round brick sides, from the top of which oak posts support a gilded dome. This pump supplied water for the villagers until the main water pipes were laid in about 1936. For some reason the metal pump was removed and the well covered.

He also started the jam factory employing many villagers and to this day one can see Elsenham jam on sale in many countries. Another sideline of Sir Walter's was the lavender fields which yielded the flowers from which was made the delightful Elsenham Lavender Perfume.

The Norman church of St Mary is built on the site of an earlier Saxon church. The feature of this beautiful church is the arch with its star and chevron decorations. In the chancel, coloured metal panels with portraits of saints were brought from France by Sir Walter Gilbey.

The Great Eastern Railway came through Elsenham in 1843 and Queen Victoria and Prince Albert travelled from Tottenham passing through Elsenham on the way to Cambridge; this must have been a very exciting journey at that time of railway travel. The original station was sited at Fullers End, but subsequently moved to its present site in 1850. A horse-drawn omnibus ran from Elsenham to Thaxted until a branch railway service commenced in 1913. This line was closed in September 1952, coming under the Beeching railway axe. Once again an omnibus, motorised this time, made the connection.

The Hon Dorothy Paget bought Elsenham Hall and paddocks in 1936 and was the owner of *Golden Miller*, the greatest steeplechaser of all time. He was the winner of five Gold Cups 1932 to 1936 and of the Grand National in 1934. He is buried at the paddocks with a stone marking his resting place.

In 1933 the population was 500, and in 1990 approximately 3,000. Many housing estates have been built, but one may still find a few beautifully thatched cottages, and lovely gardens. There is a new village hall, attached to the junior school, which caters for most social activities, and a Memorial Hall in the playing field with adjacent sports field and children's playground. There is one public house, the Crown, for the benefit of locals and visitors alike.

🍁 FARNHAM

In the early 1930s village life was bound up with farming, and many of the men worked on the land as farmworkers or estate workers. Others walked or bicycled into Bishops Stortford to work in industries such as Millars works and the match factory, both of which have disappeared. At busy times in the farming calendar many of the wives came out onto the farms to help, especially with weeding crops in the springtime, and harvesting in the summer and autumn. Children from the school also helped with the harvesting; it gave them an insight into working life, and as most of them left school at the age of 14 they knew what was expected of them when they did start to earn their living.

Various tradesmen came round with vans and sold groceries and fuel, as there was no electricity supply until 1939, and then only in some houses. Paraffin was used for lighting and heating, and some people used it for cooking as well. A Mr Bishop came with a pony and high wheeled cart selling fruit and fish, and sometimes in the summer, custard ice cream. Mr Warwick, who lived in the village, travelled around two or three other parishes as well as his own selling sweets, cottons, clothes and other things. He rode a bicycle with his goods in cases on carriers front and back and baskets on the handlebars, and because the cases were attache cases he was known as 'Tachy' Warwick He joined the RAF for the war.

The school had a headmistress, Miss Senior, and in the early days she used to ride a motorcycle and sidecar, and lived in the school house. The children spent all of their school life at the school, which is a Church of England school, and much emphasis was placed on religious education. Everyone marched down to the church on Ascension Day for a service, also on Empire Day, when the Union flag would be run up the flagpole. Other social occasions at the school were May Day, when a May Queen was chosen and a maypole erected and danced around, and at the end of the summer term there was Feast Day, held in the parish room, followed by games in the rectory garden.

The rector of the village was Canon Geare, who served for over 50 years. He drove a Clyno motorcar and was one of the few car owners in the village, while his wife rode a large upright bicycle. They descended on the school most days of the week to take religious instruction and prayers, and to make sure that discipline was maintained – the fear of God was wrought in us all!

The pace of life seems much faster now, there is no time to stand and stare. Many of the old village cottages have been renovated and are lived in by people working well outside the village; for much of the year they leave for work in the dark and arrive home in the dark. Perhaps there are some who would welcome back the allotments and the flower shows, and no mowers or chainsaws on Sunday.

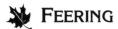 FEERING

Bypassed by the A12 for over 40 years, the village of Feering has been said to derive its Saxon name from Feringe, or 'dwellers by the road'. The old Roman road to Colchester passed through Feering.

The centre of the old village of Feering lies to the north of the Roman road. On the rising ground above the flood plain of the Blackwater lies the village green. Its post office and general store and old cottages, one with a dovecote, are overlooked by the square tower of the village church. The newer buildings on two sides of the green remind the observer of the more recent building which has occurred in the village, but the church has dominated the story of Feering.

A visitor to All Saints church enters through a beautiful Tudor brick porch which has been carefully restored. The porch was the gift of a 15th century wool merchant, and his mark is in the porch roof. Like many old churches, the building has been added to over several centuries from the 13th century nave to the 15th century tower with its eight bells. It has been lovingly repaired and cared for since, often by East Anglian craftsmen, although the present chancel arch was designed by Sir George Gilbert Scott, as a young man, in 1845.

Not far from the church, on the old glebeland, stands the original Feering village school, now a private house, opened in 1842 and in use until 1987. It is perhaps a measure of the comparative importance of education and cultivation in 19th century Feering, that the first head teacher in 1842 was the vicar's gardener.

The village inn, appropriately named the Bell, has stood near the church for many centuries, facing the village green and the old almshouses, now converted into cottages. The ten almshouses were sold to their occupants by the vicar for £300 in 1938 when the rental was not worth the cost of collection! Next to these cottages lies Church Farm, a reminder of the days when every church had its own means of support from the land around it and of Feering's dependence on agriculture until recent times.

Within the parish of Feering are many small communities of a few houses, all part of the larger village community. A new bungalow at Stocks green is the only reminder of where the stocks once stood, but Feeringbury has been the manor house since the Abbots of Westminster used to enjoy staying there.

A regular visitor to Feering was the painter John Constable. It was appropriate that the altar piece of the Risen Christ painted by him in

1822 for the chapel at Manningtree hung over the altar in the lady chapel of Feering parish church until 1998 (now replaced by a copy). This picture and a painting of Feering vicarage were included in the 1976 Tate Gallery exhibition of Constable's work.

🍁 FELSTED

Artefacts found as the Dunmow-to-Braintree railway line was being built in 1868 provided evidence of Roman occupation of Felsted. These are now housed in Colchester Museum.

Digs revealed the foundations of dwellings with timber frames and wattle and daub walls. This style of construction continued, with modifications, for many centuries. More recent buildings of a similar structure are still standing in the village. An old survey, by the Royal Commission of Historic Monuments in 1921, listed 108 timber-framed houses, largely dating from Tudor times. Wooden-framed houses in the Essex style are easy to identify in the village centre. Notably, one by George Boote, churchwarden and builder, still proudly proclaims on one of its external beams 'George Boote made this: 1596'. Some say that the figurine on its wall comes to life and wanders the street on Hallowe'en.

The Boote House, now a restaurant, stands opposite the church and the guildhall. The guildhall probably dates from soon after 1500, according to carbon dating tests. Built for the Trinity guild, it was converted to use as a school by a foundation deed in 1564. The school was intended to provide 'lernyng of Grammar and other vertues and godly lernyng' to male children born in Essex. Preference was given to boys born on Lord Rich's manors and farms, parts of his widespread and prosperous estates.

Although the original church must have been Saxon and wooden, the oldest standing structure is the Norman tower. One can see pieces of Roman brick and tile incorporated in the flint-rubble dressed with stone from which it is built. The present church was built in stages between the end of the 12th and the early 14th centuries. Amongst its treasures is the tomb of Lord Rich.

The Felsted WI banner has as its emblem a barrel wreathed by circling fish – a motif better suited to a fishing port than a village in the heart of arable Essex, one might think ... unless one knows the history of the so-called 'herring window' inside the wagon arch linking the street to the parish church.

Richard, Lord Rich, in residence at Leez Priory, endowed a chantry at Felsted in 1555, following the custom of wealthy men by making provision for the local poor and a kind of spiritual insurance for himself through the regular prayers to be chanted by its chaplain for the benefactor. The revenue from certain parcels of land was to be used by the churchwardens to provide eleven barrels of white herrings and eleven barrels of red herrings (kippers) for distribution on Ash Wednesdays, and a further seven barrels of each on every Lenten Sunday. Incidentally, 20 of each fish were to be kept for the chaplain's own use, and the wardens were bidden to keep the barrels. This custom continued, at Little Leez and Much Waltham too, until 1852, when a more realistic gift of cash was substituted.

Some poor people were well provided for by Lord Rich, who built a set of five thatched houses, with an attached meadow for six cows, a barn, a brewhouse and an orchard. On the site of these tenements one can see the modern almshouses, next to a pub, east of the guildhall. These were erected in 1879 after a destructive fire which started in the cowshed. Another fire in 1998 again destroyed some of the almshouses, but these have been restored and are now occupied by elderly people.

Beyond the heart of the village, with its clutch of shops, restaurants, pubs, church and school, one can find other interesting and handsome buildings. Felsted parish extends to nine so-called 'greens'. Some still show their commonland or pasture spaces, as at Bannister Green. There, the Three Horseshoes pub adjoins the erstwhile smithy.

On the road out of Bannister Green, towards Leighs, stands the thatched cottage, with pargeted walls, called Quakers Mount. In its garden one can glimpse the burial mound used for plague victims.

Continuing towards Leighs, the gatehouse for Leez Priory stands among the trees. The Elizabethan brick building can be better viewed from the lane which passes over the river Ter and then turns in front of the priory. The grounds are occasionally open to the public and the priory itself is now used for corporate entertaining and as a venue for weddings and special events.

🍁 FIDDLERS HAMLET

Fiddlers Hamlet lies 1½ miles south-west of Epping, in the parish of Theydon Garnon, which itself was once a hamlet of Epping. The hamlet is still surrounded by farmland, but this charming old English scene has had to be carved up for motorways. The beauty of the countryside can still be admired, but the sounds of animals and birds are no longer all that can be heard. Fiddlers Hamlet has been a centre of population since the 17th century but now comprises a dozen houses or so.

Stand at the crossroads, facing towards Epping, and on your right you will see the picturesque Home Farm and farm buildings some 400 years old, with the gnarled old trees guarding the entrance.

The Merry Fiddlers Inn is another 400 year building, but which has had a few additions built on to it. This is where the hamlet got its name. Walk past the inn, over the bridge. The medieval house on your left is Masons Bridge Farm and is the oldest building in the hamlet although it does not look it from the outside, having a modern exterior. Over 50 years ago this farm stabled race horses and there was a track here where racing took place. Later, a nine hole golf course was laid and Bridge Farm became the club house. Nowadays it is a private dwelling and the land belongs to another farmer.

Retrace your footsteps over the bridge and stop at the houses opposite the inn. It was here that an annual fair was held, but in 1872 Chisenhale Marsh, the lord of the manor, abolished it by petition. This is probably the spot where the fiddlers came and played. There was a cobbler's shop and a grocer on the corner, although many traders called and travelled round the neighbourhood. During the Second World War a Nissen hut was erected in which to hold church services and social evenings but it was later demolished. Theydon Garnon's 700 year old church lies some two miles away and until recent times parishioners always walked over the fields to attend.

Turn left and take the road to Coopersale but as you walk past Home Farm look ahead and on the right you will vaguely see the old school and the bells which rang out to summon the children to school.

If you glance to the right you will see a magnificent building on the hill – Gaynes Park, with a long curving drive with parkland on both sides. This was the home of the Chisenhale Marshes which they vacated in 1976. Happily the family, or part of it, live in Theydon Mount and still farm the land.

🍁 Finchingfield

When the Festival of Britain was being organised in 1951 it was decided by the London committee that it would be a delightful attraction to select four

The Green, Finchingfield

or five of the prettiest villages in Britain and present them to the visitors as examples of true England. Finchingfield was one of the chosen. Visitors came to the Festival and many of them found their way or were brought by officials to admire. The Festival ended but the fame the occasion brought to the village did not fade. Calendars, postcards, tapestries, paintings and crafts, all depicting the loveliness of an Essex village kept Finchingfield very near the top of the tourists' itinerary.

On the east side of the pond adjacent to the hand bridge is the old workhouse. In 1767 there were 30 inmates. Several years ago the old workhouse was a butcher's shop and today is a delightful private residence.

Past the workhouse and on up the hill, is the Guildhall, now over 450 years of age. In 1630 a school for poor children was formed by the generosity of Sir Robert Kempe. Under his will the Guildhall and the adjoining almshouses were then given to the poor of the parish. Today the Guildhall is used for exhibitions, committee meetings, lectures and the occasional social evening. It is an integral part of the life of the village as it has been for over 400 years.

The tiny museum facing the entrance to the Guildhall tells much of the hard work done by the labourers, the craftsmen and the straw plaiters.

In her book about village life and characters Eliza Vaughan, whose father was installed as vicar in 1864, tells the story of a woman who died. The corpse lay in the coffin downstairs and the relatives were upstairs sorting out the possessions of the departed. They found a box containing some strange little things that looked useless but which they suspected of being imps, so they burned them. When they went down to look once more on the earthly remains of someone who had been suspected of witchcraft they found only a heap of ashes.

If there are doubts about witches there is no doubt about the beauty of St John the Baptist church which stands on top of the hill and seems to be a symbol of strength and security. It is over 400 years old and has withstood religious wars, political machinations and gale force winds. Once a year this lovely old church is the scene of a Flower Festival.

🍁 FINGRINGHOE

Unlike many English villages, Fingringhoe does not nestle, but spreads, east and west, along a rise overlooking the beautiful Roman river valley.

Village people have worshipped for 900 years in St Andrew's church, built in 1100 and enlarged in the 14th and 15th centuries. It is peaceful, welcoming and bright with white plastered walls, fading medieval wall paintings and homely faces of 14th century local people carved on the timbers of the unusual barrel roof. Smugglers were rumoured to hide their contraband behind the battlements.

Stories of smuggling are easy to believe for the farmland slopes south down to eerie marshes through which curves Geedon Creek, often covered in drifting mists and silent except for the calls of shoreline birds. Here once was South Green, one of the three greens around which the population clustered. A census of 1881 listed many cottages whose occupants were agricultural labourers, with one shepherd who spent his life caring for the sheep grazing on the borders of the marshes. Sheep still graze there but sadly the people have gone and their cottages have long since fallen down. The Green has disappeared under the plough but some of the cottages were saved and have been restored and converted for modern living, keeping the name as a reminder of the people who have gone before.

On the west side of Church Green is another important amenity of any village, the ancient inn, in this case called The Whalebone which, until quite recently displayed the decaying jawbones of the great sea creature as its sign, perhaps brought by a returning sailor to one of the nearby quays at Rowhedge or across the river Colne at Wivenhoe. Two old cottages remain and share with the inn a most beautiful view over the Roman river valley. Church Green has only one old cottage left but recently new cottages have been built opposite especially for older residents. This scheme was made possible by gifts of land and money and the hard work of the Church Green Trust who have made this great contribution to village life.

Built in 1887 the Church school shares the Green. It is a happy school with an active Parent Teacher Association. Modern amenities include the post office, a village shop and the village hall. The Methodist church close by has an active membership.

The manor has been held by different families but reverted to the Crown until Edward VI granted it to the Darcy family in 1553, who lived here for nearly 100 years and rebuilt Fingringhoe Hall in the early 17th century. Sadly the main wing of the house was destroyed in a fire.

Fire brought destruction, again in the 20th century, when part of the mill built in Tudor times was destroyed. Rebuilt, it still functioned, though tidal power gave way to oil and the tall brown barge sails were no longer to be seen on the river. Recently, when operations ceased, the old buildings were converted into two large residences with views up and down the Roman river. The tranquil scene has been preserved.

The Nature Reserve at Fingringhoe Wick attracts many visitors. Quarrying in the 19th century left deep holes, now lakes, which attract herons and a variety of water fowl. Nightingales have returned and geese winter on the marshes.

🍁 FOBBING

Fobbing lays quietly overlooking the marshes, with Basildon to the north and the river Thames to the south, at the head of a tributary of Hole Haven Creek.

The church tower can be seen from many vantage points around the area. One Tree Hill, a local beauty spot is the highest point (in a direct line) before the North Pole, with Westley Heights being on the same ridge of hills overlooking the Thames.

Until 1953 and the east coast floods the creek from Fobbing was navigable to the sea. With a little imagination on a misty day it is easy to see the smugglers bringing in their contraband of 'brandy for the parson and 'baccy for the clerk'. It was supposed the clergy were involved and the fact the old rectory has such large cellars seems to lend credence to this idea.

The Dukes Head (Fobbing Road) is thought by many to have been a public house. Although built for that purpose, a licence did not become available in the area and it was run for many years by the Wood family as an off licence. The teenagers would congregate there and the local police requested Mr Wood's father to keep them in check; he encouraged them by forming a football team and cricket club.

On a derelict farm near the Five Bells stands an old bungalow now used as a cow-shed. Many years ago a Mr Cash lived here and it was he who started up the Vange Water Company. The company bottled water from the well between One Tree Hill and Hovells Farm. The Temple Well has been visited by many locals and their relatives. It died out after about 5 or 6 years but by then Mr Cash had made his money. The bottles were 2/6d each and people came down from London to collect their supplies. Whether it cured them or not was questionable. Towards the end of the active life of the Vange Water Company there was a dispute with a Mr Poole at Hovells Farm. He stopped the flow of water to the Vange well by digging one for himself and bottling his own brand for a short spell.

Fobbing wharf ruins can still be seen today and the tide used to come up the creek to the brickworks. The Kynocks Ammunitions Factory was down on the marshes (now the site of the Mobil Oil Refinery) and people who worked there were commuters on the Corringham Light Railway. There was a colony for workers in the region of the Mobil Pegasus Club.

🍁 FORDHAM

The parish of Fordham is separated from the parish of Aldham by the river Colne. The name of Fordham is thought to have originated from the ford across the river at Ford Street. Fordham is about six miles from Colchester, which is the main shopping town. However, about two and a half miles away, at Stanway, a new business park has been built, with several large stores, so Colchester has literally come out towards us!

All Saints' church is a 14th century building, consisting of a nave, two aisles and a chancel with a square tower containing three bells. Close by the church stands Fordham Hall, part of it as it was in medieval days. The house is of lath and plaster construction with a tiled roof. Fordham Hall is now the home of local farmer, John Jinks, and his family, who has done much for the village in the planting of hundreds of trees and has undertaken conservation work in the area, as well as farming the surrounding land.

Oak House was formerly known as Church Cottages and comprised four cottages. The cottages were thought to have been used as the village lock-up at one time and as the poor house in the 17th century and housed 13 men and 13 women. In 1924 the cottages were converted into two dwellings, and it is now one cottage.

Fordham Mill was referred to as Tower Mill on old maps. Fordham appears to have had a mill during pre-Domesday times and is certainly listed as having one in the Domesday census, but the actual mill itself was demolished in 1903. It was thought to have dated from 1780. The mill was primarily a grain mill but in 1653 records show that it held fulling stock for the woollen trade (teazles still abound in the surrounding fields – another link with the cloth trade). The Mill House as it is now called, is a private dwelling house.

Fordham has two thriving public houses. The Three Horseshoes in Church Road was first mentioned in Kelly's Directory in 1855 but is thought to have its origins somewhat earlier than this. The Shoulder of Mutton at Ford Street is a 15th century building almost unchanged from its original structure. It was first mentioned as a pub in 1859. There was a third pub named 'The Vulcan' which stood near to the village post office and shop, and which was demolished in 1998 to make way for six new houses which have been built very sympathetically to fit in with the village. Opposite is the new village green, complete with wildlife pond, village sign all nicely repainted, and sundial installed to commemorate the Millennium. The village Church primary school which was built in 1849 is to be up-graded and enlarged in 2001, increasing its capacity to over 100 children.

Fossetts and Chancers Lane is situated opposite the church and the Three Horseshoes public house. 'Fosse' is a Middle English word, derived from old French, meaning ditch or moat; and Chancers means doing something risky whilst hoping to avoid discovery! Poaching, maybe!

There are now six houses and two farms in the lane; Fossetts is a very picturesque thatched cottage worthy of any chocolate box. In the 1980s, just behind these houses, a lead coffin was found in a shallow grave, inside which were the skeletons of a woman and a child. Surrounding the coffin were pots, pans and kitchen utensils. The archaeologist's opinion was that it was probably a mother and child dating back to the Roman period, obviously from a rich family, and that if excavated the site would probably reveal a Roman villa of some importance.

The lane continues downhill with twists and bends and the sound of running water from the ditch which never runs dry, and eventually comes to the first farm, Watercress Hall, so-called because of the abundance of wild watercress which grows there. Watercress Hall was built in 1777.

Lovers Lane is a cart track and public footpath which joins the Essex Way beside the River Colne. Further up river there is a new footbridge, built in 1996, to continue the path to Eight Ash Green. Lovers Lane used to be a lonely area. Down this track were three cottages where today, over the hedge, cows graze happily down to the river edge. Yet this was the scene of a double murder some 100 years ago. No one would live in the cottages again. They became derelict and were eventually demolished. The nature of the place has changed rapidly. Dutch elm disease has decimated the ancient hedges and trees. The gravel pit, which at the turn of the last century was the source of the roadstone for Fossetts Lane, is filled in, and where the cottages were is now a productive vineyard.

🍁 FRYERNING

Fryerning, one of the loveliest villages in Essex, is situated on a hill three quarters of a mile from Ingatestone. The church of St Mary the Virgin was built in Norman times. The tower is a landmark for miles and is surrounded by a large churchyard and cemetery. Three huge yew trees grow near the building, though one was badly damaged by the October 1987 gale.

The public house, the Woolpack, is at the top of Fryerning Lane. Before the boundaries were altered some years ago, part was in Fryerning parish and part in Ingatestone. The windmill, privately owned, is in good order but has been out of work for years. At one time it was the habitat of the white owl.

Standing as high as the village does, the main stretch of road is almost, if not quite, level with the top of Ingatestone church tower. Strange though it may be, there are still three large ponds left. There were a few more but these have been filled in. The largest one left, always known as the Bob Pond, was full of carp and roach until it dried up in the warm summers of 1989–90. Fishing always began on Whit Monday and finished when the cold weather set in. Dates and seasons were not thought of in those times. Hard winters and frosts made skating possible. On moonlight nights all the village turned up with their skates.

At one time, again before the boundaries were altered, a bride-to-be wishing to be married at Fryerning church had to pack a suitcase for the rector to have at the rectory for the three weeks her banns were published in church. They also had to be called in Ingatestone, making three sets of banns if the bridegroom-to-be lived out of either parish.

The Cricketers was known by the old inhabitants as the Bat and Ball and cricket was played on the common in years gone by. Further along the road is the Viper, or the Snake as some people call it, said to be the only pub of that name in the world. Between the two pubs is the common which was a network of trenches during the First World War. There locally billeted regiments practised hand grenade throwing.

Another landmark is the water tower built to supplement the water supply for Fryerning and Ingatestone. Some years later Fryerning residents came down one morning to no mains water. The tower was empty. Hence the building of the reservoir along Beggar Hill Road. At one time the waterworks was halfway down Fryerning Lane, now new houses have been built on the site.

Beggar Hill is supposed to have got its name from the 'men of the road' who used it on their way to St Leonards where they would be given a meal and a night's lodging. Blanket Hall, for years known as Fryerning Grange, was so named because these men would call there for a blanket.

Eventually the Eastern National ran buses on Fridays and Saturdays from Chelmsford to the Viper and back. Cars came into their own and the buses were taken off the road. 'Mod cons' were the next thing. Telephones were installed, the sewer laid on, then gas and electricity. Hopefully the district will not alter too much now, as it has been declared a conservation area.

🍁 FYFIELD

Fyfield is a rural parish situated on the B184, two and a half miles north of Chipping Ongar. It is a sprawling village with a population of about 900. It has been called 'the gateway to the Roothings', the series of villages through which the river Roding flows on its way to the Thames. The Roding enters Fyfield from the north-east and leaves the parish in the south-west. Fyfield is also crossed by that ancient footpath, the Essex Way, on its route towards East Anglia. The area is mainly agricultural with high quality soil.

The village boasts its own flower, the Fyfield Pea, *Lathyrus Tuberosus*, thought to have originated in Eastern Europe. Looking rather like a small sweet pea, it is a bushy or climbing perennial two to three feet high, with crimson, slightly fragrant flowers in June/July. It grows on grassy verges and in the hedgerows in the area, but sadly it is now becoming scarce. The local primary school and bowls club have adopted it as part of their emblem and it is carved on the village sign.

Nowadays the village has a restaurant and two public houses, but the village shop and post office closed in 2000. The Black Bull on the main Ongar to Dunmow road is about 400 years old. It was once licensed for slaughtering and was also a stage coach and carrier point. The Queen's Head in Queen Street is of similar age and both are welcoming country pubs providing good food and drink.

Education in Fyfield goes back over 300 years, when in 1687 the rector, Dr Anthony Walker, endowed a free school for poor children. A transcript of part of his will can be seen on a wooden plaque on the west wall of the church. The present school, a modern building, still bears his name – Dr Walker's Church of England Primary School.

The site of the boarding school at Clatterford End, originally a truant school for West Ham in 1884, then a school for delicate children and subsequently Essex County Council Boarding schools, first Fyfield and latterly Elmbridge, has now been redeveloped as a residential site. The original Victorian buildings have been converted into 18 housing units and an estate of 34 new houses constructed.

St Nicholas' church, which is of an unusual design with a central tower, is of Norman origin with the north and south aisles added in the 13th century. It is recorded that the headless body of Henry, Lord Scrope of Masham, whose family were patrons of the church in the 12th century, is buried under the organ in the north side of the choir chancel. Henry V suspected him of being a traitor and he was beheaded at Portchester Castle, but after Agincourt he was pardoned and his headless body was returned to Fyfield.

The watermill, also mentioned in the Domesday Book, can be seen from the bridge over the river Roding, making a picturesque part of a private dwelling. Fyfield once had a windmill too, but this was blown down in a gale in 1910, though its site can still be clearly identified.

There are an unusual number of timber-framed houses in Fyfield, privately owned and not open to the public, some moated like Lampetts, and Fyfield Hall, the manor house, which contains a rare aisled hall and trussed rafter roof, said to be the oldest example in the country.

🍁 GALLEYWOOD

Although in Saxon times a settlement probably existed in Galleywood, down the years it was no more than a hamlet of Great Baddow. With the building of the fine parish church on the common, it was granted the status of an ecclesiastical parish in 1874. Not until 1987 did it become a civil parish, separate from Baddow, and administered by its own Parish Council. The name Gavelwode appears in 1250, probably deriving from the Saxon 'gavol', or rent, paid for the woods around the settlement.

Perhaps the village's main claim to fame is its historic racecourse, and it can safely be said that it is the only racecourse in the country which encircles the village church, dating back to the 18th century.

In 1890 a new racecourse with a new grandstand was formed. It twice crossed the main road, which was covered with tan made from oak bark, and all traffic was stopped during the races. Flat racing gave place to steeplechasing and the races became a great local occasion. Twice yearly a two-day meeting was held, the first mainly attended by the gentry and the second by farm workers and townspeople. Because of the danger to children from traffic the school was closed on race days.

Steeplechasing at Galleywood came to an end in 1935, as the national economic crisis affected attendances, but the grandstand was not dismantled at that time, and remained to serve as a venue for many village activities, until the generosity of Mrs Keene produced the Keene Hall.

There are many 16th century houses in Galleywood, mainly in Well Lane, where there are three wells. At one time they provided the main water supply, and indeed the piped water supply did not reach the village until 1930. Goat Hall is another 16th century house, while Wild Wood Cottage in Galley End was built in 1640, by one Louis Monsant, in peculiar style: he provided a watertight roof by inverting an old boat on the walls and covered it with pitch. During conversions some years ago the main keel and ribs of the boat were revealed, and barnacles and other shellfish were clearly visible. A similar roof can be seen in The Street.

St Michael and All Angels' church on Galleywood Common owes its existence to 'Squire Pryor' who bought the mansion of Hylands. He was the wealthy chairman of a brewery, who was persuaded by his deeply religious wife to finance the building of the church at Widford, and also one on the high ground of Galleywood Common, which is still a landmark visible for many miles. Arthur Pryor laid the foundation stone in 1872 and later attended the consecration ceremony in 1873, when bellringers rang 5,060 changes on the new bells. If Mrs Pryor cherished any hopes of attending Sunday services at Galleywood with her husband and nine children, they were soon dashed. Mr Pryor disliked the first sermon he heard there, which to him smacked of 'popery', and could not be persuaded to attend another service in the church on which he had spent £6,300.

🍁 GOLDHANGER

There is much to be seen on a visit to the village of Goldhanger. At the top of Church Street, stand on the larger grass triangle and, looking up the drive to Follifaunts, imagine how it looked when the manor was given to help found Beeleigh Abbey, close to Maldon, in 1180. Then cross to the smaller triangle and glance up the drive to the big red brick house, built in 1851/2 by a well-to-do clerical family to be the rectory. They had good parties there, and entertained Lewis Carroll. Walk down Church Street and you will see on your right a row of red brick cottages, neatly built to the edge of the road to house four Coastguards and their families. On the other side is the school building which served us well from 1875 to 1977; today the children go by bus to a school in Tolleshunt D'Arcy. The Goldhanger building is now a nursery school with a Christian ethos.

Now you are in the centre of the old village, with the 11th century church, the Chequers pub, very old and of uncertain origin, and the Square. The inside of the church has been altered over the centuries, but the two small Norman windows in the north wall give it the 11th century date. Outside, the stonework shows clearly how in the 15th century they built the tower a few feet away from the church, and when it was complete knocked down the church's west wall and joined the church to the tower.

Back by the churchyard gate, one finds that the road takes only half of the old Square, the other half, with a brick wall making the division, being the Chequers car park (and previously a vegetable garden). On the north side only the first house shows how the buildings used to face on to the Square; the next three have taken a piece for their front gardens, this again defined by the brick walls that marked out the village, probably in the latter part of the first half of the 19th century.

A Thames barge near Goldhanger

All this would have mattered more over 640 years ago, for they needed a big square with the pump in the middle, not on the pavement as it is today. In 1348 the lord of the manor got royal permission for a market every Thursday, and at the same time for an annual fair which included for sale ribbons, gingerbread and knick-knacks, held in the 18th century on 14th May and later on Whit Monday. Nowadays we block off that stretch of road and so use half the old Square for the May Fair on the first Bank Holiday in May.

Leaving the Square by Fish Street, you pass the place where, until the 20th century, a mill was still working. The Mill House, rather reduced in size, still stands in a commanding position with the main mill building converted into a pair of cottages. The mill was powered by both wind and steam, and its chimney is said to have been taller than the church tower. Walking down past these buildings you will find you are close to the wide tidal estuary of the river Blackwater, on the old road that led down to the head of the creek where fishing smacks unloaded their catch. The water has receded, and today the road ends at a large playing field edged by a footpath that is a tunnel of trimmed hawthorn bushes and leads to the creek and the sea-wall.

GOOD EASTER

Not only is Good Easter isolated by the river Can, but even its name is shrouded in mystery. A monk claimed that a lady called Godgyfu had left her Eowestras (Sheepfolds) to Ely Abbey in her will. Ultimately the lands seem to have been restricted to High Easter, higher up the valley of the river Can, and the name left to Good Easter (Godgyfu's Eowestras).

Today as nearly a thousand years ago the parish is devoted to arable farming. Commuters, the young affluent and the retired occupy the cottages and old smallholding farms. Good Easter is a very pleasant place to live. Often described as a sleepy village, here is the record of one day when it woke up:

On March 2nd 1885, coming out of Sunday School, Emily Tyrell saw the steeple of St Andrew's on fire. Running to the mill she raised the men who hastened to the site. The fire was first seen by the Rev E. J. Bicknell. His diary records that a man was sent to Chelmsford by horse to get the Fire Brigade, only seven miles away. It was 9.20 am. By 11.30 am the sweat-lathered horses had pulled up the hill and the fire engine had arrived. But it was too hot to do anything with the pump.

Christopher Matthews of Newarks and his men were dragging blazing baulks of timber into the water-filled ditches and ponds, and did so until 12.30 pm. Now that the fire was dying down the Fire Brigade was able to get close in to put it out. This took until 4 pm in the afternoon, solely by manual pumping.

By July 20th 1886 the money was raised and repairs to the steeple completed.

🍁 GOSFIELD

Gosfield is a very pleasant village of some 1,000 inhabitants surrounded by beautiful parklands. It has welcomed a queen in her glory, sheltered a fugitive king, and has the largest fresh water lake in Essex.

The first church was built in 1190 by Aubrey de Vere, when the surrounding lands were owned by the Earls of Oxford, and this is why you will find the de Vere star on the north east buttress of the church wall, facing the lychgate. The present church was built by Sir Thomas Rolf in 1435.

Gosfield Hall began, in Tudor times, with a building by Sir John Wentworth in 1545, and was added to in the 17th and 18th centuries. There is some lovely English linenfold panelling in the Queen's Gallery and a priest's hole over the salon, which was often useful for eavesdropping! The hall also boasts an 18th century well and pumping system operated by a horse or donkey harnessed to a beam. There is only one other to be found in Britain, and that is believed to be on another old estate in the village known as 'Cut Edge', or Cut Hedge as it is now.

The lake, which was a small pond in Tudor times, was enlarged in the 18th century to a mile in length. It is now a tourist attraction, and used for water skiing training and national events.

There have been many distinguished visitors to the hall. Queen Elizabeth I really did stay there in 1561 and 1569. Louis XVIII of France spent two years of his exile at Gosfield Hall at the invitation of the Marquis of Buckingham, who then owned the hall. He often walked in the village and delighted the children by throwing pennies to them as he passed. Besides this, many of the villagers liked to go to the hall kitchens on Sundays, and sometimes in accordance with the French custom of the time, were even allowed in to see the King dine.

The King and his court were not the only French people living in Gosfield at that time. There was a small community of nuns, the Poor Clares, who had fled from France during the Revolution and who occupied a house called the Nunnery or Highgates in Church Road. They did much good in the village and gave the school children one halfpenny every Christmas. Ten of them are buried in the churchyard.

The Buckinghams, who owned the hall before moving to Stowe, brought many benefits to the village. They set up a school for all the poor children of the parish, gave a weekly dole to about 20 poor persons and a dinner every Sunday to the schoolchildren and other poor people. Their greatest contribution was the setting up of a local industry plaiting straw for hats.

After a rather chequered career the hall was sold in 1854 to Mr Samuel Courtauld, head of the textile firm. He brought a great many benefits to Gosfield and the district. His works at Bocking and Halstead brought an increase in employment and general prosperity. He built Park Cottages, the present primary school, the Coffee Room and many other cottages. In 1870 members of his family built the present building at Cut Hedge, together with the two lodges and other houses at White Ash Green for the servants, including a laundry.

One very recent benefactor of the village was Maurice Rowson. A bequest by him made it possible to convert the old Sunday schoolroom to the present well appointed Maurice Rowson Hall which can be used for a multitude of functions. The rest of the money has been put into the Rowson Perpetual Memorial Fund for the benefit of the whole village.

GREAT BADDOW

Great Baddow lies on the south-eastern side of Chelmsford and grew up around the river crossing the Maldon and Southend routes. Historically it appears the village grew from two parts, the larger being concentrated round the church. Many names currently used for roads and buildings have their origins in the 15th century, such as Noakes, Rothmans, Skinners and Dines. Visitors today approaching the village from Chelmsford would be excused for finding it difficult to establish where the demarcation boundary exists.

The accepted commencement of the village from this direction is the junction of the Maldon Road and High Street. There is a convenient car park here at the side of the Blue Lion public house. Opposite the Blue Lion is Ebernezer Terrace comprising a group of small cottages, once condemned, but now attractively restored in a period style.

Going up the hill of the Maldon Road, the grassed area on the right once formed the gardens of the Vineyards, a large 18th century house, a victim of postwar development after years of neglect. The splendid trees partially screen the rather out of place office block which bears the old name. On the left of the road is a mixture of period buildings, Valley Cottages, Manor Place and Beech House which with its massive 17th century brick chimney stack, dominates this part of the road.

At the brow of the hill turn right into the Causeway. This leads past the front of the modern shopping area to a minor junction with Pump Hill. There are a couple of quaint restored cottages on the left of the road going straight on, which is called Bell Street and leads to the church and Church Street. On the right of the junction at the top of Pump Hill, is another pair of old cottages, again restored in period style.

About halfway along Bell Street on the right is a long wooden building, which is now the Bell Centre, used by different groups within the village. It used to be the library, but a bigger and very modern one has been built elsewhere.

The end of Bell Street will bring into view the junction of the High Street, Galleywood Road and Church Street with the small village green. Until a few years ago this area had a medley of small shops of varying trades. The White Horse public house, in old photographs, used to display a large sign advertising the local Baddow Brewery beer, now long since gone.

Carrying on up the slope to the left leads to the porch and pathway to the entrance of St Mary's church. The church first appears on record in 1172. Opposite the church is the newly built vicarage. The original 18th century vicarage stands by its side, showing that old and new can still live together.

From the church the road runs southerly to the village boundary with Sandon. Along this stretch of road will be found several large houses such as Baddow Place. The original Baddow Brewery building, with huge windows, built in 1868 has been renovated and is now a thriving antiques centre with small craft workshops.

🍁 GREAT BARDFIELD

In spite of invasion by the motor car, Great Bardfield still retains a goodly measure of the peaceful atmosphere of a country village which was such a feature when it was almost entirely agricultural and occupied only by farm workers or traders and craftsmen serving the farming community. Change is always going on, of course, and even in living memory there have been considerable developments and yet somehow the village retains its atmosphere. If a 15th century inhabitant could return he would at least find familiar landmarks in the church, the White Hart and Gobions, which still retain much of their 15th century appearance.

The village has many reminders of other former inhabitants. One of these was Henry Smith who was born at Great Bardfield Hall in1804, his family having farmed there for several generations. In his turn he took over the farm and in 1859 built the Town Hall, allowing it to be used for various village functions. It remained in the ownership of the Smith family until 1947 when Mr Thomas Smith, the last miller in Great Bardfield, sold it to the parish. Standing in front of the Town Hall one can see on the right hand side a small extension or outshot which is now used as a ladies cloakroom. This extension was built to house the village fire engine – another of the Smith family benefactions. The engine, a horsedrawn manual, was bought by Henry Smith in 1860 for his own use and was presented to the village by his son Henry Junior in about 1871. It remained in its Town Hall lodgings until the 1930s.

Another reminder of Henry Smith can be seen by the side of the brook in Brook Street in the shape of the fountain which Henry installed in 1861 to bring water from a spring in the Hall Meadows. Many Great Bardfield inhabitants can remember having to fetch the day's supply of water from the fountain before they went to school since mains water did not arrive in the village until the 1930s.

William Bendelow, Serjeant at Law in the time of Queen Elizabeth I, is another worthy who must be remembered. Although he practised in London and was a prominent member of Lincoln's Inn, his home was the house now known as Place Farm, and he was probably the greatest benefactor the village has ever had. The list is too long to give here but one of his gifts, a small almshouse, is now the Great Bardfield Museum and is well worth a visit. A very fine copy of his portrait can be seen in St Mary's church.

Also in the church is a funerary helm believed to be of the Lumley family who came to the village in 1623 when Sir Martin Lumley, a well known London personage, bought the manor. A cloth merchant by trade he became Master of the Drapers Company, an Alderman of the City of London, Sheriff of London and Master of Christ's Hospital, and no doubt now wanted to set himself up as a country gentleman. The old manor house, now Great Bardfield Hall farm, did not suit his purpose and he built a grand mansion in the centre of the Great Park calling it Great Lodge. The estate was sold in 1725 and soon after that the mansion was pulled down and the remaining barns and stables converted into a house. The old drive leading to Great Lodge, now called Lovers' Walk, can still be seen opposite the churchyard.

GREAT BENTLEY

Great Bentley has the largest village green in England, 43 acres; the very name means 'large green' for in Anglo-Saxon times it was a wide, flat marshy area covered in 'bent', or coarse grass, surrounded by forest, and gradually brought into use for grazing, hence 'ley' a pasture.

There has been no 'great' house attached to Great Bentley since Ulwin the Saxon who dispossessed after 1066 in favour of Alberic De Vere, Earl of Oxford, whose family were lords of the manor for the next 600 years. The De Veres were always absentee landlords, and Great Bentley never had a local Squire to run the community.

St Mary's church, on the northern corner of the green, dates from about 1135, and the font which was presented by Robert De Vere, Earl of Oxford, dates from 1221. The church has undergone much internal alteration, but the stone spiral staircase which once led up to the rood screen gallery remains.

By 1718 there was a Quaker meeting house, now a private residence, and by 1819 a Methodist chapel, later rebuilt and enlarged and still flourishing, but worshippers in both these places still kept in touch with the church. There was a Quaker churchwarden, records of the baptism of Quaker children in the church, and both Quakers and Methodists were buried in the churchyard. In the 1840s the church and chapel Sunday schools appear to have been combined, owing to lack of space in the church! In 1878 the chapel minister and congregation took part in the church Harvest Festival. This close association has continued ever since, and during the last ten years the Roman Catholics have celebrated a weekly mass in the church.

The green is, and always has been, a common, and has never been enclosed and very rarely encroached upon. The absence of a local Squire has meant that the villagers were always, to a certain degree, independent, and have guarded their rights very vigorously. In 1812 a faction, mostly farmers, wanted to enclose part of the green but villagers led by Mr Thompson (who owned a coalyard at the wharf) opposed the scheme and eventually obtained a private Act of Parliament declaring the green a common for the use and enjoyment of the villagers. Again in the 1890s a faction wanted to restrict grazing rights, but the Act was invoked by Mr Wright, a grocer (whose descendants owned the shop until it closed in the 1970s) and the green was declared inviolate. The only buildings on the green were those which the villagers wanted – a windmill from 1755 until the 1890s, and then a steam mill, which lasted until 1925. There is now little trace of these, or of a carpenter's and coffinmaker's shed, but a disused forge still stands and the chapel which is still very much in use. About 30 years ago the village was again rent asunder by a proposal to build a new village hall on the green. After much heated argument and many meetings the Parish Council organised a vote, and the motion was defeated. The village had to wait for its new hall, now built on council land opposite the railway station.

Cricket has been played on the green since the 18th century and football probably since a much earlier date, and still the teams flourish, but maypole dancing and fairs have rather fallen into abeyance, with fetes, carnivals and gymkhanas taking their place. The flourishing community spirit brought honour to the village and its people in the year 2000 when Great Bentley won the Village of the Year competition.

The southern boundary includes the tidal creek which flows, eventually, into the river Colne and from medieval times until the coming of the railway the Bentley wharfs were an important trade centre for shallow-draft vessels plying between here and London. The old wharfs are now silted up and returning to salt marsh, but one still remains reasonably clear and until the recent water pollution scares was a pleasant swimming place at high tide – if one did not mind the occasional eel slithering across!

🍁 GREAT BROMLEY

Centuries ago a stream, now the Frating Brook, carved out a shallow valley and on its gentle northern slope rose in the 14th century one of the finest churches in Essex. It is the centre of the scattered village of Great Bromley, the school, the post office-shop, the Spread Eagle, which closed as an inn in 1987, and a cluster of dwellings, some old, most new.

The road through the village comes from Dedham through Burnt Heath, a 'waste' when the church was young, but where there was the village forge. The smith was still working there 60 years ago.

Just across the brook Mary Lane branches off eastwards to Cowey Green, one of the village's three 'Green' outposts. A footpath from a bend in the lane, across the fields still exists and nearby, until they were condemned and pulled down some 60 years ago, were cottages called Guildhall and the Workhouse, which were of possibly Tudor origin.

Simon and Gregory Stone went from Great Bromley to a new life in New England in 1635. The brothers settled first at Watertown, a few miles up the Charles river from Boston, but after a year or so Gregory moved on to Cambridge, Massachusetts. Both became worthy citizens, as their memorials in their local churchyards proclaim. Some 270 years later their descendants gave them another memorial, the window in the church where they were baptised, St George's, Great Bromley.

In two lights stand St Simon the Apostle and St Gregory the Great. The increase decorates the top lights with the seals of Massachusetts and Essex, one to each side and in another stands an Indian. A Latin motto, translated, runs 'The generations pass into the coming generations', truly so of the Stones. Simon's and Gregory's descendants, though few still bear the name, now number more than 1,000. Many of them visit their ancestral home and they maintain association with (to paraphrase) their forefathers' rude hamlet. Never a church appeal goes out but there is a generous response from Massachusetts and many other states.

GREAT CANFIELD

Great Canfield, mentioned in the Domesday Book in 1086, now has about eight miles of road linking the four Ends which comprise Bacon End, Church End, Helman's Cross and Hope End. The old roads of Oak Lane (now called Cuckoo's Lane) and Boxley Lane were old drove roads.

The church, a Grade I listed building dates from the first part of the 12th century with the beautiful east wall mural of Mary and Child believed to have been completed in 1250. The mural was hidden during the Reformation by the memorial of the Wiseman family, but was rediscovered in 1879 when the memorial was removed for repairs and rehung on the south wall. The Elizabethan chalice and paten, used now only for special services, are dated 1577.

The village stocks, last recorded in use in 1860 for a case of drunkenness had disappeared but a modern copy has now been erected. The whipping post remains at Helman's Cross. Elizabeth Abbot, who lived at Helman's, was burnt as a witch in 1683.

Although Great Canfield now has no school, shop or pub, the latter closing in the early part of the last century, along with the school, the spirit and life of the village is alive and very active. Whether city commuter or farmer, the cricket club, over 60s club, indoor bowling club or Canfield Society, all make great contributions to the activities, friendliness and unity of the village. The threat to English country life and prime farming land posed by the possible further development of Stansted Airport still worries many villagers who are steadfast in their determination to try to protect and preserve the environment for the next 20 centuries.

🍁 GREAT HOLLAND

The parish of Great Holland is a small village surrounded by sea, brook and railway, south-west of Frinton-on-Sea and is set in a wide expanse of flat, mostly arable farming country.

As a small community bordering the sea, Great Holland was a notorious place for smugglers in the 18th century. When a boat came ashore, the labourers assisted in 'working the goods' and frequently became addicted to alcohol with such constant supplies of gin. Several older properties including The Ship and the Lion's Den are reputed to have cellars and passageways leading seawards for the concealment of the contraband.

Great Holland manor house was on the site of today's Manor Farm. It is known to have had a court held there in 1545 and to have been given for the use of Anne Boleyn's father, but the Ecclesiastical Court House in Little Clacton Road dated back to the 12th century.

The village has two churches. The Wesleyan Methodist church was built in 1928 at a cost of £3000. All Saints church dates back to the 13th century but, with the exception of the west tower, was rebuilt in 1866. The tower of red brick with black brick diapering is one of the best preserved in East Anglia.

Legend tells of Miss Barron, formerly a wealthy resident of nearby Walton-on-the-Naze, who in her advancing years became most eccentric and devoted to goats. Walton parish had approached the Barron Bell Trust for a peal of bells but, unfortunately for them, two of Miss Barron's goats strayed from her garden and wandered into the churchyard where they were seen by a passing churchwarden. He dispatched the goats with his boot but Miss Barron had witnessed the incident and in her indignation gave the peal of bells to Great Holland instead.

The village green, now with its swings, slide and see-saw is well patronised by the younger generation, but 150 years ago it was used by the labourers as a donkey park. As many as 26 donkeys were left to graze on the green and 'the music from them was heard all over the parish'. Here it was traditional for bonfires, annual fairs and Methodist meetings to be held. The latter, preached from a borrowed farm wagon were well attended.

In 1975 East Essex Iron Works known as 'the Foundry' by the villagers and founded by the Ratcliffe family, finally came to a halt after almost a century of the very specialised production of cast, chilled ploughshares, distributed worldwide.

The present population of 800 is steadily increasing. No longer is it a farming community. With the advent of modern machinery the labour force has dwindled to an expert few.

🍁 GREAT HORKESLEY

The lovely little 12th century parish church of All Saints, stands on the northern boundary of the village on a hill overlooking the Stour valley and Suffolk beyond.

Yet the village pre-dates the church by many centuries for Great Horkesley is one of the oldest inhabited places in the country, with Iron Age earthworks still to be seen in Pitchbury Wood and very early tiles and pottery, made from the local clay, discovered within the parish. Roman coins have turned up in field and garden and there is a legend that Queen Boadicea fought a battle near Pitchbury Wood. The long straight road that slashes through Horkesley from north to south is a Roman road and was itself superimposed upon an ancient time-worn track.

The name Horkesley means 'a shelter for lambs' and the village has always been an agricultural area and remains so today. In earlier times the houses were largely at the northern end, but building has gradually moved southward towards Colchester. Recent housing developments have brought an increase in population and local life flourishes, with an active church and thriving school, and a wide variety of clubs and organisations.

Great Horkesley has a quite undramatic history but sometimes a controversial character has appeared in its midst, ruffling placid waters. During the 18th century just such a person became rector of Great Horkesley. He was the Reverend John Brown who was presented to the living in 1756 by his patron, Lord Hardwicke. John Brown was highly gifted: a scholar, a dramatist, a poet as well as a churchman.

In 1756, the village was very small, with a population of 450. It was a place of farms and farm-workers, small tradesmen and craftsmen. With the exception of two Quaker families living at Spratts Marsh the village people were Church of England. In general life was peaceful and in step with the rhythm of the seasons.

Unfortunately such a simple rural environment did not suit John Brown's volatile temperament and soon after his arrival in Great Horkesley his parishioners were complaining that he spent too much of his time in London.

And so he did. Whilst he was rector of Great Horkesley Brown wrote two major plays, *Barbarossa* and *Aethelstane*, both of them tragedies, which were produced at Drury Lane Theatre with the famous actor David Garrick himself appearing in them.

GREAT & LITTLE LEIGHS

The parishes of Great and Little Leighs are a combination of two villages, but are one community. The villages are nestled between Chelmsford to the south, Braintree to the north, Boreham to the east, and Felsted to the west.

The church of St Mary the Virgin stands in the middle of the parish on rising ground about the river Ter, which gives its name to the next village, Terling. A hundred yards from the church is the manor house of Lyons Hall, called in the Domesday Book, Laghen Beria. Until 1726 the patrons of the church were the lords of the manor of Great Leighs (Lyons Hall), but since then the patrons have been the College of the Blessed Virgin Mary and All Saints, Lincoln, commonly called Lincoln College, Oxford, and the rectors of the church have been members of the college. The church tower is one of six round towers in Essex. The tower was probably a place of defence against North Sea pirates coming up the Chelmer and Blackwater.

Most of the land around the villages was farmland, either arable or grazing land. With the population growing, the villages were now beginning to expand further towards the High Road, which is now the A131. A new government school was built for all village children to attend. After 132 years, this also had to close in 1977, owing to further expansion to the two villages. A new modern school was built on another site which connected up with the building of a private housing estate during the early 1970s.

Another larger estate of houses was built behind the first one, and this was where Mr J. S. Wright had first started and built up a willow merchant business, employing many men since 1894. The main product of the business is cricket bats, which are exported worldwide.

A good landmark for visitors is the St Anne's Castle public house. This is right on the crossroads of the A131. St Anne's Castle appears on the Greenwood's map of Essex, published as long ago as 1824. It is also said to be the oldest public house in England, and to be haunted.

St John's church, Little Leighs, stands just off the A131 turning into Church Lane, from Blacksmith's Corner. The church was erected by the Normans after the conquest. Today's building gives an initial impression of being Victorian as a major restoration was carried out at the end of the 19th century, but it retains much of its original work and many interesting features. It is said there is a passageway underground which goes through to Leez Priory. The priory and Warrocks was founded in 1229 by Sir Ralph Gernon for Augustinian friars (Black Friars or Canons). The patronage and advowson remained in that family until Henry VIII's time in 1537. He granted it to Sir Richard Rich (afterwards Lord Rich), who was that year elected Speaker of the House of Commons, and in 1548 became Lord Chancellor. He founded Felsted School in 1546. In 1550 Leez Priory was one of the most important private residences in Essex. It was described as a worldly paradise.

As you come from the church back on to the A131 the old forge stood, hence Blacksmith's Corner. This no longer operates, but was of course very much a working forge in years past, with horses being shod and iron tyres made for the farm carts.

🍁 GREAT OAKLEY

A settlement at Great Oakley has been in existence since 3000 BC. A primitive pot dating from that period was found south of the village during the 1950s and it is now to be seen in Colchester castle. The village became known as Acley, which means 'oak pasture', when the Saxons invaded and settled in the area. Then the Normans came and the village was surveyed, and it was listed in the Domesday Book of 1086, under the name of Acclei.

There are many oak trees still standing in and around the village, even after the loss of many during the great storm of 1987. Oak trees from Great Oakley were taken to Harwich to be used in ship building, so Great

Oakley's oak trees no doubt travelled the world when ships were still made of wood and really were 'hearts of oak'.

The village still boasts an industry which sends a commodity over the world and that is an explosives factory. It is housed on an island in the Hamford Waters, north-east of the village. Bramble Island, linked to the mainland by a causeway, was acquired by the Explosives Company in 1905. It was a small affair at first. Cases of explosives were ordered three or four at a time and these were loaded on to a cart and drawn by horse to Thorpe le Soken station, six miles away and sent off by train. Later a dock was constructed and barges were used. The First World War caused the factory to step up production considerably, so it made a great contribution to the war effort. Then again in the Second World War its goods were in great demand.

There have been a number of accidental explosions at the factory, one in 1942 when three employees died and three of the workers were awarded the Edward Medal later converted to the George Cross. In the east coast floods of 1953, three employees received awards for their bravery in disposing of explosives left in a very dangerous condition by the rising tides. For their courage they received the British Empire Medal.

In the early 1900s Great Oakley was a large and thriving community, with many shops, good communication between Harwich Clacton and Colchester.

In the early 1920s there were many activities in the village, such as a football and a cricket team. There was even a ladies football team! It was reported at one time, in the local paper however, that the goalkeeper had to play for her team in a long skirt because her husband would not allow her to wear shorts. Fancy going for a ball in a skirt!

🍁 GREAT TOTHAM

Great Totham is a very large parish, which includes the Island of Osea in the Blackwater estuary. The village is long, consisting of two parts separated by about a mile and a half.

The south part of the village contains the lovely St Peter's church, dating back to Norman times. There is also the Barn Chapel, with its thatched roof, which became a chapel in 1822 when Mr Isaac Foster donated his barn for a place of worship for non-conformists after hearing John Raven, a ploughman, preaching to his fellow workers.

The village school celebrated its centenary in 1977, but by that time the Victorian building, though still in existence and used for storage, had been replaced by a large modern school on a different site. There is also a Grade II listed building known as the Honywood School founded in the mid 19th century as a church school by the Honywood family of Marks Hall, Coggeshall who had inherited the manor of Great Totham. This is still in use as the church hall.

In Great Totham North there is a United Reformed church dating from 1871, recently refurbished and used not only for services but for many other activities such as the pre-school playgroup. Just around the corner adjoining the small village green, is the late 17th century Compasses pub.

According to the old maps, before the time of the enclosures, the outskirts of Great Totham North were part of Tiptree Heath, then well known as a haunt of smugglers, this being celebrated in the name of a house in Mountains Road, Spirits Hall. The 'mountain' in question is Beacon Hill, at 83 metres one of the highest points in the county and probably the original place of settlement, giving the name Totham, possibly derived from the Saxon, meaning 'look out' or 'hill top dwelling'.

The Prince of Wales in Totham South, was completely gutted by fire in 1990, so many historic features have been lost for ever, but it has been rebuilt and reopened, the first pint pulled by Ted Newton, who was born there over 80 years ago.

Another recent change in the village is the completion of a new extension to the Norman church of St Peter, well blended in with the old building and very well used.

Great Totham has changed a great deal over the centuries, some of the crafts and trades having died out or been brought up to date. There are no longer any walking-stick makers, brickworks or saddlers, but there is a coachbuilder's and a thriving haulage business. The old gravel pits have become recreation areas for children or fishing lakes.

🍁 GREAT WAKERING

Great Wakering is one of several village communities in the green and pleasant marsh-lands of south-east Essex.

The Romans produced much of their salt here, by creating evaporation tanks, large vessels beneath which fires would reduce readily available sea-water. As this method of extraction declined, the abandoned sites and apparatus gradually disintegrated, leaving the area covered with burnt red-clay, thus giving rise to sites now known as Red-hills. The available clay was also used in brick-making, an industry that has been carried on in the village over many centuries.

The area being marsh-land, was very damp and supported many associated diseases which were particularly detrimental to women. This, plus the appalling death rate of women through childbirth etc, created a deficit of females, and replacements were persuaded to come from the more northerly counties to make up the shortfall. While being damp, the average rainfall is the lowest in the country, and Great Wakering's greatest claim to fame, is to be entered in the *Guinness Book of Records*, as the 'Driest Place in the United Kingdom'.

The sea has always played an important role in the life of the village. Apart from its harvest of fish, oysters and wildfowl, it enabled the village to transport its surplus products to various markets and to import other essentials, such as spirits, tobacco, silks etc, that is provided the Customs men did not get there first, for the winding shallow creeks were a haven for smugglers.

The area is rich in stories of witchcraft, ghosts and superstition, much of which is centred on the parish church of St Nicholas. The nave and chancel are said to have been built about 1100 while the tower, porches etc were added over the following centuries. It is thought that the church is at least the second such structure to stand on the site, replacing a Saxon church which served as the burial place of two murdered princes, Ethelbert and Ethelred.

Until recent years the village was a typical linear one. The High Street, approximately one mile long, runs directly east and west with the parish church at the eastern end. Many of the wooden cottages have been demolished to make way for modern developments, resulting in a virtual doubling of the population.

Little Wakering Hall Lane runs past the village allotments to the 15th century manor house of Wakering Hall, alleged to be haunted by the ghost of Betty Bury, a serving maid. Close to the Hall stands a large 17th century barn. Near to the lane stands the Evangelical church, formerly the Peculiar People's church. This religious sect was started in this district.

Turning into Common Road you pass the village pond, used in earlier times for the washing down of carts. The road continues through the common to the creeks at Mill Head. The surrounding creeks are a haven for many types of wildfowl and a large proportion of the world's population of Brent geese winter here each year. Here, at Mill Head, was situated the 19th century brickfield, where over 20 Thames barges were used to transport bricks to London. Gradually these were phased out due to the growth of motor transport in the 1930s. Unfortunately the beautiful sight of the barges is but a memory and the old brickfield is now a refuse tip.

The White Hart is an attractive 17th century building and stands opposite the old village school built in 1876 and enlarged over the years. The school is currently home to a Community Centre and a Youth Club. The Community Centre, run by volunteers, is used by many of the village's clubs and organisations, thus keeping this old building as a valuable asset to the village.

🍁 GREAT WALTHAM

Once known as Waltham Magna, the village lies five miles north of Chelmsford, and is about halfway between London and Cambridge. The village, which retains much of its old architecture (the Historic Monuments Commission having noted more than 80 old houses within the bounds of the parish) has extended its housing considerably twice since the Second World War, and now numbers among its residents many commuters to London, changing the pre-war, almost solely farming village into a very mixed community.

The church of St Mary and St Lawrence with its peal of eight bells, the oldest cast in 1336 and the newest in 1769, contains traces of Norman work incorporating Roman bricks. The Norman font bowl was discovered under the floor in the restoration of 1961 and is now in the porch, and the stair doorway and windows in the tower are Norman. A panel listing the names of vicars from 1361 can be seen on the south wall and includes the eminent historian Nicholas Tindal who had Philip Morant, the historian of Essex, as his curate from 1722 to 1732. It also includes Canon Hulton (1876–1906) whose benefactions to church and parish include the village hall, the almshouses, the schoolmaster's house (now a private house opposite the school) and much else.

Langleys lies in its own park to the north-west of the village. The estate we see today began when the manor was owned in 1200 by a family named Mariskall or Marshall. From the Mariskalls the house came under the ownership in the middle of the 14th century of the Langleys, the name being retained until the present day. The Everard family were there for over 200 years and it then came into the possession of the Tufnells, who were responsible for enlarging the house and converting it into a gracious Queen Anne house.

The parish of Great Waltham is said to be one of the largest in England and includes the hamlets of Broads Green, Howe Street, Ford End and North End and bounds the medieval village of Pleshey on one side. The village itself contains two large Tudor houses, Wisemans which is reputed to have a priest's hole, and the one known to the village as The Guildhall which has magnificent Tudor chimneys and can be seen just before the church when entering the village from Chelmsford. The vicarage, opposite the west front of the church is a pleasant Queen Anne house of red brick.

There are a number of old cottages, mostly surrounding the church, one of which houses the former bakehouse. At the beginning of the 20th century there was a thriving lace industry but now there is little other industry apart from the workings of a gravel pit near Broads Green. There are three public houses in the village, listed in 1769 and still selling ale and spirits.

🍁 GREAT WARLEY

Great Warley's most famous inhabitant was Miss Ellen Willmott (1858–1934), a distinguished horticulturist whose home Warley Place stood with pride in beautiful grounds in the village. Her name has been given to many species of flowers, particularly roses. She became the first woman fellow of the Linnean Society of London, also first woman holder of the Victoria Medal of Honour created by the Royal Horticultural Society to honour the Diamond Jubilee.

Warley Place at one time stood on the main road to Brentwood but later a new road was made to enable the house to overlook a large field which is a colourful sight every spring with masses of mauve and yellow crocus, and snowdrops followed by daffodils.

The old church became unusable and a temporary wooden building was erected. The present parish church of St Mary the Virgin, built in 1902 in memory of Arnold Heseltine, was erected by Mr Evelyn Heseltine, his brother. This is classed as Art Nouveau with settings of mother-of-pearl and aluminium.

Coombe Lodge, an impressive country house originally owned by the Ind family, became the property of Mr E Heseltine and was used as a hospital for wounded soldiers during the First World War. During the Second World War it was again occupied by the RAF. Great Warley was also a 'bomb alley' for enemy planes discarding their loads on return journeys and many parts of the village suffered casualties and damage to buildings, including the church hit more than once.

The village is one of the few with an active blacksmith's forge and in bygone days boasted a brick works at Stoneyhills, with a carpenter and wheelwright around the village green, which was converted into a delightful residence now known as Chestnut Tree Cottage.

GREAT WIGBOROUGH

Beautifully situated on the top of a hill at the highest point of the parish, the tree-circled tower of the church is a landmark for many miles around. The large manor of Abbots Hall belonged to the important nunnery of Barking from at least the Norman conquest (1066) until the dissolution of that monastery in 1540, and with that ownership went the patronage of the parish church, so we can assume that there was a church here from at least Norman times.

The present church of St Stephen is built of septaria and rubble with tiled roofs; owing to rebuilding and restoration it has no features earlier than the 14th century. The nave and chancel were built late in the 14th century, but the chancel has been completely rebuilt, introducing other stone. Late in the 15th century a west tower was added and also a south porch, but the tower has been rebuilt following the extensive damage done by the 1884 earthquake.

Wigborough had two martyrs, John Simpson and John Ardeley who were tried in London in front of Bishop Bonner on 25th May 1555 and burned at the stake on 10th June 1555. These two peasant farmers from Wigborough had committed no crime, but were condemned for their belief in the Protestant Church.

The other manor house in the village is Moulshams, dating from 1450 and extended in the early 16th century. It is a beautiful house, timber-framed and plastered with a red tile roof and exposed timber frame on the west side.

❦ GREENSTEAD GREEN

Greenstead Green is a small village in north Essex, three miles from Halstead and 13 miles from Colchester. There are no housing estates as such, though houses and bungalows have been built over recent years, filling in the odd spaces. There used to be a windmill in the village, but unfortunately the sails came off. For a number of years it looked like a huge pepper pot, but eventually it was taken down.

The church was built in 1845 and has played a great part in village life. The local gentry would fill the pews in the front and lesser mortals would sit nearer the back. The tall church spire is one of its outstanding features.

One vicar who made a great impression on everyone was the Rev Herbert Fasson. He came just before the outbreak of the Second World War and stayed for around 30 years. Mr Fasson was a bachelor and never owned a car. He was a familiar sight on his bicycle, his hat in one hand waving to all and sundry with a cheerful 'Hallo you!' Everything that took place in the village was of keen interest to Mr Fasson. He would run up and down the touchline during a football match crying 'Come on the Green'. He was loved and appreciated not only in his own village but in surrounding places also.

Sadly the vicarage and the village school are now private homes. The school was built in 1846 and closed in 1963. The children are taken to schools in Halstead. It is a long time now since Greenstead Green children greeted Halstead children with the cry of 'Halstead Tom Cats' and Halstead's reply was 'Greenstead Green Water Rats'!

At one stage one of the charities from the church was for loaves of bread to be given to certain people in the village. The people who were to benefit always knew when it was their turn for a loaf. Children would take the bread to the people who were unable to collect it themselves. The 'Forty Shillings' was another charity from the church which was given out twice a year. Great secrecy was observed when this was presented, but somehow the word always got around who had had the 'Forty Shillings'.

Greenstead Green is still a friendly village, though the farm workers are very few. People now commute to the various towns to their work.

❦ GREENSTED-JUXTA-ONGAR

Greensted parish is well known for its ancient Saxon church, the oldest

The Church of St Andrew, Greensted

wooden church in the world. Every year thousands of people from overseas and Great Britain visit this lovely little church. At least one service is held there every Sunday, and worship has continued for 1,300 years!

The church was probably built on the site of a pagan 'temple' by Saxon settlers before they were converted to Christianity by St Cedd. Cedd began his work in about AD 645 and the first church at Greensted was probably built soon after that date. The church is dedicated to St Andrew also suggesting a Celtic foundation. The nave was probably added about AD 845. Dark patches on some of the present upright wall timbers may be scorch marks from lamps or torches. The flat inner sides of the logs were smoothed by adzes.

The parish is small and rural and the church has a peaceful setting. At one time Greensted had two mills, one a windmill, and the other a watermill: no trace of them remain today. There was once also a large open green, and although the postal address remains Greensted Green, the green has been enclosed and taken into adjoining land.

Between Greensted church and the Drill House Inn at a T-junction is Drapers Corner. It is claimed that nearly 200 years ago a man named Draper was hanged there for stealing sheep – his ghost still haunts this corner!

Close to the church is Greensted Hall, the site of a Saxon manor. The present house dates from the 15th century and was altered by Alexander Cleeve whose initials are seen on the front facade. It later belonged to the Budworth family, descendants of the Cleeves and whose memorials are in the church.

The village has connections with the Tolpuddle Martyrs. Six Dorset farm labourers were given harsh sentences for agitating for higher wages and better working conditions by forming a trade union at Tolpuddle. After their conviction in 1834 they were condemned to transportation to Australia for seven years. In England there was a public outcry at their harsh treatment and sentences, and eventually their sentences were commuted in 1837.

They were unable to resettle in Dorset owing to the farmers' opposition, so they were granted farm tenancies in Greensted juxta Ongar and High Laver. One of their tenancies was for Newhouse Farm, Greensted Green. The land was in poor condition and difficult to farm – one of the fields is still known as 'Starve Goose Field'! While in Greensted James Brine married the daughter of a fellow prisoner, Elizabeth Stanfield. The 'martyrs' tenancies were not renewed owing to local opposition and they emigrated to Canada.

🍁 HADLEIGH

Investigations indicate that a settlement here was inhabited during the early Iron Age. The name Hadleigh goes back to Saxon times.

Hadleigh has two prominent edifices. The first is the church which was built about 1140 by the Normans and probably takes the place of an earlier timber structure. It stands on top of a hill and is older than Hadleigh castle, the other famous building. The interior of the church has some interesting features, the most important being a wall painting of Thomas a Becket thought to have been painted in 1170 or 1171.

It was Henry III who granted a Royal Licence to Hubert de Burgh to build the castle in 1231. In 1539 Henry VIII gave the castle to Anne of Cleves and later to his last Queen Catherine Parr. By the 17th century it had become ruinous. It has been immortalised by John Constable, the famous painter.

A tunnel was supposed to link the castle with the Castle Inn, a mile distant, and contraband is said to have poured into the village via this subterranean route. There is certainly an ancient cellar at the inn, but a tunnel that length would have been a major engineering feat. Its existence was probably more imaginary than factual.

It is known, however, that the Castle Inn, then called the Boar's Head, was used as a hide-out for smugglers and their goods. And when demobilised soldiers and their wives settled in the wooded district after the Napoleonic wars, smuggling and crime made the area notorious.

Things changed with the arrival of the Peculiar People, who took their name from a Bible text: 'the Lord hath chosen thee to be a peculiar people' (Deut 14 v2). They converted the populace to agriculture and a more settled way of life.

This dedicated sect is now called the Union of Evangelical Churches. Just one of their three churches remains. It is a small building, but an even smaller place of worship is the little timber-built St Michael's church at the corner of St Michael's Road and Bramble Road. About 90 years old, it can hold 50 people at a pinch. Set in a green woodland setting, it would be a tourist attraction if it were not so far off the beaten track.

Hadleigh's most famous citizen in the 19th century was Wizard Cunning Murrell who cured people's ailments by a combination of incantation and herbalism. In his working life he was a shoemaker, but colourful tales are still told of him being involved with smuggling, witchcraft, fortune-telling, magic and astronomy.

The Salvation Army has played a major part in the history of Hadleigh, and their band plays most Sunday mornings in its streets. Some 3,000 acres of wooded slopes around Hadleigh castle were bought in 1890 by General Booth and a farm colony started. Ex-Borstal boys, people on probation, and problem cases of all kinds, passed through the gates on which were emblazoned the words: 'Enter His Courts With Praise'. They were taught farming skills, and for most of them it was just the break with their past life that they needed.

Today we have Hadleigh Castle Country Park, with walks giving good views of the Thames Estuary.

🍁 HADSTOCK

Hadstock is a small village of about 300 souls, situated in the north-west corner of the county, within hailing distance of Cambridgeshire on two of its borders, and close to Suffolk.

St Botolph's is the main feature of interest and is an early Saxon building. In AD 654 Abbot Botolph started to build a monastery at Icanho. In AD 680 he died and was buried there. From ancient documents in Ely Cathedral it would seem that Icanho was the early name for Hadstock. During extensive archaeological excavations inside the church in 1974, an empty early Saxon grave was found against the east wall of the south transept. It was very shallow, so that most of the coffin was above ground and that fact, and its position, denoted that it had been the burial place of a very important personage. The body had been exhumed at a later date, and it is known that the body of St Botolph was removed and his relics distributed to the monasteries of Ely, Thorney and to the King's reliquary.

From circumstantial evidence, therefore, it would seem that this was the site of St Botolph's monastery. The chapel where the coffin was found has always been known as St Botolph's chapel. From further finds during the excavations this feeling has been reinforced.

There are many interesting features of Saxon origin in the church, but the main door is of special note. It is the oldest door in the UK to be in constant use and is mentioned in the Guinness Book of Records.

A 'holy' well is situated by the western wall of the churchyard and was said to possess healing properties. It was known as a cure for scrofula. It is fed by a spring that never dries up, and until 1939 was the source of the village's drinking water. On a certain day a young girl would drop a 'ring' into the well and she was supposed to dream of the lad she would marry. This seemed like a fairy tale until two rings were found in modern days. In the late Victorian era, the rector of the day built a new rectory on the slope above the church and installed a 'modern' drainage system. It is said that one member of the rectory staff was a typhoid carrier, and leaks from the drains trickled downhill and into the well. Rumour has it that 40 folk from the village died, although no account of the deaths can be found in registers of the period. Presumably any illusion of the water's healing powers must have vanished!

From the 1950s to the 1970s the only mounted Scout troop in the UK was based in Hadstock. The troop was used by the Chief Scout as a Guard of Honour at Jamborees and when the Royal Show was held in Cambridge they gave a display. All Scouts learnt to ride and the troop only ceased when the Scoutmaster had to retire.

The oxlip and bee orchid have always been found around the village, but nowadays in restricted numbers, although they are protected. The Essex Naturalist Trust owns a small reserve in the parish and there is a very ancient wood which is part of what was the great forest that covered the area in bygone years. It is in private hands and being well cared for. Many footpaths encircle the parish and lead to neighbouring villages, a significant pointer to the days not so long ago when journeys were mainly made on foot, whilst the bridleways were the horse 'lanes' of the area.

🍁 HATFIELD BROAD OAK

Approached along winding country roads and lanes, Hatfield Broad Oak is an ancient roadside village; a compact village with a definite beginning and an end.

Enter the village at half-light, when narrow roads blend with silhouettes of uneven pitched roofs, bulging walls and timbered buildings, and one can easily glimpse back to medieval times! A bird's eye view reveals a remarkable network of roof-tops and an intricate, misshapen patchwork of outhouses and gardens, interlocking with one another as the pattern of a jigsaw. Certainly not the dream of modern planners, but a rare insight into early building skills and craftsmanship. Missing now is the monastery with cloistered courtyard, as is the block of houses which once projected into the middle of the High Street to enclose the Town Square and Market Place.

On the approach to the village from Hatfield Heath, up Feathers Hill, one is faced by the Court House, so named because this building once contained a local seat of justice in which court sittings were held. It later became the Plume of Feathers Inn (hence Feathers Hill) but has now reassumed the name of the Court House.

In the village centre near the village pump is an archway with a 15th century gable and fretted bargeboards which used to span an old street, leading through the arch into the Chepingfield (sale ground) of olden days.

The Cock Inn is an ancient hostelry mentioned in 14th century documents. The visitor to Hatfield Broad Oak can be sure of a good welcome and excellent food here, and can usually sample the famous Broad Oak Sausage, made by the local butcher to the same recipe that has been renowned since the maiden voyage of the *Queen Mary* in the mid-1930s.

The village and surrounding countryside is of course dominated by St Mary's church with its 81 foot tower, which houses a peal of eight bells. Of prime interest is the clergy vestry built in 1708 to contain the famous library, covering such subjects as philosophy, theology, history and biography; also a Breeches bible and a Vinegar bible.

One of the highlights of the church and village calendar is the Hatfield Broad Oak Flower Festival held annually over the Spring Bank Holiday, when the church is vibrant and aglow with flowers of unimaginable contrast and beauty. Many other events and concerts take place in the church during the year – as well as in the well-equipped village hall, which nearer to Christmas time is home to the traditional and famous HBO Pantomime – a wonderful gathering point for all the family and visitors.

🍁 HATFIELD HEATH

Despite the address, (Bishop's Stortford, Herts), Hatfield Heath is four miles over the border. Upon entering the Heath on one of the six main roads you will circulate round the large village green, our pride and joy, upon which lies the cricket field spreading its green acres and stretching back in time beyond living memory.

In front of the Post Office Stores, on a grassy mound, is the ancient village pump, which used to augment the many 40 ft wells in cottages and houses around the green. From this there is a good view over the green of the church of Holy Trinity and its wooded graveyard, a little over 100 years old, small, but large enough for these modern times.

Opposite Holy Trinity is the village junior school, its foundation stone bearing the inscription: 'The Very Reverend Montague Butler, Master of Trinity College Cambridge, Wednesday 25th October 1899'. He was grandfather of R. A. Butler, Minister of Education whose Education Act of 1940 brought secondary education for all pupils. The log books, dating back to 1830, chart the progress of education in the village from the early dame school. Notably, one log book bears the signature of the famous poet

Matthew Arnold (1822–1880) whose father, so well remembered in *Tom Brown's Schooldays*, was the legendary Doctor Thomas Arnold, headmaster of Rugby School.

A large windmill once graced the village hard by Mill House and Mill Cottage on the south side of the green. It was demolished in 1908, being overtaken by progress in the shape of a new, engine-powered mill to the west end of the village on the Stortford Road. This mill in turn was superseded by the larger mill in Bishop's Stortford, about 1970. It remains smartly decorated but redeveloped into small businesses and offices.

Why so many main roads passing through here? A record number for an English village we're told! They grew in the 17th and 18th centuries when London was expanding. Flour and produce from the wheat-growing parts of Suffolk were hauled in by large horse-drawn vehicles en route to the London markets, often staying here overnight. Hence, also, four inns supplemented by the many unlicensed alehouses prevalent in those days.

Corringales, situated on the outskirts of the village, is a link with Saxon times as it was once a Saxon hall. The founder, a certain 'Curra', built a hall known as 'Curras Ing Hall' in AD 836. It would have been a large hall with a hole in the roof for smoke emission. Ongars was mentioned in the Domesday Book. Friars Farm once paid its rent to the friary which was situated at Hatfield Broad Oak. Lea Hall, on the Broad Oak Road, was a moated manor, having still the remains of a moat behind which the stock was driven for protection when raiders from the sea were in the area.

There is still a lord of the manor who owns the soil of the village green and four houses whose owners, known as 'Commoners', have vested in them some 'Rights of Common'. These individuals' rights are (1) right of loppage, to gather wood for burning; (2) pannage, the right to pasture swine on the common land; and (3) the right of the warren, the right to hunt rabbits on the common. Not, however, the 'right of chase', ie the hunting of animals. This was the prerogative of the lord only. In medieval times Hatfield Heath was but a clearing in the Great Forest which covered most of England, hence its name, Heath meaning 'a clearing surrounded by trees'. Hatfield Forest, but three miles away, is a reminder of days gone by.

☘ HATFIELD PEVEREL

Draw two diagonal lines across a map of Essex and there, almost plumb in the centre, you will find Hatfield Peverel.

Hatfield is from the Saxon 'Hadfelda' meaning 'a clearing in the wild uncultivated ground'. William I took as a mistress one Ingelrica, a lady fair, and daughter of Ingelric, a Saxon noble and court scribe; she bore the King an illegitimate son, also to be named William and later to become owner of Nottingham Castle. Eventually the King tired of her and Ingelrica was married off to one of his knights, Ranulph de Peverel. Amongst his estates in Essex was Hadfelda and when Ranulph's own name of Peverel was added to 'Hadfelda', we have the name by which it is known today: Hatfield Peverel.

It is Ranulph's wife Ingelrica, and their legitimate son, again called William, whom we have to thank for the Norman church, at some later date to be dedicated to St Andrew. This was built as part of the old priory, for after the death of the King in 1087, Ingelrica began to reflect on the misdoings of her earlier life. To make atonement, she founded in the village, on land given her by her husband, a college of secular canons dedicated to St Mary Magdalene; here she spent the remaining years of her life. After her death around 1100, William her son carried on her work, changing the order into a priory of Benedictine monks subordinate to the abbey of St Albans and dedicated to the Virgin Mary. All that remains now of the original priory is the church; the present impressive building bearing that name was built in the 18th century.

To round off the story of Ingelrica, a legend exists which says that the Devil vowed he would have her soul whether she was buried inside or outside the church. This problem, so we are led to believe, was neatly overcome by burying her in the wall itself – neither inside nor out. Believe what you will, but we all love a legend. A 13th century effigy, reputed to be that of Ingelrica lies on the window sill of the north wall, next to the organ.

Of the several old houses in Hatfield Peverel, the oldest is Vinehurst in the Street; it is directly opposite the post office (itself 15th century) and has been authentically dated to around 1350. The previous owners told of two ghostly presences, one kindly and affectionately known as Silas, whilst the other, unnamed, manifested itself, even on a warm day, by a sense of chill and a feeling of unease, and at which the dog would howl all night. On such nights the lady of the house would pull the bedcovers tightly over her head!

A further strange tale is that of 'Shaen's dog'. This creature, big and with glaring eyes, was said to haunt the road between Crix Corner and the bottom of the hill on the approach to the village from the Chelmsford direction. A waggoner who lashed out at him was consumed with fire – together with his waggon.

Whilst in the vicinity of the post office, spare a glance at Hill House, next to Vinehurst, which was reputed to have been built by smugglers and with a system of cellars. When Excise men became suspicious and organised a raid, it is said that the villagers lay on their stomachs to drink, as the spirits ran down Hatfield Hill.

On the other side of the Street and clearly visible is the tall spire of the Methodist chapel, but you will look in vain for the weathercock – on 22nd April 1884 it was toppled, a casualty of the earthquake in the Colchester area. Nearby is the William Boosey public house, formerly the Crown and mentioned in deeds dated 1607. Not only has it served as a place for refreshment, but almost 200 years ago it was a station for fish-curing. Big wagons rumbled in from Lowestoft and Yarmouth and deposited their fish at a building behind the hostelry. The owners, the Ong family, used sawdust to fuel the fires, and the villagers brought their hams there to cure.

🍁 HELIONS BUMPSTEAD

Helions Bumpstead is a border parish in many senses since it is adjacent to both the Cambridgeshire and Suffolk borders and is situated immediately below the watershed between the boulder clay uplands of Essex and the chalklands of Cambridgeshire, a geological border which once formed the northern boundary of the great forest of Essex, the remnant of which is represented today by Epping Forest.

It is difficult to assess when the village proper came into existence but the building of the church near the crossroads by the local benefactor, probably in the 12th century, obviously established the position of the village. The attraction of tradesmen such as a blacksmith and wheelwright, and the provision of a beerhouse and a bakery of course followed, thus creating the nucleus of a conventional village and a centre for the inhabitants of the outlying hamlets.

The Domesday Book records that the parish contained four manors, namely Horsham, now represented by Horsham Hall Farm at the Suffolk end; Bumpstead, now Bumpstead Hall Farm on the road, midway between

Helions and Steeple Bumpstead; Helions, now Helions Farm, close to the village centre; and Olmstead, now Olmstead Hall Farm at the far Cambridge end of the parish.

Apart from farming there was a cottage industry in the 15th century engaged in spinning, and to a lesser extent weaving. The area embracing the towns of Dunmow, Coggeshall, Braintree and Bocking became a virtual industrial centre for these activities. The villagers of Helions Bumpstead formed a guild known as the Guild of St Peter of Spinners and Weavers – a craft union – who held their meetings in their 'Yeld Hall'. But the prosperity brought to the area faded away and whereas in Colchester 20,000 had been employed, that number had dwindled to 150 by 1790. In 1750 in Dunmow the best spinners could earn eightpence per day, by 1790 they could only get fourpence. In the villages the situation was worse.

In the 19th century another cottage industry evolved, straw plaiting. It had its advantages since the raw material was freely available and all the female members of the family could participate. Since the straw bonnet was de rigueur for all females from all walks of life at work or at play, the demand was never-ending – until of course the straw bonnet went out of fashion. In the 1851 census no less than 74 women, wives and daughters of farmers and farm labourers alike, are listed as straw plaiters.

🍁 HERONGATE

Herongate has a great history. Heron Hall was the place of exile of the Tyrell family after one of them unfortunately killed William II (nicknamed 'Rufus' because of his red hair) in the New Forest, claiming that he mistook him for a squirrel! The Hall was originally moated, and in the fields behind it are the banks which formed the old heronry. The sign for the Boar's Head public house shows the Tyrell crest, a boar's head holding a peacock's feather in its mouth. There is a local legend that Dick Turpin, closely followed by those trying to arrest him, jumped from an upstairs window of the pub and got away.

Robert Graves, in one of his books about the Emperor Claudius, has the description of an ambush planned in this area by the 'Heron King' (a man on stilts) in an attempt to stop the march of the Romans on Chelmsford.

There used to be a windmill at the top of Mill Hill and the common once stretched from the south of Button Common to Common Road, Ingrave.

Lord Petre owns most of the local common land and has the right, confirmed by Act of Parliament in 1979, to hold a manor court here. According to the Act, it is 'to manage the land' he owns, and it is one of only some dozen such courts still in existence in England. The Petre family take a great interest in Herongate and Ingrave.

The old Tudor Hall, replaced by Thorndon Hall in Ingrave, used to stand in the woods west of Herongate. Instead of reconstructing it, the Petre family had it pulled down. It would have been too difficult to bring it up to the then modern standards; for instance, as at Weald Hall, all the bedrooms led off each other.

There is a letter in the London Record Office from the then rector of Ingrave asking the Government to station troops at the foot of Brook Street Hill, Brentwood, to prevent the anti-Catholic Gordon rioters, in 1780, from marching against the Catholic Petre family.

There is a Tyrell Society in the USA and from time to time various descendants of the family still come to visit Herongate, the home of their ancestors.

HEYBRIDGE & LANGFORD

Heybridge and Langford have seen many changes over the years but one thing that is unchanged are the beautiful walks by the canal and riverside. The long awaited bypass from Maldon to Heybridge opened in 1990, takes up a lot of the countryside, but the developers kept most of the footpaths where possible and in some cases have improved upon them.

At Langford, one can see an imposing red brick building built in 1879 to replace an earlier wooden building which was burnt down, and which is now known as Langford Mill. Next to it is the Mill House and the unique St Giles' church where the Norman apse is at the west end. Formerly it had an apse at each end. The church was restored in Victorian times by the Honourable Mary Byron, whose husband Frederick was the rector from 1890–1913. The family lived in Langford Hall, a large Georgian house that can be seen behind the church. Several members of the family are buried in the church grounds.

The chief occupation of the inhabitants of Langford was farming until the 1920s when the waterworks pumping and treatment plants were built and employed about 50 men. Langford today has no shop, no post office and no public house, just a small village hall that was originally a cow shed. Langford is a charming and unspoilt village.

The name of Edward Hammond Bentall, who lived between 1814 and 1898, can be remembered by the older population of Heybridge. It was because of this man's invention that many local men were employed at E H Bentall Engineers making agricultural machinery to be sold all over the world. In those days it was a familiar sight to see horse-drawn barges on the canal, loaded with the machinery that had been stored in an enormous building at the water's edge that E H Bentall had built in 1863. These were taken along the canal and through various locks to be loaded onto larger ships at Heybridge Basin and exported to many foreign countries. The barges were also used to transport coal, corn and timber in the opposite direction to Chelmsford.

The canal towpath takes you past Heybridge Cemetery where some Heybridge Basin people are buried, having travelled in a funeral cortege by canal lighter. It is only a few years ago that this procedure was witnessed, presumably at the request of a very old resident of Heybridge Basin. Today there are many boats moored by the bank and it is a haven for estuary-going yachts and cruisers. There's always someone messing about on the water.

The Basin was dug out of Heybridge Marsh in 1793 and soon after that date houses were built. There are still some attractive cottages by the locks. Unlike Langford you will find the 'Basiners' have two public houses and two churches; St George's which stands isolated and the United Reformed. A village store was opened by Samuel Purkiss in the 1900s and with his son Clifford he started a mobile shop which allowed customers to have goods on credit. Anything in the drapery line as well as boots and shoes etc could also be obtained from Sam; one could more or less tell the time by his weekly visits. Sadly all this came to an end many years ago and only a yachtsman's shop now remains by the shore.

Crossing over the footbridge on the locks, take the footpath along the sea wall heading back towards Heybridge. Looking across the river Osea, Northey Island can be seen and often flocks of birds in flight. In a short time Maldon Promenade comes into view on the opposite side with St Mary's church standing out against the skyline. The locals used to call this point of the sea wall Paddle Dock as it was a quiet and peaceful spot for taking a swim. In olden days barges en route to John Sadds timber wharf could be seen taking sawn timber to be unloaded by hand into the quayside warehouses. Timber was also transported from Heybridge Basin by horse-drawn barges along the canal to Chelmsford; sadly

Heybridge has lost that part of its heritage. Today we see timber-built holiday chalets where cattle used to graze and rabbit warrens flourished.

Eventually you leave the waterside and come into Heybridge Street, where the local shops cater for most requirements and the shopkeepers greet you on Christian name terms, which all makes for a warm and friendly community. In common with most places many changes have taken place in the village; buildings knocked down to make way for industrial sites and building sites cover many a green field. Most of the public houses and some of the shops have retained their external appearance but what was the Square is now a roundabout.

A prominent landmark is St Andrew's church, with the church hall on the opposite side of a busy narrow road. Locally known as the Waring Room, it is so called after a former vicar, Francis Waring, who died in 1833 at the age of 62. He had a son named Walter who had the original St Andrew's school built in 1869 in memory of his father. The school closed in 1900 but the Waring Room remains today as a centre for so many social events and meetings, having been brought up to date and modernised.

🍁 HIGH EASTER

The ancient village of High Easter possibly derives its name from the old English 'eowestre' meaning 'sheepfold' and the 'high' probably from its situation on the hill. The highest point in the parish is 287 feet which is about 27 feet higher than the highest point at Good Easter.

The village was well served by schools, the British school where pupils paid 1d a week and the Church of England school, now a private residence. There were general stores which included an off-licence kept by Mr Lodge who also had a bicycle shop and acted as a carrier. The butcher's shop called the Cock and Rothershop was sited on the left hand side as one enters the churchyard.

In 1995 Lodge's Coaches celebrated 75 years in business and purchased land to build a new and larger garage. The same year the old shop and post office was closed down, but by public demand Lodge's agreed to build a new stores next to their offices, and this was opened in 1999.

The workhouse, now two private houses, saw coffins carried along the back fields path to the church past the Cock and Bell. This inn had a bake house by the tap room door. Together with The Punchbowl opposite, they still bear witness to their 15th century origins.

In the beautiful nave roof above the clerestory in the church, a carved gate can be seen and it is said to be a rebus on the name of Sir Geoffrey Gate, who died in 1526. The illustrious family of Gate lived at Great Garnetts, in an old house since pulled down and of which only the moated site remains. The last of the family to live there was Sir John Gate, appointed Gentleman of the Privy Chamber by Henry VIII in 1535. He was made Knight of the Bath, became Sheriff of Essex in 1549 and three years later became Chancellor of the Duchy of Lancaster. On the death of Edward VI in 1553 he supported the celebrated devise of succession in favour of Lady Jane Grey. For that he was arrested, tried and found guilty and was beheaded on Tower Hill on August 22, 1553.

A late example of witchcraft in the country is the case in 1880 of Charles Brewster and his son Peter versus Levi Sharpe, a labourer of High Easter on behalf of his wife, Susan. They accused her of bewitching the son's wife and said that to prove her guilt, which she stoutly denied, she must submit to being thrown into one of the village ponds. If she sank, they would be satisfied she was not a witch 'for witches could always swim'.

Father and son were told by the chairman of the court they had been guilty of 'a very foolish act' and each was bound over in his own recognizances of £5 to keep the peace for six months!

🍁 High Roding

The Rodings (or Roothings) are a group of eight villages said to take their name from a Saxon chieftain named 'Hroth', and from the Saxon 'ings' or 'meadows' by the river Roding, a small stream which eventually flows into the Thames at Barking Reach.

High Roding is so called because it lies further upstream than the other Rodings, and is on slightly higher ground. It was at one time considered to be the most important of the Rodings and on that account is sometimes referred to in ancient records as Great Roding. This may account for the fact that High Roding church is larger than the others in the Roding group. The village consists of several old thatched cottages.

At the beginning of the 20th century Gowers Farm, as it is known today, was connected with Tryphena Mission, a holiday home for East London's poor children, and was supported by voluntary contributions. So was the clock on the school tower, which was purchased and erected in commemoration of Queen Victoria's Diamond Jubilee. The building is no longer used as the village school and is now a private house. The Youth Hostel in the village has also been made into a private dwelling.

In the early 1900s High Roding had several public houses, a post office and two general stores, a bakery and butcher's shop. Today there is just one public house and, like so many other villages, the shops and post office have gone, but village life continues to flourish.

HOCKLEY

The ancient village of Hockley stands on high ground, commanding a view of the river Crouch. It has two high points; on Plumberow Mount Roman remains have been found and the other is dominated by the parish church.

Hockley, which means mallow field, was purely agricultural and has survived the Saxons, the Danish invasions, the Normans and the Black Death as so many other Essex villages have done. The present church of St Peter and St Paul was built in 1220 on a Saxon foundation. During one of the restorations an ancient Norman altar stone was unearthed and it is now used as a requiem altar. During the reign of Mary Tudor, the curate William Tyms was burned at Smithfield, martyred for his faith.

With the coming of the turnpike road in 1747 a tollgate was erected and the stagecoaches came through on their way to Rochford from Shenfield, and the village began to grow. The old fountain, although only a symbol now, still stands at the top of Fountain Lane, where the horses could drink before going into the village.

In 1838 a 'curing' spring was discovered and three years later a spa was established. An imposing Romanesque pump room was built. Unfortunately the spa failed, mainly as the fashion was now for sea bathing. The Spa Hotel was built, but there were not enough amenities to sustain the popularity of taking the waters and the enterprise failed. The spa building still remains, now a listed building and in the care of Guinness Brothers who make billiard tables.

Nearby stands a thatched cottage, built in 1635, now known as the China Cottage, which was decorated by a former owner, Mr Harry Prior with pieces of smashed china. Mr Prior, member of a well known local family, spent much of his time purchasing odd china to add to his decorative cottage.

The National school, which stood next to the church, was moved to the main village in 1904. The old schoolroom has been converted into a private house, but still keeps the school bell in the roof.

The railway, which arrived in 1889, cut the parish church off from the main village and signalled the growth of Hockley. Farms were sold and more houses were built. There are still some farms left although most residents now commute to London, Southend or Chelmsford.

Most of the development has been to the north as Green Belt regulations have restricted building to the south, and this, thankfully, has preserved Hockley's greatest glory, the woods, changing constantly and yet unchanged since the end of the last Ice Age. They have been designated an area of Special Scientific Interest and are the most extensive area of ancient woodland in the county. They contain many species which are only found where the soil has been undisturbed for hundreds, if not thousands, of years.

Despite the changes, from Plumberow Mount with magnificent views over the Crouch valley, it can still be appreciated that Hockley is built in woodland as the house-tops barely emerge from the surrounding trees, and across the great field (no hedges now) on another hill the top of the octagonal tower of the 13th century church is just visible above the trees, as it has been for nearly 800 years.

🍁 HORNDON-ON-THE-HILL

There are many ghost stories told in this ancient and historical village. One 20th century ghost story recorded in the parish register concerns a lady called Mrs Oman, who used to rise out of a pond riding on a donkey. This apparition would cross the road and disappear into the coppice on the other side of the road, causing many cyclists to swerve and have accidents. Her haunting was about 300 yards north of the old road junction at Rookery Corner. Another ghost, a man, used to ride a horse at speed from Orsett Road down along Blackbush Lane; this apparition was also blamed for accidents at this junction.

Thomas Higbed of Horndon House, in March 1555, met his death by burning at a stake in the centre of the village. Thomas Higbed was a yeoman with a very puritanical outlook. When Queen Mary succeeded to the throne, she was determined to re-establish Catholicism, aided and advised by Bishops Pole and Bonner. Bishop Bonner held an estate at Orsett and George Tyrell betrayed Thomas Higbed to him.

Situated about 150 yards to the east of the 12th century church of St

Peter and St Paul, is the 15th century inn called The Bell. It is here since about 1900, that on Good Friday each year, a hot cross bun, freshly baked, is hung from one of the original oak beams. This task is usually performed by one of the oldest residents in the village, as a mark of esteem. The row of buns now extends for the length of the beam and many of them are blackened with age. In 1941, during the Second World War, no buns were baked due to a shortage of ingredients but a replacement bun was hung, made of concrete.

The origins of the annual Feast and Fayre date back to the granting of a Royal Charter to Robert Gifford and his heirs in perpetuity by King Edward I. Although changing form throughout the centuries the Fayre continued until the early years of the 20th century. It was revived by the Horndon Society in 1974.

🍁 HUTTON

There is evidence of Roman occupation in Hutton, as coins have been found near the church. The Domesday reference mentions Hutton as a place where many pigs were kept. Epping Forest then covered many square miles, and Brentwood (a charcoal area – Burntwood) and nearby Hutton were all in the forest clearings.

The church of All Saints stands on the site of a crossed spring, which suggests pagan rites even before the coming of Christianity to Essex. The list of rectors begins in 1325, when Hutton was part of the Benedictine foundation of Battle Abbey. Unlike most village churches this one stands alone, away from the old properties and in recent years a new church (St Peter's) has been built nearer the 'new' population. Because the church is away from the mainstream of human activity it is a refuge of peace and has remained undisturbed by the 20th century's upheavals.

A moated house, Hutton Hall, has existed from medieval times with its cottages nearby and, until the 20th century, many farm lands and tenant farmhouses. The Hall was rebuilt in 1720, using local brick. Hutton had good clay deposits for brickmaking and some are still to be seen in the present house. The moat can still be seen around the pleasant grounds and house, now a private home but a walk round the lane in daffodil time is quite an experience.

There is evidence of education in the village from the 1600s and by 1807 there was a day school with nine or ten pupils, supported by the lord of the manor and the church. Six poor houses were sold to raise money for a school and the old school (1844) is now a modern nursing home but retains the facade and one original building. In 1900 records show that, where possible, parents contributed one penny per week to their child's education. In 1840 William Offin who lived at Hutton Park gave £500 for the school building and the Cross family at the Chequers public house built the school. The thriving village, still so small, enjoyed much care from the community. Interesting church records reveal how much was given to parishioners in difficulties.

At the beginning of the 20th century, changes loomed on the Hutton and Shenfield horizon. Hutton was a very small community, in green fields far away from city influences. Its row of cottages, its farms, the few larger houses, the Hall and church moved into the 20th century but even now remain slightly aloof from the busy commuter world.

In 1907 Hutton Poplars was built as a large institution for orphans from a London Borough. The population of Hutton literally doubled when George Lansbury decided on this site, with 500 children to be housed and educated. It stayed for over 50 years but when legislation decreed that children should be cared for in smaller units the homes were demolished. The school remains for adult education, the land developed with houses suitable only for the wealthier 'commuter' pockets.

The word commuter is the clue to the tremendous post-war growth in population, together with another jargon term 'Metropolitan overspill'. The railway at Shenfield meant wholesale disposal of lands; Hutton Mount, once all farmland, became the mecca dwellings of the railway bosses. Hutton and Shenfield became part of a great movement east of the capital. Since the Second World War many estates have been built near the main road, near to the station, and the population has risen dramatically. A good example of this is the change in education. In Hutton alone one small village school was outgrown by 1961, when five schools were opened and another was being built.

In 1986, Hutton village was designated a conservation area, ie the ancient grassland and fringe of older houses. Opposite the church is an open space, the centre of village life once. Queen Victoria's Jubilee tea was held there, a path from it is an ancient bier path. There are ponds and lakes near the church and clay from the area made bricks.

🍁 INGATESTONE

It was reported as hurricane force winds that night in October 1987, which had torn and smashed the trees to the ground. The local residents of Ingatestone viewed the scene with unbelieving shock and a feeling of helplessness. Those beautiful, majestic sentinels had stood tall with

The clock tower, Ingatestone Hall

history passing beneath their outstretched branches for possibly hundreds of years.

It is possible those same trees stood there in 1742 when the physicians rushed to attend the 8th Baron Petre, who was dying of smallpox. Though only 29 years of age, he was a brilliant botanist and garden expert. His interest starting as a young boy, he later travelled to all parts of the world in his search for specimens, and we have him to thank for many of the trees and shrubs to be found in our gardens today, to name but one, the michaelmas daisy.

Smallpox was once rife in Essex – hundreds of families suffered and were wiped out. In the year 1766 Ingatestone villagers may have had their doubts about 'cures' for the scourge. However, there was one man who moved into their midst who had discovered otherwise. He was Daniel Sutton, England's greatest inoculator and his treatment had brought about the decline of the dreaded disease.

John Troughton must have felt gratitude for the strength of the oak's timber which had built his ship *The Lioness* as he crashed through the thrashing waves of the Mediterranean Sea, in engagements against the Spanish and Portuguese in the 1600s. Then a Commander he had started his career as a page to the Petre family at the Hall. A plaque placed in the parish church by the family, to his memory, can be seen today.

A warning to each generation has been not to stand under a tree in a storm for fear of lightning striking, but did those turkey drovers hesitate to do so, as they journeyed in all weathers from Norfolk to Romford market? Some of them might have been lucky and been given shelter for the night in stables, perhaps at the Bell Inn or one of the others of which there were many.

Dawn would find them making an early start on the highway, keeping a careful watch on the livestock and listening for the resounding trumpeting of a horn, which would announce the rapid oncoming of the Royal Mail coach, on its way to London from Ipswich at 12 miles an hour!

🍁 INGRAVE

The village of Ingrave is two miles south of Brentwood. It lies by the lovely woodlands of Thorndon Hall, the former family seat of Lord Petre, who remains closely interested in the manor.

The present church of St Nicholas, built of red brick, is one of the most remarkable 18th century churches in the county. It has a massive west tower, holding six bells. It was built by the Roman Catholic Lord Petre of the time for the Protestant workmen on his estate, which was compulsory as the previous two churches, both dedicated to St Nicholas, had fallen into ruins.

William Byrd, the famous Elizabethan composer and organist, one of the fathers of English music, is recorded as having stayed with Lord Petre at old Thorndon Hall three times. He later settled at Stondon Massey, where he died in 1623. Vaughan Williams visited Ingrave in 1903 when collecting old folk songs for posterity. His lovely song *Bushes and Briars* was recorded here.

The second of the old churches stood in Rectory Lane, now Middle Road, opposite which still stands the old rectory (circa 1600). It was renamed 'Heatleys' after the Rev Henry Heatley, the last incumbent to live there.

Rising above the Southend Road is the medieval church of All Saints, East Horndon. It is steeped in the history of the Tyrell family and contains an incised slab of the tomb of the Lady Alice Tyrell dated 1422. The church, falling into disrepair, was saved by the All Saints' Society and is now in the care of the Redundant Churches Fund.

In the woods surrounding Thorndon Hall is a chantry chapel, erected in 1870. In it was re-interred, on 16th October 1874, the remains of the executed Earl of Derwentwater. James, 3rd and last Earl of Derwentwater, having been taken prisoner after the battle of Preston when the Jacobite army was defeated in 1715, was beheaded on Tower Hill on 24th February 1716.

Dr Earle of Brentwood, medical man to Lord Petre, was present when the coffin was opened for identification. His daughter later described the scene: 'The body was in three coffins, first an oak one. Then one covered with crimson velvet and then a leaden one. When the lid of this was raised they looked on the perfect face and figure of a young and very handsome man fully dressed with a lace cravat bound tightly round his neck. And even as they looked he was not, face and figure faded from before their eyes and in its place a skeleton, the air had done its work, and they asked each other had they really seen this very man, dead for over 150 years. The next day he was laid to rest in the chantry chapel'.

❧ KELVEDON HATCH

Kelvedon Hatch lies astride the A128 between Brentwood and Ongar. The village may perhaps not seem to be worth a second glance when driving through and yet it has quite a story to tell. Take 'Brizes' for instance, a mansion house standing on a small estate and seen from the main road. A medieval house once stood in these grounds, built by Thomas Bryce, a dealer in fabrics in 1498. The house was named Bryce. The existing mansion was built in 1720. In 1882 Bryce was held by a Mr Royd. A certain gentleman, Mr Randall, went shooting one day and shot a pheasant on Mr Royd's land, who went so far as to bring the gentleman to court to fine him. Mr Randall was so angered at being brought to court and declared he owed Mr Royd a grudge. In 1906 he built a row of cottages, placing them in full view of the Manor so that they caused a blot on the otherwise open landscape. To this day they are known as the IOUs.

The name Bryce was changed to Brizes and later owned by the Hon Simon Rodney, a descendant of a distinguished family line dating from 1140. He was also a cousin of Winston Churchill. His parents were friends of Sir William Baden Powell who, when he was forming the idea of a scouting movement asked permission to borrow Simon Rodney and his three brothers. He took them away and taught them the art of camping out. The Hon Simon Rodney was always proud to boast that he was the first ever Boy Scout. After his death Brizes was sold and is now a private school.

The village can boast of another mansion, a rather imposing entrance gate with a lodge either side is the entrance to the Kelvedon Hall estate. A long driveway leads to a stately mansion built in three sections and set in extensive grounds. A certain John Wright possessed the estate in 1538. Kelvedon Hall was held by his descendants for nearly four centuries and there were ten successive John Wrights. The eighth John Wright entirely rebuilt the Hall which has remained unchanged to this day. In 1836 a member of the family, Samuel Wright, emigrated to America where he became the ancestor of Wilbur and Orwell Wright, pioneers of the aeroplane. There are Americans who bear the name of Wright and make a point of visiting Kelvedon Hall as the home of their ancestor!

There was no day schooling recorded in the village, but during 1812–16 the rector taught reading to 30 children on Sundays. A kindly lady also gave lessons. A school was built and opened in 1879. The building contained two classrooms and the schoolhouse which still remains.

Because of the increase in population a modern school was built in the grounds behind the old school and was opened in 1968.

Gas did not come into the village until 1955 and electricity much later. Employment was mainly found on the local farms. Today most of the villagers commute.

Kelvedon Hatch has a 'Secret Nuclear Bunker' – now open to the public and well worth a visit.

🍁 KIRBY LE SOKEN

The small village of Kirby le Soken has a long and chequered history, dating back to the Romans and believed to have been used for shipping as far back as 1326. Certainly by the mid 1800s Kirby was a thriving area with Kirby quay handling everything from sand, gravel, chalk, lime and fertilisers to wheat, copperas and of course fish. In fact, everything needed for a population of around 900 people, at that time more than Walton on Naze itself whose population had only reached 500.

Apart from the legal trade, Kirby was a great place for smugglers, very well organised and quite extensive, not just the odd bottle or 'baccy'. If today you walk along the high path of the sea wall on the backwaters, it is not difficult to imagine it would have been a perfect place to carry out 'private' business. It can be a wild and lonely place on a winter day.

The fine Norman church of St Michael set spaciously in well kept grounds has many beautiful windows. Its polished pews and tapestry kneelers give a warm feeling of a church well used. The full peal of bells rings out for Sunday services and on Tuesday for practice. Quite often visiting bell ringers ply their hands and once again the lovely sound rolls across houses and fields.

Like most villages there is a mix of lovely old houses, small cottages and two reasonably new estates. Luckily there is a sub post office, which is also a mini supermarket, and two pubs, without which no decent village could boast existence. Both the Red Lion and the Ship, like the village itself, have long histories, and were certainly suspect in the smugglers' days. Now of course both offer good food, good beer and pleasant atmosphere.

The stretch of backwater upon which the village grew is no longer used commercially, but is much used and loved by naturalists and watersport users. Yachts, rowing boats, windsurfing boards and light craft take the place of the barges. It is a tidal river running to the east of the village and at its source has Walton one side and Harwich the other, where of course it remains very commercial. The walk along its bank to Walton is ever changing.

The backwater area is unique as it is totally salt, having no river sources or entries of fresh water. It is regarded as a 'Jewel in the Crown' of Essex, is a national nature reserve and a registered wetland of Europe. Apart from the wildfowl which include Brent geese, pintail and shelduck, the flora and fauna is prolific. To add to the interest, it boasts oyster farming and on an island called Horsey, thoroughbred horses are bred, reared in an ideal situation and exported around the world.

🍁 LANGDON HILLS

Langenduna (long hill) is recorded in Domesday Book as consisting of one manor held by Suene of Essex while adjacent Leindune (Laindon) took its name from a stream called the Lyge rising near St Nicholas' church. Between the two stood Leam (Westle and Eastle) held by the Canons of St Paul's. Records here are confusing and in 1432 Eastle was combined with Laindon and Westle with Langdon.

There are no very old buildings left in the area. A house still stands on the site of Westle manor which had belonged previously to Edith, Queen of Edward the Confessor and there are timbers in a barn reputedly from the original house. Hall Farm now stands on the site of the manor of Langdon and Goldsmiths, once a farm in the parish of Horndon-on-the-Hill and ceded to Langdon at some unknown date, has been much altered over the years. All three are now private dwellings.

The old church was built in the 16th century but traces in the walls suggest that it was the site of an older building. Standing at the entrance to Hall Farm, it is reasonable to suppose that this was the original church of which there seems to be no records. This church has now been declared redundant and has been converted to a private dwelling. The new church was built in 1876 on top of the hill, an impressive building backed by beautiful woods.

The bulk of the residential part of Langdon Hills developed after the coming of the railway, and in the closing years of the 20th century many more changes took place. Most of the houses along the High Road, for instance, have been demolished along with the small shops which used to serve the community and replaced by new housing. Towards Basildon, expansion is resisted by the Conservation Area and the Country Park, but at the other end of Langdon Hills, building is still on-going out towards the A127.

🍁 LANGHAM

Langham is a long narrow village of 2,977 acres, lying six miles north of Colchester. It is about four miles from north to south and not much over a mile wide.

At the northern end of the village is the church of St Mary, standing in the private grounds of Langham Hall. The earliest parts of the church date back to the 12th century. One of its ancient possessions is an oaken dug-out chest, said to be the oldest church chest in Essex and one of the oldest in the country. The solid baulk of timber measures 4′ 7″ × 1′ 6″ × 1′ 3″ but the cavity inside is only 13″ × 7″ × 6″. Its lock, plate and hasp have at some time been broken from the heavy iron-bound lid.

Langham at one time had three working mills, including two windmills. One windmill in what is now Old Mill Road near the Boxted boundary is recorded as belonging to Charles Whiley in 1822 and members of the Whiley family were practising millers there over a long period in the 19th century. The mill is thought to have been demolished in 1907. About the other a rather wonderful tale was recorded in the *Ipswich Journal* of 1st November, 1800. This stated that a post windmill, of a large dimension, the property of Mr Baines, was moved nearly three quarters of a mile over five ditches and a road, the operation taking six days and the mill was kept working the whole time. This must have been some feat in those days! The mill was situated near the top of Nightingale Hill and was moved to be nearer the Ipswich Road for the convenience of the farmers and merchants. The third mill was a water mill on the river Stour. This was working up to the First World War and was bought by the South Essex Waterworks Company by whom it was demolished when the Langham Valley Waterworks project to supply water to the Southend area of Essex was started in 1928. A large reservoir was built in the valley with houses for the workforce and a large pumping station was built a little further down the river at Stratford St Mary. Water is pumped from here via reservoirs at Ardleigh, Abberton and West Hanningfield to Southend. The whole concern, since water privatisation, has now been sold to a French company.

The impressive Victorian house in School Road was built in approximately 1888. In 1936, it became the Adelphi Centre, a pacifist community under the leadership of Max Plowman, a founder member of the Peace Pledge Union. Max died suddenly on 4th June 1941, and is buried in the churchyard at Langham. From 1937 until 1939 a group of some 60 Spanish refugee children from the Spanish Civil War stayed here. Some of these 'children' returned in 1987 to commemorate the 50th anniversary of their first arrival. From 1943 to 1956 Langham Oaks was an approved school for boys run by the Society of Friends. It has since been taken over by the Essex County Council as a special school for boys and has been renamed Homestead School.

The Langham scene was changed drastically when Boxted Airfield was built in the Second World War. Householders and landowners received a nasty shock in January 1942 when letters were received from the Air Ministry giving notice of their intention. It was called Boxted as there was already a Langham Airfield in existence in Norfolk. The first planes, American Marauders, arrived in May 1942. It was closed in 1947 but Park Lane, which had been closed because one of the runways extended across it, was not reopened until 1954. The present owners of Langham Lodge, a farm of over 300 acres which was completely swallowed up by the airfield, still get frequent visits from American airmen who flew from there.

Other changes that have taken place in the village are the disappearance of the local pubs and shops. There is still the Shepherd and Dog, standing on Blacksmith's Corner but the Greyhound and the Fox have gone as have three of the general stores. There used to be Lilley's on the corner of Perry Lane, Pickering's at Blacksmith's Corner, and Biggs' in Moor Road. The Biggs' shop did not close until the early 1980s, when the sisters Florrie and Phyllis Biggs retired. It had been in their family from the time it was built at the end of the 19th century. Fortunately, the post office and village stores run by the Forder family is still flourishing but Thorpe's, the butcher, closed in February 1995.

A great loss was the ancient oak which stood on Langham Oak Corner, the turning into the village off the main Colchester to Ipswich road. This had to be removed when the A12 was widened to dual carriageway. A new oak tree has been planted at the junction and the Coronation Oak at Pond Corner, planted to commemorate the coronation of our present Queen, is developing into a handsome tree.

🍁 LANGLEY

Langley is a small village of about 500 people. There are two distinct parts of Langley, upper and Lower Greens. Upper Green is high and breezy, almost the highest point in Essex, nearly 500 feet above sea level. Lower Green is more sheltered along the valley of the Stort, here only a small stream.

'Langley' means long lea or pasture. According to local tradition cattle and horses on their way to market from the north were put to graze in the rich meadows by the meanderings of the stream. The Bull, on Lower Green must always have been prosperous from the drovers and graziers congregating there. Opposite the Bull the cottage which was once used for the Langley poor carried on its wall the constable's warning that beggars will be whipped.

Up the lane from the Bull, near Upper Green, are the parish church and the ancient manor house. From the churchyard the wide views into Essex, Hertfordshire and Cambridgeshire, are of big arable fields, but still with patches of woodland, tucked-away cottages and isolated farms. The fields each side of Bull Lane have always been enormous. Until the mid 19th century they were the two great open fields of Langley, North field and Peaseland field, divided into innumerable strips with pathways in between. The view to the west beyond Lower Green to Langley Lawn Farm would, in the Middle Ages, have shown a great enclosed park for hunting and until the Second World War it was all rough grazing and woodland. Now it is all arable, but deer still live in the remaining pockets of woodland round Langley.

The church is very small but beautiful, with its Norman porch, Norman and 14th century windows, 15th century hammerbeam roof and brickbuilt chancel with the Stuart coat of arms in the east window. Next to the church there has been a manor house, Langley Hall, since the Middle Ages, when part of Langley was made into a separate manor from the much bigger manor of Clavering, and given to the priory of St Bartholomew, Smithfield, London. Today Langley Hall is a stout 17th century farmhouse. In front of it the ample yard and outbuildings include an 18th century dovecote and at the entrance is a big duck pond.

Langley cricketers were flourishing in the 19th century and they have gone on to acquire fame beyond Essex, reaching the final stages in national village cricket competitions. Fielding may be hazardous because the pitch on Upper Green is bisected by the road to Duddenhoe End, but the turf has always been first class. The old men used to complain that they could not find a bent to clean their pipes when they came to watch.

🍁 THE LAVERS

The three villages which comprise the Lavers lie to the north-west of Ongar, on high ground which is well drained by many streams. This accounts for the name Laver, derived from an Old English word meaning 'stream passage'. It is a rural area and the main industry is farming which is evident from the well maintained farms throughout the area.

Each of the three villages, High, Little and Magdalen Laver retains its own identity and parish church, although they share the same rector.

To the east lies Little Laver, one of the smallest villages in the neighbourhood. There were only 15 inhabited houses in 1801 and the current electoral register lists only 78 souls. The church, rebuilt in the 14th century, was added to in Victorian times and stands in the grounds of the old manor house.

In the north is High Laver where in the 18th century the philosopher John Locke spent the last years of his life with the Masham family at Otes, a red bricked Tudor manor house. He lived there from 1691 until his death in 1704. He is buried in High Laver churchyard, having written his own epitaph which is now inside the 12th century church on the south wall.

An interesting listed building is Mashams, a 14th century hall house, very little altered through the years, and which, on the death of its owner was left to the Mashams' Trustees. Each year a garden party is held in its grounds for the Lavers residents, raising money for local charities.

Magdalen Laver lies to the south and is a parish of scattered houses with an unusual number of ancient timber framed farmhouses, many of which stand on or near moated sites. One of the most attractive of these is Bushes, a 15th century farmhouse.

The parish church of St Mary Magdalen is most picturesque, constructed in the 12th century with a 16th century wooden tower. It stands, almost hidden, in a field near the manor house, approached by a tree-lined chase, although prior to the Second World it could only be reached via footpaths. A former rector was William Webb Ellis who, whilst at Rugby school, picked up the ball during a football game and ran with it, thereby establishing the game of Rugby Football. He also founded the village school in 1862, this was closed in 1960.

To the north of the church is Pole Lane, an ancient byway reputed to be the main street of the medieval village, deserted at the time of the Black Death.

In the three Lavers villages there is now only one public house, the John Barleycorn in High Laver. There are no post offices and the village shop closed in 1969. This would seem to indicate a dying community but this is not so. The village hall in Magdalen Laver, although isolated, serves as a centre for all the Lavers and is in constant use. There is also a flourishing Horticultural Society which, although only a few years old, secured a Gold Medal at Chelsea Flower Show at their first attempt.

🍁 LAYER DE LA HAYE

The name Layer de la Haye has changed over the centuries. The first known name is from Saxon times – Legra meaning 'lookout', from the hill top settlement where the church now stands. Later the name becomes

A typical cricket scene

Leire, which means mud, which may have described marshland around the village. During Norman times Layer was used with 'de la Haye' added when Walter de la Haye was Lord of the Manor. The name was recorded in 1128 in the charter of the Benedictine Abbey of St John in Colchester.

Some of the place-names speak for themselves: the Roman River; the Charity Wood, so-called because firewood for the poor was cut from it; the Kiln, the site of a medieval kiln; Blind Nights, according to legend, was a hospital during the Crusades. Malting Green, where the maltings were, was the site of a tollgate now known as the Greate House. The 16th century Porter House was said to be the haunt of smugglers. The porter business moved to the Donkey and Buskins in 1840. The previous year the Fox Tavern moved to the crossroads from the south end of New Cut.

The village was once small and well scattered. In 1959 the population was barely 700, today it is a thriving community of nearly 2,000. The village school has grown apace too with a roll of 211 today. The village is still an attractive mix of old and newer houses surrounded by woods, fields and farms and edged by the natural boundary of the Roman River Conservation Zone.

Essex and Suffolk Water has a pumping station at the reservoir on the eastern boundary. This has one of Europe's best wildfowl areas and a Site of Special Scientific Interest, with a Visitors' Centre run by Essex Wildlife Trust. There is fishing nearby at the gravel pit.

Village amenities today include a recreation ground with football pitch, a play area, tennis courts and the Queen Elizabeth hall, scene of many social occasions. To celebrate the millennium, members of the village embroidered a tapestry as a pictorial record of the year 2000. This has pride of place in the hall. Five of the old church bells have been taken from the tower to be returned and a new one is being cast. All six will soon turn full circle and ring again over this ancient landscape.

🍁 LAYER MARNEY

Layer Marney lies south west of Colchester, between Birch and Tiptree. It is a village of about 80 dwellings, with no real centre, comprising dispersed farms and small clusters of houses.

Very little development has taken place over the years, because of planning restrictions, however there have been about 15 dwellings built since the 1950s. Comparatively few of the once numerous Tudor cottages survive today. The most permanent entities in the area are the farms, despite the changes in farming methods which have resulted in the removal of hedges and the consolidation of some farms into larger units.

The village once boasted a school, rectory, bakery, workhouse, off-licence, grocery and butcher's shop, slaughterhouse and fruit farms; a vet, blacksmith, wheelwright, bricklayer, and a dressmaker, although not all at one time. Alas, the majority of these have long gone, leaving only Parish Records as a testament to their existence. The school closed during the two World Wars 'in consequence of the decrease in child population of the parish', and now Layer Marney's only amenities are a garage and the church.

Layer Marney is situated in a very pleasant, rural part of North Essex. Its country lanes and flat open fields are complemented by the Tower – the enormous gatehouse built by Henry, first Lord Marney in the early 16th century. The Tower itself is 80 feet high and was to be the entrance to a central courtyard of a house to be built to the north. Unfortunately, Henry died in 1523, bringing the building operation to an end and leaving the Hall much as it is today, with East and West wings to the gatehouse and an isolated South range, but no completed courtyard. During September 1579, Queen Elizabeth I stayed two days at Layer Marney Tower during a progress through Essex. Both Tower and church are open to the public, and can also be enjoyed when the grounds and buildings are used to host Country Days and Antiques Fairs. The Tower is also used for wedding ceremonies.

The church of St Mary the Virgin, built at the same time as the Tower, and within the extensive grounds, replaced an earlier Norman church on the site. The Marneys were a Norman family, who followed William the Conqueror, and the Marney chapel contains the tombs of Sir William, Lord Henry and Lord John Marney, as well as an original Tudor fireplace.

❧ LITTLE BADDOW

The village of Little Baddow is located either side of a ridge of land between Danbury and Boreham. The main road continues down the hill to cross the Chelmer and Blackwater Navigation at Paper Mill. In the 18th century paper was made at the mill site. The waterway was built for trading purposes but is now used mainly for pleasure.

The village is surrounded by lovely woodlands, some owned and managed by the Essex Naturalist Trust or the National Trust, and by agricultural land.

Although many people commute to London there is a strong community spirit, with many clubs and activities in existence. Among those very active are the Conservation Society and the Historical Society; the latter society produced an excellent booklet *A Century of Village Life*.

On the other side of the road from the village shop and post office stands St Andrew's Meeting Room and Chapel. This used to be the village school until it closed in 1960 when the last headmistress retired.

There are two churches in the village, St Mary the Virgin, which dates from Norman times and contains two very rare wooden effigies and two wall paintings, and the United Reformed church dated 1708 which is one of the six non-conformist chapels in Essex listed by the Royal Commission for Historical Monuments in England.

Nearby is Cuckoos Farm where Thomas Hooker and John Eliot ran a school. Hooker was one of the early dissenters and ultimately he fled to America where he helped found the state of Connecticut and establish the first written Constitution. Eliot preached to the Indians and translated the Bible for the Algonquin tribes.

There are other interesting properties; Old Riffhams constructed in 1308, Bassetts on the site of an old manor and Little Baddow Hall, originally the Norman manor house. Much of interest is kept in the Parish Chest; application to view this can be made through the Historical Society.

🍁 LITTLE BURSTEAD

Little Burstead is a rather straggly and widespread village south of Billericay, the boundaries of which have changed over the years. It has been designated a Green Belt area, and the main part of the village has been created a conservation area, so there has been very little new building and the appearance of the village has not altered since the early 1920s.

There are several fine large old Elizabethan houses in the village (including the Old Rectory) which are privately owned. The most prominent one is Stockwell Hall, dower house of the Mexborough family. Lady Mary Savile, a lady in her own right, lived there until after the war, when it was sold. This house is also known as Clock House, so called because of the large clock on the end of the house, and it is said that the hands and figures were made from human bones, but were later changed to sheep bones. The house belonged to the Earl of Mexborough, as did a lot of properties in the village, farms and cottages.

Up until the first half of the 20th century these houses provided employment for many of the villagers, as did the farms and other local enterprises. Among these were a wheelwright, blacksmith, bakers and a general store. Also in the village were several poultry farms, a piggery, market gardens and an orchard, so people lived and worked in the village.

Unfortunately only the blacksmith remains (now called an agricultural engineer). In several instances, two or three small farmworkers' cottages have been made into one large house. Originally the village had two public houses, the Wheatsheaf and the Duke's Head. The latter is still open to the public, but the Wheatsheaf is now a private residence.

The village school closed around 1947 and is now used for activities connected with the church. Just past the school is the village pond. Children once played hop-scotch, skipping, ball, whip and top and hop in the main street, mostly by the village pond which was the favourite meeting place. Another favourite pastime in the spring was catching newts and tadpoles in the then clean pond, and in mid-winter sliding on the ice was great fun enjoyed by all the youth of the village.

Almost next to the pond stands the property which used to be the village shop and post office. This business ceased in 1973, although many villagers found it invaluable. Opposite the old shop stands the village hall. This was built by Mr Weedon in 1926, on land donated by the Johnson family from Hope House. Many happy hours are spent in the hall by the villagers participating in the whist and beetle drives, parties and coffee mornings; and of course the Christmas party.

The church of St Mary the Virgin is quite an interesting small church, the structure being a survival from late Norman times, although most of the church dates from the 14th century and is well worth a visit.

As the road rises towards the church of St Mary the Virgin, it takes a sharp bend. This is Broomhill and there are still some properties called 'Broomhill' or 'Broomhill Cottage'. The records show that there has been a church on this hill since about 1142. The rectory is further along Rectory Road towards the village of Little Burstead. In the late 1950s one could stand in the churchyard and look towards London, Grays and Southend without seeing a single light. Now the whole area is one mass of lights.

Another pretty place is opposite the Duke's Head, part of Laindon Common, an area of woodland which is much explored by people from the surrounding district.

🍁 LITTLE CLACTON

Little Clacton is a pleasant and popular place to live and has a steady increase in population.

The open space in front of the Blacksmith's Arms was once the site of an annual fair held to celebrate St James' Day. In 1806 the Blacksmith's Arms was the setting for a fight between villagers and some of the Cameron Highlanders who were stationed at nearby Weeley. The men of Little Clacton chased the soldiers along the street until one, Alexander McDonald, who had hurt his foot, was struck down and died. Legend says that where his head hit the roadside a hole appeared which resisted all efforts to fill it. The event is recorded on a tombstone in Weeley churchyard where the soldier was buried.

The church of St James the Great dates mostly from the 14th century but the chancel, which has a Norman window and priest's door, is thought to be 12th century. The font dates from 1190 and one of the three bells housed in the wooden turret was cast by Robert Crouch in 1437. This is thought to be the only one of his bells to remain in Essex.

In 1596 William Hubbard who lived at Bovills Hall left £100 14s to be used as a charity fund for the poor of the village. A farm was bought at St Osyth Heath and although sold in 1944 the profit was invested by the trustees and the income is still distributed at Christmas time. There is a brass on the wall of the church in memory of William and three of his four wives!

🍁 LITTLE WALTHAM

'So silently they one to th'other come,
As colours steal into the pear or plum,
And air-like, leave no pression to be seen
Where e're they met, or parting place has been'.

Robert Herrick.

However secret the meeting place, someone knew where they met, those lovers, and the story has passed down through the generations of Little Waltham villagers for 450 years.

What was Little Waltham like in those days? St Martin's church was there of course, though smaller than today, and one of the Mildmay family lived at the old hall which then stood between the lake and the modern Pond House. Some of the very old houses in the village may have been standing at that time, and most of the farms, Pratts, Longs, Powers, Belsteads and Channells amongst others. There was some arable land, but a lot more grass than there is now and there were many acres of woods and gorsy heathland.

In 1517 Sir Thomas Boleyn, father of the famous Anne, gave to Henry VIII his house called New Hall in Boreham. The house was rebuilt in the next years. Henry was very well-pleased with New Hall and renamed it Beaulieu. The people of Little Waltham must have been in contact with all this. Park Farm, at that time called New Lodge, was within the Park of the New Hall, and the tenant had to carry loads of straw to New Hall as part of his service.

At that time, one of the park-keepers or wardens lived in Little Waltham at a cottage on Blasford Hill. The building is still there, on the left as you go to Chelmsford and was once, possibly, the old manor of Blasford's Fee. It is very old and has a thatched roof. This is where Henry VIII and the young Anne Boleyn used to meet in secret, arriving it is said, from different directions, to avoid suspicion!

A very different story about Little Waltham comes from the 1930s. What on earth is a Flapping Track? The track, or stadium was, in fact, announced on a large board erected next to the Little Waltham Garage – 'The Waltham Greyhound and Whippet Racing Club'. Flapping meant that it was un-licensed. It was one of many such tracks that sprang up locally in the 1930s. Others were at Braintree, Thaxted, Stondon Massey and on the King's Head meadow in Chelmsford.

The track was started in 1930 by Bill Cass who owned the Little Waltham Garage with the land behind, and by Frank Stewart, builder of Roman Road and Manor Crescent. The grass track or stadium covered the whole area of land which is now occupied by the Chelmer Avenue houses and gardens.

The track closed down about 1938. After the Second World War there were requests to start the racing again, but the Parish Council did not give permission for this to happen and a few years later the land was built over.

🍁 Little Wigborough

Little Wigborough is a small village overlooking the salt marshes and the estuary of the river Blackwater, eight miles south of Colchester between Great Wigborough and Merea.

Little Wigborough is mentioned in the Domesday Book under the name of Wigheberga, with the land belonging to Hamo Dapifer. The manor of Copt Hall, now owned by the National Trust, was held by the Earls of Gloucester. In the early 17th century, Sir John Cotton sold the manor to the Governors of the Charterhouse and it was held by them until recent times.

Being so close to the sea, it is appropriate that the church is dedicated to St Nicholas, the patron saint of sailors. There has probably been a church here from Norman times; the list of rectors goes back to 1272. The parish is now united with Great Wigborough (since 1878) and this parish was joined to Peldon in 1975. The church is small but attractive consisting of chancel, nave and west tower. It had probably been rebuilt in the late 15th century. Much restoration work had to be done between 1885 and 1888 following the severe damage caused by the local earthquake in 1884, especially to the tower.

Little Wigborough's other claim to fame relates to the German Zeppelin L33 which crashed across the lane at 1 am on Sunday 24th September 1916. This was one of the first airships to fall on English soil in the First World War. The countryside was suddenly lit up by flames from the huge gas bag as the commander fired his ship. Nearby cottages at New Hall Farm narrowly escaped being hit or burnt. A framed account of the destruction of the Zeppelin hangs in the church together with a section of the airship.

🍁 Littlebury Green

Littlebury Green is a small hamlet four miles west of the town of Saffron Walden, in North Uttlesford.

The houses, 52 in all, are a mixture of architecture, mainly modern which is an indication that most have been constructed since the early 1970s. This is nevertheless a much older settlement, shown as a well-established hamlet in the 1777 map of Essex published by John Chapman and Peter Andrew and on view in Saffron Walden Museum.

The main feature of the hamlet is the small church, dedicated to St Peter, clad in corrugated iron, painted green with a single bell tower. It is a chapel of ease, sitting at the top of the rise into the hamlet, built in 1895 and purchased in kit form from Birmingham. The church is lovingly cared for by a local family; brass gleams and the pews are polished, the linen is laundered and the churchyard regularly mown. The kneelers, Lenten cloth and tapestry, and other official garments have been beautifully sewn by a group of local ladies.

In 1983 the church was in trouble when attendance was down to only two or three regulars. This prompted the change of use to a community centre was well as a church. The idea worked, the community has a focal point and this in turn has influenced attendance at church services. The St Peter's Community Centre was born. The proudest moment for the community was the Centenary Celebration held in 1985 and conducted by the Bishop of Colchester.

The oldest residents can recall walking up a dirt road into Littlebury Green in the 1920s. The Harvey family at Howe Hall employed most of them. The women were cooks and maids, stating at 6 am and finishing at 9 pm, with a half day off a week. For this devotion to duty they received twelve shillings a week, wore a uniform at all times and attended to the many functions, tennis and shooting parties. A reward for hard work was being let off duty on Friday afternoon and walking into Saffron Walden. The hamlet, it seemed, bustled with people walking to and fro, attending to allotments or going to the two pubs, the Hoops and the Old Rose to play dominoes and darts matches with friends from Catmere End and Strethall. Howe Hall still stands as an imposing house with its dovecote as you enter the village, but long gone are the beef cattle, horses and pigs that were driven to market in Bishop's Stortford down the dirt road. The two pubs are private houses and the only other public building is the red telephone kiosk! The children in the 1920s walked to school in Littlebury and school buses did not appear until 1937. Consequently an ancient feud still survives between Littlebury and Littlebury Green. The Littlebury children were always warm and snug around the schoolroom stove when those from Littlebury Green arrived cold and wet and, it seems, remained that way – they have not forgiven! The road to Littlebury was eventually surfaced in 1931.

Littlebury Green is still a thriving community. The village fete is being held again; the Jumble Sale, Barn Dance and Games Evening have become part of the yearly pattern of life. The local landowner is Audley End

Estates and the Littlebury Farming Partnership farm most of the fields that surround this beautiful, still unspoilt corner of North Essex, where arable has largely overtaken livestock farming. An increase in aircraft noise from Stansted Airport is noticeable year on year and we have only one 'village elder' to inform us of times past, memories that reflect the rapid change in our lifestyles.

🍁 Manuden

Manuden, or 'common valley', was an established village community at the time of the Domesday survey when it was known as Magghedana, one of over 40 variants. The tiny village of only 200 houses nestles in a valley, four miles north of Bishop's Stortford, where its picturesque thatched cottages and timbered buildings hug the main street which meanders through the village almost parallel with the river. Although for centuries unchanged, the last 100 years has seen Manuden transformed from a sleepy, Essex village dependent upon agriculture, into a haven for commuters.

The large houses like Manuden Hall and Manuden House with their once large staffs of servants, cooks and grooms belong to a past era, although there are still villagers who can remember their heyday. Gone too is the mill, the maltings and the whitening manufacturer, all employers in their time.

Occupying a central position in the village is the stone and flint church of St Mary, officially dated from 1143 but largely medieval and much rebuilt between 1863–67. It contains a magnificent, early 15th century, carved oak choir screen, complete with little green men, and a splendid pipe organ given by Rev. J. B. Forster in 1912. On the north wall of the vestry an impressive wall tablet commemorates Sir William Waad, a notable diplomat and Officer of State to Elizabeth I and James I, and who as Lieutenant of The Tower of London was custodian of Guy Fawkes and Sir Walter Raleigh. Sir William's residence was Battles Hall, 1½ miles north west of the village where his grandson Capt William Waad was brutally murdered in 1677. The assassin was later executed in Chelmsford but Richard Savill, who robbed and killed villager Thomas Bray in 1789 suffered hanging on Manuden Downs facing his mother's cottage.

In common with other villages Manuden's clergy and parishioners suffered persecution throughout history. In March 1431 vicar Thomas Bagley was burnt at the stake in Smithfield for heresy. Two hundred years later Thomas Crowley of Manuden Hall was being persecuted for his Catholic belief. However, this good man obviously forgave his tormentors as he bequeathed a charity to the poor of Manuden which, along with several others, is still administered today.

❧ THE MAPLESTEADS

Great and Little Maplestead lie two miles north of Halstead between the A1017 and the A131. At the heart of each is an attractive and interesting church. Little Maplestead has one of only four round churches in use in England and was built by the Knights Hospitaller of St John, c.1335, probably following the ground plan of an earlier round church on the site. The church of St Giles, Great Maplestead is believed to date from about 1100 and much early Norman work has survived, together with two exceptionally interesting monuments of the Deane family, formerly of Dynes Hall, in the parish.

The two villages differ in their geology and architecture, but they have in common the fact that the beautiful, rolling countryside is predominantly given over to the cultivation of arable crops with some livestock, where once had grown coriander and caraway, teazels and hops. The former were sent to London to be used in drug-making and for flavourings and the teazels were sold to Halstead cloth manufacturers. Hop-growing, centred on the Hedinghams, was also important until the 1850s when the advent of the railways brought supplies from Kent. There has been a strong tradition of progressive agricultural method in the two parishes, which continues to the present day.

In 1863, Mrs Gee, a local benefactress, built the school in Great Maplestead at the top of Church Street. The Victorian buildings have been extended recently and the school is flourishing, drawing children from surrounding villages. The school at Little Maplestead, built in 1874, closed in 1933 and was used for a while as parish rooms, but is now a private house.

A nunnery was built in Great Maplestead in the 18th century and in 1867 the so-called House of Mercy, a 'penitentiary for fallen women' was built on the same site. It continued in religious hands until 1959 when the building and chapel were demolished. All that remains of the nunnery is a massive, red brick wall, which now encompasses a small modern development.

 Margaret Roding

Margaret Roding straddles the busy road from Chelmsford to Dunmow. In ancient times there were two places here, Roding Masy and Margaret Roding. Roding Masy or Marcie Fee (Monks Hall) paid its tithes to Stondon Massey, and hence the Masy. It also had a private chapel. Margaret Roding consisted of Garnish Hall or Olives and Garnetts as it was then known. Nestling hard by the grounds of Garnish Hall is the beautiful little church of St Margaret with its magnificent Norman doorway. This little church has inspired a tale as the following letter will tell.

It was sent to the Revd G. F. Bartlam in 1986 by James Shepherd, of Victoria, Australia:

Dear Sir,

This bible was preached from by Rev William Shepherd at Margaret Roding for many years preceding 1851. In that year, it was presented to his son 'James' who, as a midshipman was wounded at the Capture of Rangoon; was invalided home and in the same year, set forth with his nephew and two brothers to seek his fortune on the Australian goldfields.

Upon arrival at Melbourne the party equipped themselves and set out on the muddy road to the famous and wild diggings of the Buckland Valley, some 120 miles distant. Here it was, eventually, that James was called upon to press the bible in to service...

Wild as they were, those diggers were extremely pious and, they gathered around the Shepherd campfire for the 'reading' as the boobook owl hooted on the ridge, night after night. This was later to become standard practice during the fifteen years of James' domicile on the incredibly rich fields of Ballarat and Bendigo; his ramblings to the Foster and Turton's Creek nearer Melbourne and on the fabulous field at Walhalla in distant Gippsland... The conditions in which bush people lived in those years and continuous usage and handling, are reflected in the condition of the bible itself as I return it to its Margaret Roding home, 135 years after the commencement of its colonial sojourn.'

🍁 MARKS TEY

In Saxon times, Tey was owned by Uleric. Geoffrey de Mandeville later had the manor, which was then called Tey Mandeville. Later on, the village was rented to a family from Calais, called de Merk, hence Marks Tey. It has also been called Tey ad Ulmos (Tey with the elms), and there is an Elm Lane in the village. Sadly, like everywhere else, the elms have gone.

Marks Tey's main importance was as somewhere to go through on the way to somewhere else! The road between Marks Tey and Colchester was turnpiked in 1694, between Marks Tey and Chelmsford in 1726, and between Marks Tey and Braintree in 1765. This resulted in an improvement in transport by road and the inns flourished.

Situated between Colchester and Coggeshall, which were both major wool towns, Marks Tey was bound to be involved in the wool trade in some way. There were almost certainly outworkers here, but Marks Tey's main contribution was in the growing of teasels. These were used during the finishing process, after fulling, when the shearmen would bring up the nap using teasels, before clipping it off neatly. They were grown where the present playing field is now situated, and the odd wild teasel can still be found growing there.

During the Civil War there was a famous Siege of Colchester. On successive days the Royalist armies and the Cromwellian armies each marched through Marks Tey. It is reputed that due to its being in the line of fire, the church tower was hit by an errant cannon ball. The tower had to be demolished, but as funds could not stretch to providing stone, it had to be rebuilt in wood. This has provided Marks Tey with a very interesting church tower, clad with wooden shingles.

🍁 MATCHING

The original site of the village was at Church Green. Later the community spread to form two villages – Matching Green and Matching Tye – and three hamlets, Newmans End, Housham Tye and Carters Green.

By the time of the Norman Conquest there were many manors in the parish, of which three remain – Matching Hall, Housham (formerly Ovesham) Hall and Stock Hall.

Until the early 20th century, Matching people experienced near-primitive conditions by present standards – no water or electricity and very low wages.

There were shops around Matching Green (none now) – a cycle agent, a saddlery/shoe shop, a forge, a draper, a grocer, a bakery, two butchers and a maltings with oast house and kiln. At one time there were six public houses!

In 1886 the village school was built but prior to this there was a penny school (now Green Edge Cottage) which, as the name suggests, required pupils to pay the teacher one penny per week.

During the Second World War, farm land was requisitioned and an airfield built by the Americans for the 391st Bomber Group of the US 9th Airforce. Most of the land used for this airfield has been reclaimed.

One resident of Matching Green was Augustus John, the artist. He lived at Elm House, next to The Chequers, with his wife, children and mistress. One elderly lady still living in the village, recalls he was disliked because he painted nude ladies, which was definitely 'not done in those days'.

Mention must be made of the Marriage Feast Room. It stands at the west end of the church and is said to have been built by William Chimney (about 1480) for use of local brides for their wedding breakfast. It was last used for this purpose in 1936 but the privilege remains. In the 18th century it was used as an almshouse, and, more recently has provided living accommodation for the church organist. Today it is used for church functions.

The spread parish of Matching has of course seen changes, but today Church Green remains virtually as it was at the time of the Saxon settlement. The lovely church of St Mary the Virgin stands on the site of the original wooden church, the ancient Marriage Feast Room to its west, and Matching Hall on the other side of the Green. It is an idyllic spot.

🍁 MAYLAND

Mayland is a widely spread community of which the larger part by far lies along the southern shore of the river Blackwater. This area is known as Maylandsea, as distinct from Mayland proper which consists of scattered houses spread over Mayland Hill to the south.

Mayland was originally a manor dating from the 12th century, when it formed part of the endowment of St Osyth's priory. In the time of Henry VIII it was bestowed on Cardinal Wolsey, until his fall from grace, and then passed through various hands, until in the 18th century it was acquired by St Bartholomew's Hospital. They it was who built the present church of St Barnabas in 1866, after an earlier church had fallen into decay.

This early history may explain why Mayland has no visible ancient centre. Within almost living memory the community consisted of a few scattered farms: Parsonage Farm, high on the hill, with the benefit of the church close by, Marsh Farm and Nipsells Farm, down by the lonely Blackwater estuary. In the midst of them stood a windmill, long since demolished, which is commemorated in the name of the Mayland Mill public house. The Mill House still stands, in its garden a large rockery reputedly built with stones from the old mill.

In the early years of the 20th century Mayland might well have become a model co-operative agricultural community. A certain Mr Fels, an American who had made a vast fortune from Naptha Soap, sought to do something for the exploited working class of the East End of London. Mayland seemed the ideal spot to establish two rows of smallholdings. The venture foundered when the ground proved unsuitable for intensive cultivation and the smallholders discovered they could earn more by working for someone else. A few of the original homesteads still remain.

Another phase in the chequered history of Mayland came with the establishment of Cardnells Boatyard, where boats of all varieties were built and repairs carried out, including the refitting of lifeboats. In the Second World War the yard employed between 80 and 90 men turning out motor torpedo boats for the Admiralty. Since then Maylandsea has blossomed into a sizeable sailing centre, with imposing clubhouses and a forest of dinghies, some hauled up on the riverbank, others at anchor in the creek.

Between the wars Mayland had been 'discovered' by Londoners seeking a retreat where they could build, usually with their own hands, a chalet or bungalow in which to spend weekends and holidays. After the Second World War the community grew apace, but it was still largely a holiday and retirement area, until the developers arrived, buying up the old plots and finding room for several houses where once a tiny shack had stood.

Life is much easier these days, with electricity and gas laid on, made-up roads with bus services and many car owners. Lots of people commute to London and to other towns. The population at Maylandsea continues to increase. There is a new church, St Luke's, with a family centre, and a new primary school in The Drive, which even when it opened was already inadequate for the growing number of newcomers.

❧ MIDDLETON

In the Domesday Book, Middleton was known as Midletuna, 'middle farm' being the literal translation. It was midway between Liston and 'Alphamstone', so was named for its situation.

The village church dates from at least the 12th century, as the list of priests hanging just inside the door demonstrates. Inside the little church there are many windows and plaques commemorating the Raymond family. This is a well known name locally, and indeed Oliver lived to be 95 years old and was priest here for 70 years. The Royal Arms of Elizabeth I are displayed on the chancel wall. It is said that there was a tunnel from the church to the big house, but no actual proof has ever been found.

The squire, of course, once lived at the big house and there was a time when every villager would have to mind his manners and touch his cap when the squire went by. However, there are many more tangible reminders of the past – the Ice House Meadow where food was once kept fresh and ice made; the sign in front of the lake 'Cave Stagnum' which was a warning to carriages coming up the drive and was erected after one driver made a mistake and went straight in; the old archway in the field commemorating the birth of a past Prince of Wales; the old school bell which still hangs outside the school door.

Villages everywhere have changed, and the saddest part of this change is the departure from the village of the old families. A farmworker leaves the village where his great-grandfather worked and his father and grandfather, covering well over 100 years between them, and the pleasant Essex accent is being overlaid by importations. The Tuffins have gone, and the Galleys have died out – Fred the horseman, friend of all the children, and his father Nathan, who was sexton for 40 years. When he retired he was presented with a cheque and the rector praised his long service. 'I can't rightly hear what you say,' said Nathan, 'but I thank you all the same.' However, when something stirs public opinion, there is still a corporate voice to Middleton.

✤ MISTLEY

Mistley is a unique village – the old part mainly Georgian with a street, a green, cottages and fields to the church. That is Mistley Thorn. Then comes New Mistley, Victorian cottages and houses, and then the modern developments. In between are the Maltings, and behind is the river Stour. It is tidal here and there are quays, with boats loading and unloading, and at low tide many wading birds and always the swans, and the ever-changing reflections on the water, with the Suffolk shore on the other side.

The walk to Manningtree, the shopping centre, is along the beautiful 'walls' – a stretch of wide grass along the river, and past the famous Mistley Towers. These were built in 1776 by the well known Adam brothers to enhance and beautify the new church built in 1735. The towers are now the only remaining part of this church, but are landmarks, and well worth seeing.

Mistley has had, like most other villages, a somewhat chequered history, but its worst period was in the middle of the 17th century when Matthew Hopkins the notorious Witchfinder General, waged his ruthless hunt for simple women he could condemn as witches. It is understood that some 3,000 were put to death in England between 1640 and 1660 and Matthew Hopkins caused 60 people to be hanged in Essex in one year alone.

But to better things . . . in 1785 John Wesley visited Mistley on one of his tours and stayed in one of the houses in the High Street. He preached here, probably by the river, and now there is a little Methodist church in Chapel Cut, and in Manningtree one of the oldest Methodist churches in Essex.

In the late 1840s Mistley Hall was demolished and the estate sold to pay debts, but the woods are still there, and the huge oak trees to stand beneath and wonder.

A newer wonder is the Secret Bunker, built in 1951 as an Army Operations Centre. In 1963 it became the main County Nuclear War HQ, and gives a chilling insight into the Cold War. It is now open to the public.

In 1869 a new St Mary's church was built and consecrated in January 1870 with great ceremony and a public luncheon where 350 people sat down to a repast. No one goes to church now in a chaise or governess cart, and there is no coal club or night school for men and boys. The dame school and the genteel lending library have long since closed, as have several of the shops, although there is still an antiques shop, grocer's and general store, and a post office.

The quietness has gone too, with the advent of the car and buses to

Colchester and Harwich, and the lorries loading at the quayside, but the neighbourliness is still there, the chatting, the visiting and the cups of tea.

🍁 MORETON

Moreton is an attractive village situated to the north of the A414 between Epping and Ongar. The name implies that there was a settlement here in Saxon times and indeed, in 1039 the church was presented to the monastery of St Albans by the lord of the manor. The present church was built on the same site in the 13th century, with the tower added in the 16th or 17th century.

Many of the buildings date back to the 15th or 16th century including one of the two public houses, The White Hart. The other, situated opposite, is The Moreton Massey (formerly The Nag's Head) and this is 18th century. These two hostelries enjoy a friendly rivalry which is manifested each Boxing Day, since 1969, when a team from each competes in obstacle races and other games in the main street, culminating in a tug-of-war across Cripsey Brook, the losers finishing rather wet! This draws many hundreds of spectators from whom a collection is taken for a local charity.

Another interesting building is a timber framed 15th century hall cottage, built as a Guildhall in 1473 for the Guild of All Saints which paid 4/4d annually to the rector for masses to be said for the souls of the deceased guildmen. It is now called Black Hall.

Although the main industry in the area is farming, other local industries played an important part in village life. The first of these is the extraction of gravel from a pit within the village boundaries which was of significant economic importance, and was originally owned by a prominent village family. It was closed in 1998. The second industry involving many local people is the mill. Originally there was a postmill, erected about 1715, and in constant use until 1931. Gradually the mill fell into disrepair and was finally demolished in 1964. However, the site is still used as a mill and a few years ago was sold to Dalgety Spillers.

At one end of the village street there is a First World War hangar which houses several traction engines. These were used for threshing until modern farming methods took over. In the 1920s the teams of men who travelled around the farms at threshing time were so unruly that the village policeman had to carry a revolver to deal with the fights that occurred.

All these industries were, and in many cases still are, owned by local people whose families go back many generations. This, together with the fact that the main buildings including the church, manor house, school, village hall, public houses, post office, and until recently, the village shop, are all situated within a quarter of a mile of each other has resulted in a close-knit community where everyone works together.

🍁 MOUNT BURES

Mount Bures lies in north-east Essex, enclosed on the north by the river Stour and on the west by its tributary the Cambridge brook, raised above both on the 46 metre contour.

The mount is a tree-grown mound, nearly as high as the church tower, believed by the local children to be the burial place of Queen Boadicea's warriors. It is in fact the remains of a great moated Norman motte, built by Roger of Poitou, one of the sons of Roger of Belleme, a companion of William the Conqueror in many battles. A wooden tower would have been placed on the summit of the impressive mound to form a rapid defensive point, essential during the early years of the conquest.

The church itself, near to the mount, also has an early Norman origin. It is dedicated to St John the Baptist, so perhaps it was erected by Roger of Poitou in memory of his mother, Mabel, who was foully murdered in 1077. She was decapitated by a vengeful neighbour whom she had wronged. Unlike many churches in the area the church was not extensively rebuilt in late medieval times. It is not a typical 'wool church', but still shows its early origins.

Glimpses of the lives of the people who lived in the village can be found in old records. Perhaps the one with the greatest claim to fame is Hugh Constable, great grandfather of the famous painter John Constable, buried in the churchyard in 1715 (though no one knows exactly where).

Nowadays the village occupies 1,400 acres and has about 400 inhabitants. It has always been based on agriculture, and farms and houses are scattered throughout these acres, many of a great age. Records exist for over 400 years and are confirmed by the ancient timber-framed construction of the buildings.

The largest cluster of houses is around the village hall, stretching to the level crossing where the Sudbury line crosses the main road. These houses have mostly been built in the last 60 years but one very old house shows signs of having held an important position in the village, perhaps a court room, and the wheelwright's shop used to be nearby. At one time there was a shop near this and in living memory there was another at the south-east end of the parish, conveniently opposite one of the windmills, in a road which terminates near the war-time Wormingford airfield.

Now there is no shop but beyond the mount and the church the water tower stands out as a landmark on the road to Chappel, though the two windmills which used to serve the parish have both gone.

🍁 MOUNTNESSING

Time was when the traveller from East Anglia to London recognised the approach of this village by its most obvious landmark, the windmill, standing high at the crossroads in the centre of the village to catch the prevailing westerly winds. Today's traveller passes at high speed by train or along the A12 by-pass.

The existence of a mill on this spot can be traced back to at least 1580. The structure you can see today is the restored postmill constructed in about 1807. In 1937 the mill was taken over by the Parish Council and the site was given to the parish by Lord Arran, the then owner of Thoby Hall. Restoration was completed in 1983 by the county millwright and the mill is now regularly open to the public during the summer.

Thoby Hall was built on the site of Thoby Priory, the home of the canons of St Augustine. Their first prior was Tobias and the charter, which dates from about 1151, was witnessed not only by Michael de Capra their founder but by Robert de Mountney. The 'lands of the Mountneys', is modernised as Mountnessing.

It is likely that Robert de Mountney lived at Mountnessing Hall, an imposing manor, some two miles from the centre of the village standing adjacent to the village church dedicated to St Giles, patron saint of beggars and cripples. The church dates from Norman times having evidence of puddingstone in its walls. There are two explanations to consider for the remoteness of this church. The hamlet may have existed around the church and hall and subsequently disappeared, alternatively the church may have been the private chapel of the manor. The latter gains credence as there was a small door in the north wall, now bricked up, which was most likely the entrance for the lord of the manor. The

The windmill at Mountnessing

most interesting feature of the church is perhaps the tower, supported by huge wooden beams.

The village of 100 years ago was based on agriculture but today's inhabitants are commuters to neighbouring Brentwood and the capital.

But the same community spirit exists. The village hall is set adjacent to a recreation field, tennis courts and the windmill, whilst across the road is the Prince of Wales, one of three public houses in the village. The others are the Plough almost next door and the George and Dragon some way towards Brentwood along Roman Road, a rightly named thoroughfare, straight as a die through the village.

🍁 MUCKING

Mucking is a small village near the river Thames, one and a half miles from Stanford-le-Hope and about the same distance from Linford.

In 1959 an important discovery was made from an aerial survey, which demonstrated the continuity of occupation in this area. In some fields at Mucking, now destroyed by quarrying, identified by the colouration of ripening barley, was an integrated pattern of rectangular and circular markings. Excavation showed that the area contained hut circles, iron-working hearths, and graves, in a chronological sequence from Neolithic to Roman times.

There is a bird sanctuary between Mucking and the nearest small town of Stanford-le-Hope, with fishing and sailing on what are disused gravel pits. This makes a pleasant stroll and is the quickest way to walk if one has no transport.

Years ago Mucking was a busy village with a 12th century church, school, pub and many more houses than it has today. The last children were christened in the village at the end of 1981, when people came from several surrounding villages to sing in the choir. Now the church has been sold and is a house. Some of the Bibles and kneelers are at Great Braxted church.

The school used to be next to the church but as the population declined it was no longer needed and was used instead as a village hall. Sadly it is now disused. Illegal bareknuckle fights once took place in or near the old Crown pub, with people escaping over the marshes when police arrived. It is also said that a secret passage ran from the Hall to the pub, used long ago by smugglers who came up the creek to hide their contraband.

One of the vicars, Rev A. M. Morgan, wrote the words of several hymns. One of these, *The Name Of Our Village*, was based on the mistaken belief that Mucking meant 'the place of much grass'. This hymn achieved some fame and was published in New York.

✿ MUNDON

Mundon lies about three miles south of Maldon. In the centre of the main street is a public house and further on the village hall, where cars may be left and the village explored by foot. Next to the new Victory Hall built in 1993, is a small wood that was dedicated to the parish council in 1990. There are a number of easily walked footpaths to navigate; one of which leaves the wood opposite West Chase. Walking in an easterly direction, this footpath represents part of the ancient St Peter's Way, and leads to the old parish church and beyond.

The building of a parish church was begun in the 13th century within the moat of Mundon Hall, the Lord of the Manor's old home. In early Tudor times, the timber west belfry was erected, together with a chapel to the south and the fine north porch. By 1684, the church had fallen into disrepair, and it was not rebuilt until the early 18th century. It once again fell into disrepair and in the mid 1970s, the Friends of Friendless Churches started to restore St Mary's church to something of its former glory. An annual service is held in early September and the church is open all year round for interested visitors.

Near to the church and Mundon Hall, is a plantation of oak trees to supply wood for battleships. The last one to be built from Mundon oaks was the battleship *Jersey* when Samuel Pepys was First Lord of the Admiralty.

In the mid 19th century, the population was recorded as 287, a figure which has not changed much over the years to the present day. Then the country community supported a wheelwright, a boot and shoemaker, a blacksmith, a baker and shopkeeper, a curate, a parish clerk and a postmistress.

The village suffered a great deal from the depression of the 1930s and from enemy action in the Second World War. A village hall was constructed on land given by the then owner of Mundon Hall, a little to the west of the church, a symbol of victory and continuity after the ravages of war.

Today the village has some 40 businesses within it, many of them occupying redundant agricultural buildings as farmers seek ways in which to diversify.

✿ NAVESTOCK

Navestock has a long history dating from Roman times and is mentioned in the Domesday Book as having three manors, woods sufficient to feed 900 pigs and four hives of bees.

Part of the old forest remains at Curtis Mill Green bounded by the M25 and by Richards Stone and Navestock Stone, two ancient stones marking the edge of the royal forest. In 1858 Curtis Mill Green was allotted as common to the villagers. Present day inhabitants have re-registered their rights to herbage, estovers and grazing. Water and electricity are available to most homes but oil lamps were the only light and water came from the public hand pump until well after the Second World War.

The parish church dating back to Norman times has many memorials including those to Elizabeth, daughter of the 3rd Earl Waldegrave and lady of the bedchamber to Queen Charlotte. The Waldegraves held the manor from 1554 and in 1776 enclosed Navestock common. Their 18th century mansion was demolished in 1811.

From 1900 to 1940 Navestock was still a village of country people. Five gamekeepers and 8 to 10 gardeners were employed on the estate. Roads were bad and often flooded. In those days the village had a baker. In Sabines Green a delicious smell of baking bread came from Mr Goodwin's bakery; later it became a post office.

The church has survived all these changes including in 1644 the theft of some brasses, probably by Cromwell's soldiers. In 1940 a noise like a train came through the sky. The parachute of a land mine became entangled in the churchyard trees and the mine exploded. The tower timbers withstood the blast.

The cricket pitch at Navestockside has one of the longest traditions in the country of cricket having been played continuously. In the pavilion a fixture card is displayed for Essex Cricket Club in 1790, matches to be played opposite the Green Man. Several famous players have played there: the square was levelled for Charles Kortright, the awesome Essex and England fast bowler.

Many Navestock people work outside the village but three farmers remain. The two public houses cater for all, serving pub lunches to increasing numbers of visitors. Above everything, is the steady drone of the traffic on the M25.

🍁 NAZEING

The parish church of All Saints is an ancient building sited on a headland overlooking the Lee valley. Hence the name of Nazeing, originally Nazinga, meaning headland and meadow.

Proceeding along the lane to Nazeing common, one passes several cottages and the old post office, all listed as Grade II buildings. Lodge Farm standing remotely on the edge of the common dates from 1777. Legend has it that Boadicea, in approximately AD 61, drove her chariot down the common to be massacred, with 80,000 men, by the Romans.

In the Domesday Book, the common is mentioned as part of the Waltham Hundred, and was disafforested in 1285 for the men of Nazeing to have the rights of pasture. An Act of 1657 gave use of the land to the tenants of 101 ancient houses. This was further regulated in 1778. In the Second World War, the land was ploughed for food and a further Act of 1947 allowed the copyholders to let the land for farming. Thus, the Nazeing common is *not* a common, but private property, through which a public highway runs, and the correct name is Nazeing wood or park.

As the village is five miles long, it is divided into Upper Nazeing, Middle Street and Lower Nazeing. In Middle Street, at Nazeingbury, ancient crossroads bisect the village where, in 1404, stood the Bury Cross. The present house of 'Nazeingbury' dates back to Tudor times; in fact it was the home of Katherine Parr, the sixth wife of Henry VIII.

The affix 'bury' to Nazeingbury, applied to the communal graves dug to contain the bodies of plague victims, brought down by river barges from London. This area seems to be the extent of the funeral journeys, as graves were also dug at Broxbournebury and Wormleybury, within the district.

Down by the river Lee or Lea, at the turn of the 20th century, the glasshouse industry was established, as the river valley soil was good and there was plentiful spring water. So tomatoes, grapes and cucumbers were grown and the produce taken overnight to Covent Garden by horse and cart. This industry attracted many Dutch, Danish and Norwegian immigrants and their surnames are now part of our heritage. This industry was at its height in the 1950s, but declined with the importation of cheap foreign fruit and the soaring price of oil needed to maintain the high temperatures. It revived partially in the 1970s, due to another group of immigrants – Italians. One famous name became a household word from this industry – Thomas Rochford's house plants. He also has closed down now.

Today, the Lee Valley Regional Park Authority is developing the banks of the river by transforming them into parks and leisure centres, marinas and picnic areas.

🍁 NEVENDON

Nevendon has had many different spellings of its name throughout its long history which dates back to Saxon times. Neutenden and Nezenden were two of these, and in the reign of Edward the Confessor it was called Newenden.

Cranes Farm and Cranes Farm Road owe the origin of their names to the Hugh Le Crane family that farmed it in 1272. Apparently the family of Sandell lived there in the 16th and 17th centuries. William Sandell in his will dated 1542 left bread and cheese and 20 shillings as alms for the poor at his burial and for a month after.

Nevendon's church is dedicated to St Peter and it still retains its original lancet windows, the existing chancel walls being 13th century. Great Bromfords (that also gives its name to a road nowadays) was a large house over 500 years old and said to have contained a priest's hiding place. It was the local meeting place of the hunt and at one time had a moat surrounding it. Unfortunately it was demolished in 1951 after being damaged by enemy action in the Second World War.

The Old Tithe Barn was built in Nevendon somewhere about the 1500s; villagers took a part of their produce there, where it was collected for the lord of the manor as part of their dues that they had to pay to him. At one time it was used as a local school, possibly in the middle 1800s. The old school stood to the west of St Peter's church and was built in 1886 as a National school, it later became a private house and was finally demolished in 1972. In the 18th century Elizabeth Kirkham (who died in 1788) was mistress of Nevendon's school for 27 years, she is buried in the local church.

🍁 NEWPORT

The Domesday Book (1086) shows Newport as an agricultural community of some 200 people, centred on a royal estate. 'Port' at this time meant any market, even though it be inland, under the control of the King. This particular 'port' must have been 'new' sometime in the 10th century and perhaps was even created as one of a series of fortifications against the Danes. Like other fortified towns of the time, it has a triangular shaped village green, which is overlooked by the church.

How though did this triangular centre of the village get the extraordinary name 'Elephant Green'? The tale goes that one year a visiting circus passed this way and an elephant died as it crossed the green. One can imagine the problems and the excitement this event would cause, which would justify commemorating it down the years by naming the spot after it.

Newport has a large boulder, at its northern end by the side of the busy B1383, which is called locally the 'Leper Stone'. Here food was supposedly left for the sufferers, in the Middle Ages, who were lodged at St Leonard's Hospital nearby. Excavations for the new houses that stand on the site near the stone, did reveal human bones but although these were, thankfully, proved ancient, they did not show any signs of leprosy.

Near the centre of the village, in the High Street, stands a private house Monks Barn, which has an interesting ornamental carving of religious theme. The house is thought to have been given its name because it was once a resting place for travelling monks.

In 1692, the owners of the Crown House, in Bridge End, had their hostelry refronted the way it is today, with a crown design in the pargetting. However, the actual building is much older. Folklore has it that this was where, when Charles II stayed 'down the road' at Audley End House, he arranged for his 'friend' Nell Gwyn to lodge in Newport.

An important and venerable part of Newport life and one still thriving, is the Free Grammar School, which began in the year of the Armada (1588). The school was founded out of tragedy, when 'Mistress Joyce Frankland' lost her only son in a riding accident. His memorial has lasted 400 years with the present building dating from 1876. Designed by William Nesfield, this 'heart' of the present collection of buildings is of considerable architectural interest.

🍁 NORTH BENFLEET

The name Benfleet goes back to Saxon times. It is derived from Beamfleote which means an inlet of creek with woods close by. North Benfleet was probably named when some of the original settlers moved further north to form a new settlement. It was also known as Little Benfleet or Benfleet Parva.

In the reign of Edward the Confessor, the manor of North Benfleet belonged to Earl Harold, later King Harold, and at the time of the Domesday survey was owned by William the Conqueror. By the 13th century it was owned by the de Benflete family, and it was probably at this time the church, All Saints, was first built. It is situated on the ridge of the hill, close by the farm of North Benfleet Hall – 'the church by the duck pond' as it is sometimes known locally. An interesting feature of the church is a memorial stone to John Cole, a soldier at Waterloo who was wounded by a musket ball during the famous battle and died 21 years later with the musket ball still inside him.

North Benfleet is a rural area with good farm land which has always supported several well appointed farms. North Benfleet Hall was built in late Tudor times. A priest's hole was discovered there in the 1920s and there was a substantial well built tunnel from the hall to the Sadlers Farm area which may well have been intended as an escape route for Roman Catholics during the troubled religious period of the late Tudors. There is still a farm on the site but the hall was demolished in the 1950s and all that remains is the pond which was once part of the moat. There were several moated buildings in the parish. Bradfield Farm which is now predominantly a dairy farm, has a substantial amount of its moat surviving.

At the turn of the 20th century parts of the large estate running from North Benfleet to Tilbury were sold off as building plots and thus the Plotlands were born. Many Londoners bought these 'little bits of land in the country' and eventually built small huts, shacks and houses on them to enable them to spend time away from the town.

Between the two World Wars, the area became more developed and more permanent buildings were erected, although it was some time before amenities such as drains, sewerage, drinking water, shops, buses etc were forthcoming. Many of these Plotland roads are still unmade and because most of them have large gardens the effect is now one of individuality and spaciousness within a still rural setting.

There is now no centre to the village as such, but many of the older buildings remain, giving a sense of history. At the corner of Pound Lane and Burnt Mill Road stands Pump Cottage which is about 400 years old, named from the nearby village pump. At the corner of Harrow Road stands Horseshoe Cottage, once the village smithy, probably about 300 years old.

🍁 NORTH OCKENDON

North Ockendon is a ribbon development village situated on the outskirts of the London Borough of Havering, at its south-eastern edge. One claim to fame is a ghost that appears along St Mary's Lane in the form of a hooded monk. There is also Stubbers Outdoor Pursuits Centre.

The history of Stubbers goes back to 1334, the date on title deeds of the land. It was named after William Stubbers, a yeoman farmer who lived there around 1440/63. One of its owners, William Coys established a botanic collection preceding Kew by 100 years and it is from there that many plants were first introduced into this country, for example the yucca, rhubarb, yellow figwort, tomato and Jerusalem artichoke. At a later date it passed to the Russell family (one of whom introduced the variety of lupin) and this family made various alterations both to house and gardens. Unfortunately, the house, which had survived right up to 1955, was then demolished and all that remains now is the walled garden and a crinkle-crankle wall – a rare construction in Essex.

There are many monuments and memorials in the church which relate to residents and landowners throughout the years, among them the family of Poyntz who have life-sized effigies in the lying position, carved in great detail in the costume of the period, circa 1600. There are also some fine memorials to various members of the Russell family. It is thought that the original church dates back to St Cedd who was Bishop of the East Saxons around AD 630, who used the well on the churchyard boundary as a place of baptism.

The village hall is known as the 'reading room' and was originally provided by the lord of the manor for his workers to read the papers. It is over 100 years old and was purchased by the villagers for the princely sum of sixpence per household to cover the cost of £20 (negotiated down from £2,000) plus expenses. This was in 1964 and was from the estate of Mr H Benyon whose family had been landowners in the area since 1758.

There only remains the Old White Horse, which is relatively young compared to the general history of the village. Nevertheless, there are villagers who remember horses being tethered together outside while the workers went in to quench their thirst by quaffing a cup.

North Weald Bassett

Few people would claim that North Weald Bassett is a pretty village. In fact it is no longer truly a village, so much building has taken place over the past few years. About 4,500 people now call it home. There are a few buildings of note in the parish, the most attractive the King's Head public house which is a fine Tudor building.

Only a few minutes walk and you can be in open countryside. This is probably why many residents were ready to fight British Telecom's attempt in 1988 to build 900 houses on land where the radio station was from 1921 until 1985. From here there was a marvellous view of the village and surrounding people. The buildings on the old radio station have since been pulled down, and although the Redoubts are listed buildings they are full of water as there is no one to maintain them.

People who live in the centre of the village can now feel safer when there is a sudden downpour of really heavy rain. For years North Weald (few people give the village its full title; Bassett came from the principal landowner in the 13th century named Philip De Basset) has suffered from flooding. A huge flood alleviation scheme has taken place. There is also now a reservoir which should be a real nature reserve in a few years time.

A new hall has been opened on the Memorial Playing Fields which will be a great asset to the village. It has replaced the Queen's Rooms, two smaller halls that stood in the centre of the village and were built to commemorate Queen Victoria's Jubilee. Recently 13 acres of land has been donated to the Parish Council, for the enjoyment of people of all ages. The village is fortunate to still have a school and a sub post office, a chemist and a few small shops.

St Andrew's church is worth a visit. The inside will surprise visitors. The building dates from around 1330 and the tower was added in the 16th century. There was a fire in 1965 and the inside of the church was rebuilt in a much lighter modern style.

Those old enough to remember the Second World War may have memories of North Weald as a famous fighter station. On Sunday, 3rd

September 2000 an Airfield Memorial and Debt of Honour was unveiled at the main gate, dedicated to the 260 men and women, including civilians, who lost their lives here in times of war and of peace.

Each Saturday there is a market on the old runway. It is said to be one of the biggest in Europe and free buses are run for people in the area.

There is still a Horticultural Society and an Allotment Association, so there are still some rural aspects to the village. The Horticultural Society has been in existence since 1902, and they once held a really big annual show that attracted people from miles around, rather like a miniature Essex Show. There is still a fine Annual Show usually in August, where people show their talents not just for growing vegetables, fruit and flowers, but for many other crafts.

Thornwood Common and Hastingwood are the other two villages in the parish. The most direct way to Thornwood Common is past the Tollhouse, now a stone's throw from the M11 motorway, and along Woodside which is an attractive route, especially in the spring when many gardens are colourful with bulbs. The two public houses were named after the trades of many people of the time, the Blacksmith's Arms and the Carpenter's Arms. There used to be a Methodist chapel until just before the Second World War and the only church was pulled down in 1979.

Hastingwood still has its church building but it has been converted into a really attractive home. Hastingwood is a pretty village, but it is so near Harlow that it is doubtful whether it will remain so for many more years.

🍁 ORSETT

In a modern parlance Orsett would be described as 'The Gateway to the Fens', and here that old chestnut can genuinely be told that the proprietor of the Foxhound sells his beer by the pound, that is if you have noticed the tiny stockade on the green that once sheltered stray animals. Adjacent to this product of a bygone age stands a rural lock-up, which must have seen its last drunken customer sometime at the beginning of the 20th century, and together, they make an unusual spectacle in Essex. Lost to present day view is the quoits pitch which was situated immediately behind the Foxhound, formerly the Swan, and until the advent of licensing hours, quoits was a very popular sport in rural areas. The cause of the decline of that popularity has been attributed to there not being enough 'open' hours in the day in which to complete a good game of 41 up.

Basketry, a smith and a fruit farm which produced amongst other things Orsett cider, seem to account for all of Orsett's industrial efforts, but these enterprises have long since gone. Orsett was one of those villages that possessed every advantage, being the administrative centre for the area, but as the years passed so did its importance, and Orsett, although the first village in the district to have street lighting, became a back-water. Lying off the main road the railway companies after failing to master the technology needed to cross the fens, totally ignored it, whereas all the villages hugging the north bank of the river Thames were connected by rail to both London and Southend. In many respects this isolation has helped to preserve the general aura of peace and quiet.

The main roads in Orsett boast of only two shops, a general store, and a post office. Any other requirements of the household can be obtained from a number of shopping centres surrounding Orsett, including Lakeside.

Orsett Hall was once an imposing and, for Essex, an important edifice. Time and circumstance has changed all that since the death of Sir Francis Whitmore, Lord Lieutenant of Essex. Francis Whitmore was lord of the manor from the early days of the 20th century and he died in 1962. His son succeeded and worked hard for the estate. He was known as a racing driver and aviator, using the grounds of the Hall to take off and land, to the consternation of the owners of chimney pots in Maltings Lane. After six years he decided to sell up and the old house is now a restaurant, where one has the privilege to eat where once only the privileged ate. The gates are passed with a feeling of regret for the loss of its former glories.

In honour of the family, the local innkeeper changed the name of his hostelry from 'The George' to the Whitmore Arms, and the inn sign proudly sports the red, blue and gold colours.

Following the road on from the village hall, first farmhouses then ribbon-built bungalows and houses are passed until Baker Street is reached. Named after a former lord of the manor, Baker Street must at some time in the past have been a main thoroughfare, because alongside is a restored sail-less mill, with a machine house adjacent. The present buildings replaced a much older edifice in the early 1800s, which went into dereliction until quite recently. Here, at the crossroads, stands the King's Arms. Opposite is the lane to the fen, a narrow, lonely way, passing through reclaimed wet-lands until it finishes at the edge of the fen.

🍁 PAGLESHAM

While only a few miles from Southend, Paglesham still has a feeling of being remote. The tidal waters which surround it on north, east and south have protected it from development, so that visitors find a peace and space remarkable to the town dweller.

The tide has influenced the development of the village from earliest times. 'Redhills' indicate salt manufacture back to Roman times. A Saxon, Paccel, may have started the village. Certainly there was a church before 1066, the living was given to Westminster Abbey in that year. Norman windows remain. Sheep grazing the flat marshlands probably paid for the handsome 15th century tower which ends the road at Church End. Waterside Lane appropriately takes the other half of Paglesham – East End – back to the sea wall and Shuttlewood's Boat Yard.

Paglesham's fame came from smuggling, the large oyster industry and boatbuilding. In the early 1800s, there was a famous smuggler called 'Hard Apple', William Blyth, who kept the village shop at Church End and was also churchwarden. The river and creeks round the parish provided ideal conditions for smuggling. Several houses were also said to have been used for storing smuggled goods; Cupola House, a three-storeyed Georgian house near the Plough and Sail, was said to have been built with money from smuggling.

In early days, some of the smugglers were oyster merchants and dredgermen and their boats would have been used. Oyster cultivation was big business, both here and on the Crouch. In 1870, 80 to 100 boats and 160 to 200 people were engaged in the fishery.

For many years people came for miles – even from London – to eat oysters in the Plough and Sail. Between the wars they cost three shillings and sixpence per dozen. For a long time the tradition at the Village Produce Association supper was steak, kidney and oyster pudding. Paglesham is the Essex village to still hold an annual Village Produce Association Show started, as they all were, in 1946.

Boatbuilding has been carried on at the river from 1848 when White's Directory gives Kemp as the boatbuilder. William Hall was there in 1883. Then James Shuttlewood took over. He built the *Ethel Ada*, a 48 ton barge, still to be seen, but converted to residential use. Many fishing smacks and some private yachts were built there by James and later by his son, Frank. Today it is no longer owned by the Shuttlewoods, but the name is still above the boatshed.

Farming has also seen many changes. From the sea wall, at one time you could look out over many acres of grassy marshes grazed by cattle and sheep. These have now been drained and ploughed. Dutch elm disease brought the biggest change to the village scene. When the elms were cut down many hedges went as well and the picture of a shady lane through the village disappeared. However, new trees were planted and are growing and so are the hedges.

🍁 PELDON

Peldon is a pretty, sprawling village with parish boundaries running down to the marshes and creeks of the river Blackwater estuary. There was a church at Peldon, or Peltenduna as mentioned in the Domesday Book, in 1086.

The present Norman building has a nave dating back to the 12th century with the tower being added at the end of the 14th century. The church of St Mary the Virgin stands on the hill overlooking the surrounding countryside.

In 1086 there were two manors in Peldon, and it is clear that the Saxon freemen were dispossessed by William the Conqueror's Norman men who had come over to England with him. The most grasping of these was William's brother-in-law, Odo, the Bishop of Bayeux who received much land in Kent and vast estates in Essex, including land at Peldon. In 1282, Walter de Peltindone conveyed the manor to the De Neville family, who in the 12th and 13th centuries were the chief foresters of the King. Later in 1545, King Henry VIII granted the manor to Sir Thomas (later Lord) Darcy and Peldon remained in the Darcy family until 1647 when it was acquired by Mr Thomas Reynolds, who became Mayor of Colchester in 1654.

The Peldon Rose, standing at the edge of the Roman road, the Strood, to Mersea, was a famous old smugglers' inn. Peldon was close to the centre of the earthquake that shook this part of the country on 22nd April 1884. Much damage was done to the church and local houses.

Various investigations have been made into the famous Red Hills discovered in the parish and it is commonly believed that these had the dual purpose of being not only early salt workings, but also sites for pottery making.

✿ PILGRIMS HATCH

In the parish of South Weald were three small hamlets, Bentley, Coxtie Green, and Pilgrims Hatch which was originally a stopping place for pilgrims on their way to the St Thomas à Becket chapel in Brentwood and then to Canterbury.

Seventy years ago Pilgrims Hatch was a very pleasant village within walking distance of Brentwood. It was quite rural with several farms and many orchards. There were two very old public houses, the Rose and Crown and the Black Horse, frequented mainly by the local men who could walk to them easily. There was a very small dark post office situated in a room at the side of a farmhouse with a bell that tinkled when the door was opened, alerting the postmistress that a customer had arrived.

Local employment was mostly on farms and seasonal work was in the orchards, fruit farms, flower picking and at two large greenhouse sites where bedding plants were grown and transplanted into wooden boxes for sale to the public. A huge site covering many fields belonged to Cable and Wireless Ltd, who had erected four huge 200 foot metal towers and five T-shaped beam masts supporting dozens of aerials which received radio telegraphy signals from all over the world and was used for relaying information, news items and cablegrams to London. Quite a number of local workmen were necessary to keep all the equipment in good order.

After 1945 village life changed. Council house estates sprang up on some of the fields and orchards to provide accommodation for the expanding population. A new post office within a grocery and greengrocery shop was built on part of the old farmyard. In 1951, instead of having a curate-in-charge at Bentley church, it became a separate parish from South Weald and is now known as Bentley Common. Private housing was built on the allotments, orchards and greenhouse sites and eventually the village policeman and the district nurse went. The radio station closed down in 1967, the aerials and masts were dismantled and all the services were transferred to Goonhilly in Cornwall which is an earth satellite station.

In common with many other hostelries, the character of the Rose and Crown and the Black Horse has changed and they have become mainly eating places with extended car parks. There is another village store (originally a paper shop) which opens seven days a week, a fried fish shop, a hairdresser's, an off-licence and a curry restaurant. Although cars are parked outside nearly every house and little 'hopper' buses have replaced the old green double deckers, we still consider Pilgrims Hatch to be a village.

 PLESHEY

Pleshey is the only Essex village which has the distinction of a mention of some substance in Shakespeare. In *Richard II* the Duchess of Gloucester says to her brother-in-law, John of Gaunt:

> 'With all good speed at Plashy visit me,
> Alack, and what shall good old York see there
> But empty lodgings and unfurnish'd walls,
> Unpeopled offices, untrodden stones?
> And what cheer there for welcome but my groans?'

This is an allusion to what had happened shortly before the time covered by the play. Events at Pleshey were headline news in 1397, when Thomas, Duke of Gloucester and youngest son of King Edward III, was seized forcibly at Pleshey Castle, his residence, and carried off to Calais, where he was put to death on the orders of the royal governor. All this, it was well known, was done at the behest of the young king, Richard II, Thomas's nephew.

Pleshey was probably built by the Earls of Essex in the early part of the 12th century and remained one of their principal castles and residences for many generations.

There had been a church built for the villagers inside the town moat, but Thomas replaced this by a grander foundation which he built and endowed just outside the earthworks. Residences were built nearby for the college of priests.

As a collegiate foundation the church and its endowments fell to the crown when the chantries were suppressed in 1546. In the 18th century the Bishop of London and the Tufnell family, by now lords of the manor, rebuilt part of the church, but a full restoration had to wait until 1868 when Frederick Chancellor of Chelmsford fully rebuilt the church.

Pleshey is probably best known now, at least among Anglican churchgoers, as the home of the Diocesan Retreat House. This is next door to the church.

A different, but also well-known, institution in the village is Mr

Clements' smithy. He is well-known over a large part of Essex as a specialist in the production of decorative ironwork.

In 1991 Pleshey won, not for the first time, the top award for 'very small villages' in the County Linen 'Best-Kept Village' competition. This was a most well-deserved award for a village that is not only historic and beautiful, but whose strong corporate loyalty ensures that it is always lovingly cared for.

✤ PURFLEET

Local legend has it that Purfleet received its name in 1588 when England was threatened by the Spanish Armada. Local children are usually told one or other of the tales relating to this at their mother's knee.

In 1588 Queen Elizebeth I had to take steps to defend her country. On her way from London to review her troops at Tilbury, the Royal barge was caught in a severe thunderstorm causing her to take shelter on the north side of the Thames, near a village. The Queen is reputed to have landed and climbed the beacon hill – a very steep hill overlooking the river. From its summit she looked towards Tilbury, and, seeing her fleet tossed by the storm, exclaimed 'Oh, my poor fleet!' The other story is similar but the ending changes. Apparently the Queen had a predilection for wearing high heeled shoes, and after climbing to the top of the beacon hill she is purported to have wailed 'Oh my poor feet!' Purfleet then, according to these stories is a corruption of 'poor fleet' or 'poor feet'!

These stories, although they add colour and romance to an otherwise rather drab place, are of course complete fabrication. It is known from documentary evidence that around the 1300s the village was called Pourtfleet, although there were many variations in the method of spelling. It appears that the name is derived from two Saxon words – 'port' meaning a haven and 'fleet', an arm of the sea, or bay.

The fortunes of Purfleet have since come and gone, first with a military garrison and as a popular destination for London trippers, to the riverside industrial developments like the Thames Board Mills and the various petroleum sites. Nowadays Purfleet is becoming engulfed by the spread of people who are constantly searching for somewhere to live which is within easy commuting distance from London.

With the closure of the London docks and the development of the docks at Tilbury, Purfleet no longer sees naval and merchant shipping plying up the Thames to London, as was once a common sight. However, Purfleet has found itself on the the map again as it is the departure point on the Essex side for the Queen Elizabeth II Bridge which now spans the river between Essex and Kent.

🍁 Purleigh

Purleigh is first mentioned in a Saxon will of AD 998 but, like most parishes, no detailed information is available until 1086, when it appears in Domesday Book. Purleigh was then a typical rural community consisting of eight manors in the ownership of four Normans.

During the reign of Elizabeth I, Purleigh's population began to increase, but the remaining woodland was too valuable to be cleared for homesteads. Consequently new cottages were built on the commons at Cock Clarks, Howe Green and Farther Howe Green. The amount of land allocated to these cottages was too small (half to two acres) to sustain the occupier by farming alone, although they usually had grazing rights on the remaining commons. Consequently, many of these new cottagers resorted to other trades to make a living.

Towards the end of the 17th century the population again declined, then rose again during the late 18th century, and stayed high for the next 100 years; in fact the 1,213 people recorded in the 1841 census was not surpassed until 1981. This time however, the rising population coincided with a high level of prosperity in arable farming. Consequently many of the newcomers were employed on the farms, although again many new trades appeared in the parish. By now the commons had virtually disappeared (the remaining areas being almost entirely enclosed by 1801) and the high value of arable land meant much of the woodland was cleared to enlarge existing farms rather than to create new holdings. The only remaining areas available for cottage sites were the wide roadside verges, hence the landscape of Purleigh today is one of dispersed farmsteads, small hamlets and frequent roadside cottages.

It is from the last phase of expansion that many of a parish's traditional assets survive in Purleigh. A church has obviously been here since the Middle Ages, but the earliest Nonconformist chapel did not arrive until the 1850s (now Chapel Cottage at Howe Green). A redundant cottage had been used as the poor-house since around 1700, but a purpose built workhouse was provided in 1740 (now the Queen's Head at Rudley

Green). In 1769 the rector, Samuel Horsmanden, left an endowment to provide for the education of Purleigh's children, which took effect in 1800 on the death of his wife. Shortly after this the then rector, John Eveleigh, financed the building of a schoolmaster's house and school room (now Eveleigh House). Another rector, Edward Hawkins, financed the establishment of a second school in 1842, Hawkins House at Cock Clarks. By the 1770s a grocer's shop with adjoining bakery had been built on Purleigh Hill, which, although no longer a shop still retains its original bow window. Purleigh's principal bakery further down the hill was converted in the 1830s, functioned until modern times and is still called 'the Steam Bakery'. Valley Stores on the opposite side of the hill had been functioning as a shop since at least the 18th century.

🍁 RADWINTER

Radwinter is a large parish about five miles east of Saffron Walden; it includes the hamlets of Stocking Green, Maypole End and Radwinter End. There is evidence in the form of innumerable fragments found in the fields that settlement has existed here since at least the Stone Age. The Romans were at Radwinter and many pieces including coins, abundant oyster shells and two human skeletons have been unearthed in recent times. Settlement continued through Saxon times and at the time of the Domesday Book, Radwinter was recorded as having 8 beehives, 18 cattle and 13 goats.

In about 1450 Lower House Farm was built; this is the oldest surviving house. The later Manor Houses of Radwinter Hall, Brockholds, Radwinter Grange and Bendysh Hall also remain standing to this day, the latter having once been contained within its own parish of Radwinter End.

In 1577 the Rector of Radwinter, William Harrison, wrote a *Description of England* which gives an insight in the ways of folk in Elizabethan times. On the south side of his parsonage house he had painted on a window 'the sun in his glory, within which was a hare'. This was a rebus, a pun on his name, hare-in-sun. Sadly the window no longer exists.

Harrison referred to Radwinter's river, the Pant, as having been wide enough for corn boats to pass from Maldon. The Pant in its present day form is little more than a large stream and past navigation requires considerable imagination.

In 1874 a great fire razed much of the centre of Radwinter to the ground, including the 13th century church. The rector at this time was Rev J. E. W. Bullock who instructed the architect Eden Nesfield to draw up plans for the village hall, almshouses and cottages of Church Hill. Once completed, these were decorated with a type of pargetting. The present day church of St Mary the Virgin was completely rebuilt in 1887/8 to Nesfield's design, the tower and spire being added by Temple Moore. The village school was built following completion of the church.

The Great War of 1914–18 had its impact on Radwinter, the names of 28 men killed are recorded on the war memorial in the churchyard. The Second World War saw the hasty construction of buildings to accommodate airmen stationed at nearby RAF Debden. A satellite aerodrome, for use in case of emergency at Debden, still exists. Also, still showing on the brickwork of the village hall, is a white arrow indicating the direction in which to run in the event of enemy attack.

RAMSDEN BELLHOUSE & RAMSDEN HEATH

Ramsden Bellhouse and Ramsden Heath are now two separate villages, but until the first part of the 20th century they were one village, which stretched from Stock in the north to Nevendon in the south. The village was centred around the crossroads, where today the war memorial stands in Ramsden Heath, but confusingly it was known as Ramsden Bellhouse. Here were the blacksmith's and the wheelwright's shops, while not far off were the mill, the parish workhouse, the bakehouse and later the school and the shops. The name Ramsden Heath applied only to an area of heathland to the north of the village.

About 1910 Homesteads Ltd bought Ramsden Bellhouse Farm and built an estate centred around St Mary's church about a mile from the old village. This became known as Ramsden Bellhouse, and gradually the old village became Ramsden Heath.

St Mary's church porch rafters date from the 14th century, whilst the rest of the porch, the wooden tower, the font and the nave roof are 15th century. The church chest is dated about 1480. The rectory was probably sited near Pump Hill but was demolished in 1734. Thomas Cox, the rector of Stock, was presented with the living of Ramsden Bellhouse, and from then until 1967 the two parishes shared their rector. The Congregational church at Ramsden Heath and the Peculiar's chapel (now gone) were built in the 19th century. St John's, sometimes called the Tin, or Iron church, was demolished in 1999. Ramsden Bellhouse Baptist church was built in 1927.

The parish workhouse, which was near Mill Lane, was sold about 1837 while the post mill, from which Mill Lane takes its name, came to a dramatic end. On 22nd November 1873, at about mid-day, while working, the mill blew down with Mr Richard Hamilton, the miller still inside. Fortunately he escaped with only bruises, being between two beams, but it was the end of the mill. A year previously in 1872, the church school was opened almost opposite the mill, and educated the local children for some 50 to 60 years. It was later converted into two houses, called somewhat wittily 'Eton' and 'Harrow', but has now made way for modern development.

The railway divides the village now into 'up the Heath' to the north and 'down the Bellhouse' to the south. The first passenger Great Eastern train went through on 1st January 1889. A station was promised, but never happened. It is interesting to note that in the census of 1841, Ramsden Bellhouse with 462 residents had more people than Wickford with 445 residents. It can only be that the coming of the railway station to Wickford turned it into today's little town. Perhaps we are fortunate the station wasn't built in Ramsden, for in spite of extensive building in both villages, we proudly believe that we still live in the country.

🍁 RAYNE

Rayne is an ancient village situated on the Roman road, Stane Street, two miles from Braintree and seven miles from Dunmow. Stane Street is where Roman soldiers progressed along the route to link Colchester and St Albans.

Rayne is in the heart of Essex farmland, sprinkled with attractive Tudor farmhouses, and in the Street itself are fine examples of clothiers' houses of a slightly later period. The village green and war memorial are well kept and close by are several Grade II listed buildings, the oldest being Rayne Hall and Tudor Cottage.

The population has remained static for several years since the new housing developments were completed in the late 1970s. Many people commute to London either by train from Braintree or by commuter coach from the village. The growth of Stansted airport has also provided employment for local people.

Since the Rayne and Braintree bypass was completed a more peaceful atmosphere has returned to the village. The Flitch Way, linear park, passes through the centre of the village and enables young and old to walk or cycle east or west along the site of the old railway line. The station, station house and platform have been restored to their former glory.

Hopefully Rayne will retain its peaceful rural characteristics well into the future. It has its farms, Rayne Foundry and many other small industrial undertakings, its church, school, modern village hall and many clubs and societies. Sport has always been an important part of village life and this tradition carries on today with the football and cricket teams. There is also a thriving table-tennis club, which was founded in 1976. More recently the village has been twinned with Verberie in France and many exchange visits have taken place. Young people from both villages have enjoyed activity holidays and many friendships have been formed.

🍁 Ridgewell

Ridgewell owes its name to its first settler Riddes, not as many think to the existence of the 'well on the ridge' – even though there *is* a well on the ridge! The Roman road from Colchester to Cambridge passes through the village by means of the Causeway, from which you descend to the river Stour, the highest point on the river. It was here that river and road came together and the Romans made a military camp. In the field on the left as you enter the village from Colchester are the remains of a Roman villa, marked today by a single oak tree. A spring of fresh water used to form a stream – now piped – which flowed down to the river Colne through Ashley Meadows. The first house on the left still shows its moat and is one of several moated houses on the hillside between the Stour and Colne.

In the early days it was a place of some importance with its own Trade Guild. The Guild for many centuries had its own Trade Chapel on the north side of the church. Records show that this was demolished at the Bishop's direction in the 17th century. The church, dedicated to St Laurence, in whose honour a fair was held every 9th August, was largely rebuilt in the Perpendicular style. Part of the north wall is of Norman origin and probably owes its preservation to the existence of the Trade Chapel alongside. You can still see the entrance in the strange shape of the east wall of the north aisle. The glory of the church is in its roof, despite the destruction in Cromwellian days of the carved angels that carried it (some of the angel wings still remain). The carrying bier is probably England's oldest, dated to the 14th century, as too is the base of the rood screen. Discerning eyes can find a 14th century graffitist's prayer scratched on the pillar near to the steps of the rood screen.

The chapel stands at the north end of the village green. The present building is the third on the site. The first dated from the third quarter of the 17th century and obeyed the 'Five Mile Act'. Round the green itself are many listed houses.

This was at one time a self supporting village, but now suffers from the usual malaise of village life – the closure of village shops in favour of supermarkets. Before the First World War there was Dutty's for groceries and haberdashery, a newsagent's, Nimble's which sold everything ('Nimble' Barnard and his van was known in all the local villages and Blossom, the horse, when not pulling, like his master grazed wherever he could), a butcher, baker, shoemaker, coal merchant, blacksmith, hurdlemaker, wheelwright, carpenter/joiner and painter, not to mention three millers and a milliner.

The village had nicknames for everyone. One old inhabitant can remember Busky, Dordy, Bluey, Hutly, Turk, Suggy, Squd, Ticker, Tot, Fingy, Porky and Chinaman (at one time a churchwarden)! If only we knew how they came by them.

There was at one time a Tuesday market in the village but it must have been discontinued in the 19th century. What did survive until the First World War was the Whit Tuesday Fair and the traditional dinner that day – roast beef followed by plum pudding.

There has been a great change in the village in regard to agriculture. All the small farms have gone, where the farmer and his family worked hard but were happy enough, and the farmhouses sold. Farm buildings too, unfortunately, have been pulled down. Wash Farm still has its c1880 (now listed) pump and there are another two in the village which are preserved.

❧ ROCHFORD

Just over three miles north of Southend, Rochford is steeped in history. It was mentioned in the Domesday Book and the first village settlement was by the Romans in the 2nd century.

Along South Street you will come to the cruciform where the four roads converge as on the compass – North Street, South Street, East Street and West Street. This cruciform is one of the few remaining in this country. South Street itself can boast many old and well maintained properties dating back many years. The Old House is a beautiful building, dating from c.1270. It has been restored by Rochford District Council and is used as a Heritage Centre.

Weir Pond Road, aptly named many years ago, still has several of the old original cottages, now listed buildings and revelling in such delightful names as Lilac Cottage, Rose Cottage, etc. You can turn right into East Street, again passing many fine old houses. On the right is King's Hill, once known as the 'Lawless Court', and the home of the Whispering Post, one of the well known features of Rochford.

The hub of Rochford is the Market Square. Originally it housed many old wooden buildings and every Thursday a cattle market was held. This was a feature for miles around and continued until 1959.

There were two fires here – one being accidental but causing a great deal of damage. The second was on the occasion of the Relief of Mafeking when a bonfire was again lit, causing much damage. According to records there was also an execution in the Square. The victim was a religious martyr by the name of Henry Simson. A plaque still exists to commemorate this and can be seen in one of the alleyways leading off the square.

Down West Street, past the station, on the right are the almshouses, built by Lord Rich, and still occupied. The lovely old parish church of St Andrew stands in the middle of Rochford Golf Course. This truly is a beautiful church, kept in immaculate condition.

Standing opposite the church is Rochford Hall, with its twisted chimneys and one of Rochford's most historic buildings. It was originally the home of the Boleyn family where King Henry VIII held many trusts with Anne Boleyn.

🍁 ROWHEDGE

The village of Rowhedge, part of East Donyland, lies three miles south of Colchester. It was compactly built in Victorian times, when the men were kept busy with fishing in the winter and sailing the big yachts in the summer. Fishermen always kept an eye out for ships being wrecked on the treacherous sands, outside the river Colne. Often carried shoulder high through Harwich after rescuing a shipwrecked crew, they would go hurrying back to the wreck to salvage as much of the cargo as they could, officially to be handed to the Receiver of Wrecks, but often it was easier to bring it straight home! Many of the houses had a cellar or smugglers' hole, which were used to hide the hard-won goods, until they could be sold.

Visitors entering the village are attracted by the unusual shape of the octagonal church of St. Lawrence. The 150th anniversary of the church was celebrated in 1988, during which year parishioners worked and donated new kneelers. Being worked in tapestry with a red background to many different designs, the kneelers give a welcoming warmth to the well-kept atmosphere in the church.

During the 1920s the village children used the marshland as their playground and the lads used a farm field for football and cricket. However, a group of hard working villagers formed a committee and raised enough money to purchase a farm field in the centre of the village. This was made into a splendid recreation ground with a pavilion, and trees were planted in an avenue each being a living memorial to a village man who was killed during the First World War. Sadly 18 of these trees were destroyed in the 1987 hurricane but all have now been replaced and are flourishing.

Rowhedge's High Street is in fact the lowest and the oldest street, following the line of the river Colne. Many of the old cottages have been demolished, public houses have been converted to houses, the shipyards have also been demolished awaiting 'development', but the atmosphere of a 'fishing village' still lingers, perhaps because Rowhedge has never been 'fashionable'. The waterfront has always been the focal point of the village and there are two pleasant public open spaces. At the turn of the 20th century these were busy quays, where tons of sprats, coal etc were off-loaded from boats. Masts and spars lay on trestles, while the boats were being overhauled, the whole area being packed with fishing smacks. Repairs must have been continuous. Every year at the end of the summer the men came back from sailing the big yachts and a Regatta Day would be arranged. The wealthy yacht owners supplied fireworks for evening entertainment.

In the heyday of the large racing yachts many men from the village crewed and sailed for rich and famous people, including the King's yacht *Britannia*. This is evident when walking round the village, especially up Church Hill, where the older cottages have names of famous yachts.

Several sail lofts still survive, and many of them have a yacht mast doing duty as a pole for the humble washing line.

 ROYDON

Roydon is situated on the edge of the Green Belt west of Harlow. The station is a mere 100 yards from the Hertfordshire border.

Not far from the station, opposite a well kept village hall, stands the 13th century parish church of St Peter ad Vincula. There are Roman tiles in the walls and the roof timbers inside have been dated to before 1250. The first incumbent in about 1190 was one William the Chaplain, who witnessed a document at Natteswell in 1198. The church has six hatchments, armorial bearings which by custom were placed on a deceased person's house and after the funeral hung in the parish church. The goblets in the Butler arms are an allusion to the family name, whereas the hogs' heads in the Booth arms have reference to the family business of gin distilling. There are several interesting wall monuments, one of which records Thomas Lord who 'drowned in a rivulet in the sight of his friends in the view of his house in the 72nd year of his age October 31 1771.'

Near the church, by the side of a 15th century cottage, are the stocks and a small wooden padlocked shed which served as the lock-up in the 19th century.

The manor house of Roydon Hall was demolished in 1864 but in 1531 it was acquired by Henry VIII for Anne Boleyn in exchange for Bromhill

Roydon church with its 15th-century village stocks

Priory in Norfolk. In 1538 Henry was at Roydon Hall with his infant son Edward by Jane Seymour, and the child was presented to the people of Roydon who were apparently delighted and trooped down to see the baby Prince.

Years ago, when horses and carts were a common sight in the village, a big galvanized iron horse trough stood at the T junction at the top of the High Street. Young men used to collect there on warm summer evenings, talking and watching the passing show.

In those days the High Street had several shops. A double-fronted draper's shop sold everything from pins to dresses; this later became the Co-op but that too has gone and the building pulled down. Across the road was Hickling's, a big grocer's shop, and there was another grocer's called Brown's further down the High Street. There was a village blacksmith's, which ended up as a wool shop, and two butchers, one of which had a slaughterhouse at the back where they used to kill the pigs. One of these shops belonged to a Mr Hill. Once Mr Hill was very ill and the farmer from the Temple Farm, old Mr Abbey, brought a load of hay in his horse and cart, and spread it on the road in front of Mr Hill's house so that the noise outside did not worry him. The village policeman made him take it all up again, an act considered very brave as many were in awe of Mr Abbey, but of course it could have been very dangerous to traffic.

The river Stort runs through the end of the village, and there are many fishermen in the season. It is lovely and peaceful along the banks of the river. One way there is a lock, through which in days gone by barges and longboats would be raised and lowered. Now there are only pleasure boats on the river. Going the other way, the river passes an old mill.

🍁 RUNWELL

Situated on low hills near the river Crouch to the north and east of Wickford, Runwell is approximately 12 miles from Chelmsford and a similar distance from Southend-on-Sea.

At its south-western end, close to the Wickford boundary, lies the parish church of St Mary. Its grey, stone tower dates back to the 15th century but the round columns of the arcades are from a church which was a place of pilgrimage in the 12th century, Thomas Becket's time. Decoration of the timber of the porches bears Tudor roses and on one of its doors, now curtained, is a strange burnt mark which legend says is the mark of the devil's hand when one summer's day he was shut in the church by a corrupt priest, Rainaldus, who dabbled in the 'black arts'.

Rainaldus, it is said, vanished in a bubbling, hissing pool of evil-smelling black liquid, which sank beneath the brick floor of the south porch, leaving a circular stain wherein could be seen a strange skull-like flint. Doubtless on account of its superstitious connection this was subsequently thrown away, but in 1944 a stone was discovered in the churchyard shaped as the legend described. Until recently it was set into the south wall of the church surrounded by an inscription in Latin, the translation being 'The wages of sin is death'. This flint is now housed in Southend's central museum.

Monuments to members of the Sulyard family grace the walls of the chancel including brasses of Eustace Sulyard and his wife in ruffs facing each other across a prayer desk. The Sulyards lived in what is now Flemings Farm, the present building consisting of the remnants of the north-east wing of a once extensive Tudor mansion. Sited in the north of the parish, it is close to Poplars Farm, due east of which is the Running Well from which Runwell received its name. The spring which feeds the well has never been known to fail and the well can be found at the highest point in the parish where three fields meet.

Despite the village's proximity to Wickford and an enormous increase in population, it has a strong community spirit and links with Chelmsford, the county town, are cherished.

🍁 ST LAWRENCE BAY

Ramsey Wick, Steeple Stone, The Stone, St Lawrence Bay – not many places in south-east Essex could have boasted four names, all acceptable to the Post Office!

The map published by Colonel Colby in 1840 shows Ramsey Island surrounded by Ramsey Marsh with just one building, Wick Farm, in the centre of the island. One lane leads directly from the B1021 in and out of the island and this has not changed today; the lane now named Main Road leads directly to the Blackwater estuary past the site of Wick Farm which was, until recently, a very attractive thatched farmhouse. Alas it is now a small housing estate called Wick Point.

So in 1840 we have a back-of-beyond island with all the charm of deepest Essex. 'Island', of course, is an academic word as the only time it could be called an island was at high tide and then a small bridge crossed a dyke called The Wade. Thus it remained until the 1890s when with the coming of the railway to Southminster six miles away, the Dengie Peninsula began to open up. People would put their cycles on the train in London and explore. For Ramsey Wick this was birth and at this time Mr Winterbon and Mr Cauldwell began to develop the Oyster Cottages, a small row of wooden two up two down fishermen's residences and by 1902 there were eight standing in their own ground behind the sea wall.

By 1903 Riverview Guest House was built and in those early years Burnham-on-Crouch was becoming a yachting centre and so yachtsmen began to explore the estuaries and creeks of Essex. Two families from London, the Huttons from Regent Street and the Haywards from Berkeley Square, admired Ramsey Wick from the water, 'especially as one could get a cup of tea at the Riverview'. They decided to rent one of the newly built fishermen's cottages whilst exploring the area and eventually bought some land to the west of Ramsey Wick which they named Scarlets. Mr Hayward, a builder, had put up three identical country houses on the site by 1910. Scarlets, being out of the parish of St Lawrence and in the parish of Steeple, caused the first name change to Steeple Stone.

After the First World War the Bebbington family sold building plots. This began the development with sheds, garages and tents. The population between the wars rose in summer to 1,200 and in the winter dropped to perhaps 30. With no main drainage or electricity many acquaintances were made at five am in the morning whilst burying the previous day's effluent!

Tinnocks estate was developed by Mr Winterbon, a private estate facing the Blackwater and to this day it is still run by the trustees. By 1938 Steeple Stone was being referred to as 'The Stone', probably due to the fact that the Ramsey Wick part had almost joined up with the Steeple / Scarlets part and at the outbreak of the Second World War in 1939 quite a village atmosphere had grown up.

Riverview was to see a number of changes over the years after 1948. It gained its licence by becoming the Stone Yacht Club although precious little yachting was carried on from its portals. In that year the returning soldiers, sailors and airmen began to see that there was something in this boating lark and so from within the Riverview was born Stone Sailing Club. Wick Farm by this time had also regained its licence as the St Lawrence Bay Yacht and Country Club.

Written records of St Lawrence's church begin in the 12th century, though most of the present church dates from the rebuilding of 1877. The site is one of the high points of Essex with a view of 25 miles. It is used regularly for worship and it was kept open every day until 1988 when there was some vandalism and an unsuccessful arson attempt.

The development from sleepy hamlet to full-blown village was inevitable. Electricity came to The Stone during the war and with main drainage in 1975 this made the Stone think in terms of 'St Lawrence Bay'. With the advent of the caravan sites and the inevitable expansion of the modern plot land, St Lawrence Bay has become an organised conurbation, with as many holiday people as residents. The crunch on the stones and the whispers at five am are long gone. That's of course if you've got main drainage.

🍁 St Osyth

This waterside village has great charm and is just eleven miles from Colchester.

The village is enhanced by the imposing Priory and Gatehouse, St Clere's Hall (a rare example of a 14th century aisled hall) and many other listed old buildings. There are a number of 14th and 15th century timber-framed cottages with weather-boarded elevations and pantiled roofs. The owners of these cottages have maintained their character by retaining inglenooks, low ceilings, oak beams and braces.

Fronting the Priory is a large green known as 'The Bury' (bury being a derivation of the word 'burgh' and the site of the original village). Mill Street leads from the Bury downhill to St Osyth Creek and a small quay. In days of yore many sailing barges carried a variety of cargoes from this quay and returned with coal and loads of London 'muck' for the fields. This small area was the scene of smuggling as intensive as that of Cornwall or Kent in the 16th century. These pirates, without doubt, were assisted by the locals. The quay is now a flourishing boatyard and the Dam is a popular venue for water-skiers and other water-sport enthusiasts.

St Osyth has a long uncrowded beach, one section of which, away from the main activities, has been reserved for naturists. The large recreation ground, beyond which you can glimpse the sea, is kept in immaculate condition and boasts a fair-sized sports pavilion, picnic tables, tennis courts, football and cricket pitches and a well equipped fenced playground for the tiny tots.

St Osyth Priory is the most well-known and the most impressive feature of the village – it has a fascinating history and much remains to be admired. During the Civil War, a Puritan mob attacked the Priory ransacking the house and gatehouse, inflicting considerable damage. The incumbent at the time, Lady Rivers, fled for her life to Long Melford.

In its long history the Priory has had many distinguished visitors. Queen Elizabeth I visited the Priory in 1561 but on the first night there was a terrific thunderstorm and Elizabeth hurriedly departed for London the very next day. But she did return 18 years later. In the 1920s and 1930s the late Queen Mary, Arthur, Duke of Connaught and many others of the Royal family were entertained at the Priory by General Kincaid-Smith, the owner at that time. There are various trees planted around the gardens to commemorate their visits.

The original priory church of St Osyth was actually in the priory grounds and was replaced in the 12th century by a stone Norman church on the present site of the parish church of St Peter and St Paul, which dates mainly from the 16th century when the nave and aisles were rebuilt in brick with a hammerbeam roof.

About 300 years ago St Osyth village was notorious on account of the number of witches reputed to dwell there. There is a book in the British Museum, published in the year 1582, which contains a report of evidence given by Brian D'Arcy JP against a number of women who were suspected of witchcraft. During the Civil War (reported in a volume dated 1645) the Justice of the Peace for the County of East Essex found time to conduct a witch-hunt in the country east of Colchester. Twenty-two women are mentioned in this volume and were indicted for witchcraft. Many of them confessed to possessing 'imps' and to evil doings by witchcraft, possibly in the hope that by confessing they would be pardoned. One, Ursula Kemp, never confessed, but strongly defended herself, able to read and write. Her trial was held at St Clere's Hall.

🍁 THE SAMPFORDS

The village of Great Sampford, and the larger parish of Little Sampford are the archetypal example of English country life. Although many people work outside the village, even commute to London, farming is still the lifeblood and mainstay of the community.

The origins of the Sampfords, meaning sandy ford, are still awaiting discovery but it is known there was a Saxon settlement about the river Pant, where the kingfisher is often seen. Mentioned in Domesday the names were Sanford (Magna) and Sanforda (Parva), when the population numbered between 275 to 325. Nine hundred years later there are around 650 residents.

The two churches are still in use. St Michael the Archangel at Great Sampford dates from the 13th century. St Michael's setting is idyllic, at the heart of the village, above the river Pant, surrounded by a flint stone wall and bordered by an avenue of lime trees. The view to the west is across miles of undulating Essex cornland and woodland.

St Mary the Virgin at Little Sampford is enchanting. Set in a fold of the land its churchyard must be one of the most picturesque. Local artists often sketch there and villagers and visitors alike seem to savour its special peacefulness with the view across the river valley. The present building is believed to date from early in the 1300s, although there has been a church on the site since well before the Norman Conquest. Great efforts were made by parishioners to raise the thousands of pounds needed to restore the beautiful east window.

The Sampfords have a school, a village hall, a post office, and the Red Lion pub. There is also a flourishing tennis club, as well as a cricket team and drama group.

Some of the old farms have names dating from the original owners in medieval times. The oldest, Free Roberts, is named after Walter FitzRobert, who annually paid 1d or a pair of white gloves for land at Great Sampford. The oldest name in Little Sampford dates from 1280; Hawkes Farm, on the lane to Cornish Hall End. The beautiful Tewes is named after Richard Tewes and dates from 1483. It is in a secret valley just below the woodland known as High Trees which leads to Little Sampford church.

🍁 SANDON

Sandon is a small village, to the south-east of Chelmsford, with a Norman church dedicated to St Andrew.

Runaway brides in the 17th century did not all have to dash to far away Scotland in order to obtain a quick wedding as the rector of Sandon, the Reverend Gilbert Dillingham, was only too ready to oblige.

As news of his willingness and cooperation spread through and beyond the county, weddings at Sandon, which had averaged four per year, increased enormously. Between 1615 and 1635 the Reverend Dillingham married no fewer than 511 couples, including a daughter of the rector of Chelmsford, using an assumed surname as apparently did lots of others. The parson undoubtedly grew fat on the wedding fees.

His successor, the Rev Brian Walton, who later became chaplain to King Charles II and was eventually made Bishop of Chester, put an immediate stop to these irregularities, to the intense disappointment and grief of those runaways who still turned up expecting to obtain the services of Mr Dillingham!

 SEWARDS END

Like so many East Anglian villages, Sewards End has changed almost beyond recognition during the past 60 years. What was once a selfsufficient farming community, with its own cottage industries and craftsmen, now is almost entirely residential.

There are several interesting buildings along the first stretch of main road – Hopwoods, a Tudor farmhouse; Campions, reputedly the oldest house in the village and famed for its wall paintings, some of which are in Saffron Waldon museum; Gaytons, a half-timbered Elizabethan farmhouse; and Everards. Although much renovated and extended, this dates back to the 14th century, and was the first privately owned yeoman farmhouse in the village.

Nearby is the church, which in fact is neither a church nor owned by the Church authorities. It is the chapel of ease, built in 1847 by a wealthy local farmer, Thomas Gayton.

Until the Education Act of 1947, the chapel was also the village school for many years, not only used by the village children but also those from Saffron Walden workhouse, or the 'Grubby', as it was called. Some of the senior residents can still recall the children in their grey workhouse uniforms being marched along the main road, which then was little more than a wide cart track. On occasions, as many as 90 children squeezed into the tiny chapel school, to be taught by just two teachers and the headmaster.

Up to 1915, Sewards End also had its own windmill, a site now occupied by three modern, neo-Georgian houses. The last miller, George Jarvis, also ran the bakery, and such was the poverty at that time, he knew if he did not get the money immediately, he would never get it. Being a generous man, he frequently did not get paid, either for bread or the use of his ovens at the week-end to cook the villagers' meat.

Near the first corner in the main road, although not visible from the road, is The Towers, a magnificently foolish edifice built during the 19th century by William Gayton, the brother of chapel-builder, Thomas. Also on the first corner is another tower – the water tower, built in 1905. This may not seem important to those who are used to unlimited water gushing from their taps, but in those days finding water during the summer could be a real problem for the people of the village. The bucket brigade had to set out early each morning, working their way from pond to pond. Often their search ended at a spring-fed pond at the western edge of the village, followed by a half-mile trudge home.

In Redgate Lane stands a group of historic houses. The oldest is Swain's Farm, which still bears the name of the original medieval landholder, Sir Walter de Swayne (1292), and it is probable that part of the house dates back to that time. Later, it had strong Quaker connections and at the back of the house there lies an old Quaker burial ground. Next door stands Sewards End Farm, originally Fibe's Tenement, a comparative youngster of a house but nonetheless much older than its Victorian facade would suggest. These days, Victorian ideas of 'restoration' would be considered pure vandalism! Brewery Cottage, one end of which is the old oast-house, Birbecks and the Old Fox complete the group. The Fox was the village's second public house, but is now two private residences. A few years ago, when one came onto the market, the estate agent's blurb described it as 'an older style semi-detached'. It is, indeed. It was built in 1560!

🍁 SEWARDSTONE

Sewardstone lies on the river Lee between Chingford and Waltham Abbey. It sits astride the Greenwich Meridian and part of it comes within the area of the Lee Valley Regional Park.

The manor of Sewardstone comprises the hamlets of Sewardstone, Sewardstonebury and that part of Epping Forest that is called High Beach – the 'Cockney's Paradise'. The earliest houses date from about 1600 with all styles and periods being represented. Nobable buildings include the parish church, a primary school that caters for about 70 children, two village halls, a conservation centre run by the Field Studies Council, a youth hostel and seven pubs!

Sewardstone has worldwide connections through Gilwell Park, which has been a training centre for the Scout and Guide Associations since 1919. The park itself is much older than that, and one of the buildings, the White House, is supposed to be haunted.

Many interesting people have lived in the area. The most famous was Alfred, Lord Tennyson, who wrote part of *In Memoriam* here. The 'wild bells' referred to are said to be the bells of Waltham Abbey. An earlier poet, John Clare, was a patient at Dr Matthew Allen's progressive lunatic asylum, which was spread over three large houses at Lippitts Hill.

The infamous Dick Turpin is supposed to have lived at Sewardstonebury. Certainly he had several hideouts in the area and did some of his most dreadful deeds here, too! His ghost is said to ride down a nearby hill with an old woman clinging to his back. The story is that he once tortured an old woman by sitting her on her own fire to make her tell where her valuables were.

Sadly, no traditional customs or pastimes have survived, but villagers do have the right to graze cattle in the forest and to gather fallen wood – no longer than a man's arm and no thicker than his wrist.

During the Second World War there was a POW camp here. Many of the prisoners were Italians and when the war ended some of them stayed here to establish themselves in the local glasshouse industry. This still provides employment for a number of local people.

For several hundreds of years, the Royal Gunpowder Works has been established in the area. Indeed, the gunpowder which was used in the Gunpowder Plot was probably made here. The famous Enfield rifles certainly were. This site is to be a museum and heritage park.

🍁 SHALFORD

Whenever visitors come to Shalford they invariably comment on the beauty of the area. Lying as it does in the valley of the river Pant, Shalford is one of a string of pretty North Essex villages stretching towards the Cambridgeshire border.

It is surrounded by farmland which, in most cases, has belonged to the same families for generations and must seem rather sleepy, possessing only a police station, a school and one pub.

However, the appearance of inactivity is deceptive as there are many clubs and organisations catering for every age group and making life busy for the local inhabitants. From the first rummage sale in the spring, through the shows, fetes and barbecues of the summer to the Christmas carol concert.

The church is small, simple and beautiful, the oldest building in the village which has a mixture of architectural styles from the 12th century to the new. Most newcomers quickly take their places in the community, their children attend the village school and become welcome new villagers in the changing countryside.

❧ SHEERING

Even before Roman times where was a settlement in Sheering. This was discovered and confirmed when, in 1989, plans were submitted for the building of a meeting room in the field next to the church. An archaeological survey was required before any disturbance was made to the site. Here were found small pits containing pottery, bones and worked flints, suggesting that the village was settled in the church area in pre-Christian and prehistoric times.

Round about 1160 the Fitzwalter family had the patronage and began building a church, the Norman tower of which still stands. Later, Robert Fitzwalter Marshall of the Magna Carta Barons (1215) was represented in sculpture, his head and that of his wife Lady Gunnara can be seen beside the main door. The church also has a 14th century stained glass East window which glows beautifully in red, blue and yellow colours.

There are a few lovely old houses, listed buildings tucked away, timber framed 16th and 17th century, pargetted, wattled-and-daubed, weather-boarded. There are no really large houses.

In 1816 the rector, Francis Tutté, gave £100 in trust to teach twelve poor girls of Sheering to read, spell and sew. By 1827 the school was a National Sunday and Day School with 15 boys and 35 girls. The present attractive, London-stock brick building, was begun in 1851, enlarged in 1874 with a school house and outside conveniences, and finally modernised and further enlarged in 1966. The school began to receive government finance in 1880. It is interesting that girls were first to receive formal education. Children took time off to help with the harvest and often left school when ten years old.

In Victorian times the Glyn family occupied the Manor of Sheering Hall. They took an active part in village life and have two family memorial stained glass windows in the church. Elinor Glyn was famous for her steamy romantic novels.

The old village of Sheering has acquired a lusty offspring. Lower Sheering is about a mile away nestling the border between Sheering and Sawbridgenorth – between Essex and Hertfordshire. This growth began with the advent of the railway. A small industrial area grew using the River Stort and the Great Eastern Railway, later to become the green-liveried steam London and North Eastern. Here thrived the Joinery Works using timber coming by river barge; the Maltings specialising in malt and codliver oil – delicious stuff like toffee – also making special malt in a separate kiln fired using bundles of faggot twigs for very special Scotch whisky.

These industries have all closed down. The Maltings are converted into unusual flats and workshops, the Joinery Works site now attractive with houses and flats bordering the River Stort. With the railway began the development of houses for commuters. These days there is a greater population in Lower Sheering than in the old village. The M11 motorway separates the two parts of the parish.

🍁 SHOEBURYNESS

Shoeburyness is a somewhat divided place from the geographical point of view as the Garrison lies between 'Shoebury Village' and 'Cambridge Town', the latter deriving its name from the public house named after the Duke of Cambridge.

In the middle of the 19th century there was very little here apart from a few farmhouses, hardly any of which still exist. In 1851 the total population of the parish was approximately 151. The area, like so many parts of the South and East Coasts, was probably one in which a lot of smuggling took place, the marshes and hidden creeks lending themselves very well to such activities.

It was of course, the coming of the RA Garrison and School of Gunnery that very gradually led to the development of the area. The coast curves quite sharply at Shoebury and the army took over quite a bit of the coastal area together with some inland ground to form the Garrison and some years later the War Department took over the land further east which formed the New Ranges.

The Garrison came in the middle of the 19th century and Shoebury began to grow. Houses were built at the Garrison end of the High Street and Rampart Street. Shops began to open and then more roads leading off the High Street, but even then it was not completely built up until the 1920s and 1930s. Cambridge Town began a little later than the first part of the Village High Street. Residents became used to the firing of the extremely loud and heavy guns. The soldiers were always an integral part of the area and many with their families remained in the town after retiring from the army. The splendid horses belonging to the Garrison were a sight some older residents still remember. They could be heard clattering down the High Street early in the morning. Harry Wheatcroft, the famous rose grower, live at North Shoebury, and you can guess where the good manure came from; several local people were always to be found at the ready with bucket and shovel!

In the years between the wars, Shoebury was quite well known as a holiday resort. The beaches are good and safe for bathing, and it has always been a source of enjoyment to walk out on the mud at low tide, provided of course one is sensible enough to learn how quickly the tide comes in. Sailboarding and water-skiing are now often to be seen.

In the latter part of the 19th century and up until the Second World War, Thames barges used to carry refuse from London which was used in the local brickworks. The barges were then reloaded with bricks and taken to London and other parts of the country. Children used to love to watch the barges being unloaded.

Across the land from the beach to the brickfields (now nonexistent) were two narrow gauge railways used to draw the refuse and bricks, at first pulled by horses, later by a small engine. Both lines cross the High Street, but there was no level crossing. Up until the 1930s there was a blacksmith's forge on the beach, just above the sands – another great source of local entertainment.

The main sources of employment over the past years were the brickworks, Garrison and railways, as well as farming. One local resident remembers how she and her brothers used to watch the men working in the brickfields. First they would see the clay (marm) and sand put in a grinding wheel, and then see it come out the front and be moulded and cut into shape. Then the bricks were stacked criss-cross to dry. She now wonders how much money the brickworks lost by the spoilt bricks caused by curious little fingers being poked in to see if the bricks were dry.

There are a number of historic and fine buildings in the area. St Andrew's at South Shoebury is a Norman church started in the 1100s, and the timber porch which is said to be the finest example in Essex was added to it in 1400. St Mary's at North Shoebury is a 13th century church. Other listed buildings include South Shoebury Hall, where the manorial courts used to be held. It is a medieval timber-framed house dating from the mid 15th century.

🍁 SIBLE HEDINGHAM

Sible Hedingham, with a main street approximately one mile long, is situated on the main Colchester to Cambridge road following the valley of the river Colne, and in terms of area is the second largest village in Essex.

There as been much development but the early village is still evident in

The Colne Valley Railway, Sible Hedingham

the clusters of cottages around the 14th century church and the three streams that feed into the river Colne. The village's most famous son was Sir John Hawkwood. Son of a tanner, he was born at Hawkwood Manor about 1320. A soldier, he fought under the Black Prince and Edward III, receiving his knighthood for outstanding services at the battle of Poitiers. After the war he formed a company of mercenaries known as the White Company and was hired by various independent Italian states, finally settling down as the official army of the Florentine Republic. He died in 1394, was given a state funeral and his memorial in Florence Cathedral can still be seen. Tradition says his family brought his body back to Sible Hedingham but this is doubtful although there was a memorial in the church of which only the canopy remains.

For many centuries agriculture was the main employer and the convergence of roads made the village a mini market town with many shops and businesses. There were once three windmills, two watermills, eight maltings and a tannery. There are now five public houses; once there were twelve and some had their own hopfields and breweries. Sible Hedingham was one of the last places in Essex where hops were grown and they can still be seen growing wild in some hedgerows.

Women have always played a large part in the local economy. Working in their cottages, many were employed in the early cloth trade and upon its demise turned to straw plaiting. In 1871 about 380 people, mostly farm labourers' wives and daughters were doing this. Straw plaiting schools were set up to teach not only the craft but also some basic education. Education has always been important and once many small schools were in existence. St Peter's church school being one of the earliest has stood the test of time and is now a centre of primary education along with Hedingham School which is a centre of secondary education with a catchment area of all the surrounding villages.

As time passed two industries became the mainstay of the economy, brickmaking and woodworking. Local clay had long been used for bricks and the arrival of the railway in 1861 opened up new markets at home and abroad. The industry flourished until the Second World War with the last yard closing in 1954. The joinery works of Rippers Ltd established itself alongside the railway yards in 1899, eventually becoming a major employer for the surrounding villages. 'All roads lead to Rippers' was a well known local saying. These two industries were responsible for a considerable amount of building in the village, providing their workers with affordable accommodation.

Rippers was always a family business but eventually it was sold to an international company that now has only a small factory on the site. The old woodyards, plus the railway land made redundant by Dr Beeching in the 1950s, have been partly used for houses. The remainder is now the site of some small industrial units. The railway station was dismantled and moved over the border into Castle Hedingham where the Colne Valley steam railway is a major tourist attraction. Today most people are employed away from the village, many commuting to London but there still remains a good selection of shops catering for most needs and farming continues in the outlying areas.

🍁 SOUTH HANNINGFIELD

At the time of the First World War the village consisted of the school, the Windmill public house, the post office and general store, the blacksmith's forge and the parish church of St Peter. 'Bearmains', the big house, was lived in by Mr and Mrs Gray, employing many servants and gardeners etc, and there was a scattering of cottages mainly occupied by the farm workers and their families. Later on Mr and Mrs Walter Hills took up residence.

The Church of England school had two classrooms, the large room built in 1874 and the small room in 1912, and two teachers. The headteacher taught the children from eight to 14 years old and the younger ones from five to eight years were taught by Miss K Bright, who worked there all her life and was respected by a good many families. It was heated by an open fire which was usually the standing point for the teachers to keep their backs warm.

The Windmill public house was a small country pub with a tap room, the floor of which was covered in sawdust, and it was run by a Mr Tom Hunt and his sister Peg, together with a housekeeper Mrs Aspin. All three were very deaf but managed to keep the locals happy, especially in wintertime with a large fire in the tap room which had seats built in the side of the fireplace. The post office and general stores were run by the Clarence family. You could always purchase lovely hand-cut bacon and cheese, and all perishable goods were kept in a back room with a brick floor, slate shelves and no heat. The blacksmith's forge was run by the two Smith brothers who were kept busy with the farm horses. When anyone wanted the doctor to call from Wickford, a white flag was placed on the smithy's wall and the doctor on his motor-bike used to call there to see where he was wanted (there were no phones in the village until the 1930s). The smith was popular with the children, making iron hoops to fit the size of the child.

When motorized vehicles began to come on the scene the church choir hired one to take its members by charabanc to the seaside once a year, mostly to Clacton, Felixstowe, Walton or Margate. The maximum speed of these was 15 mph, so they left early in the morning, arriving home late at night, causing much worry and concern to their families. Gradually things began to improve. Buses began to get more frequent, lads brought motor-bikes, taking the girls on the pillion, water and electricity were laid on and generally life improved until war broke out again in 1939.

On the whole the village escaped lightly. The end of the war was greeted with a huge bonfire and social evening in the village hall and things seemed to be settling down until a huge reservoir was planned and built on many acres of farmland. Completed in 1954, it completely altered the face of the village. New houses were built and a new road linking West to South Hanningfield. The school was demolished and the Windmill public house was rebuilt.

SOUTH WEALD

South Weald is less than two miles from Brentwood but a world away from its busy High Street. The church is large for such a small village and stands proudly on top of the hill. The Saxons settled here and the place is mentioned in the Domesday Book.

St Peter's is the mother church of the neighbourhood and until the middle of the 19th century, Brentwood, with its chapel, came under the jurisdiction of South Weald. The present church dates from about 1150, although the south door, with its chevron ornamentation, is the sole remaining Norman feature.

Opposite the church is the Tower Arms, a splendid example of early 18th century architecture. Above the entrance are the initials ALAA and the date 1704. The house was originally called Jewells. In earlier times, the village public house was on the west side of the church and was known as the Spread Eagle until about 1878, when it was renamed the Tower Arms. The licence had been transferred to the present house by 1921.

Following the road to the right outside the lychgate, there are two entrances to Weald Country Park. Between them, on the right, is a house now know as Queen Mary's chapel. In the 16th century, Weald Hall was surrounded by a series of walled courts and gardens and included this garden house, built in the same style as Weald Hall. There is a tradition that Queen Mary worshipped there secretly before her accession, but there is no contemporary evidence in support.

Enter the park at the second of the two entrances and you will be near to the visitors' centre with information and literature about Weald Hall and Weald Park. The Park was formed as a deer park in the 12th century, when the monks of Waltham Abbey held the manor.

Returning to the village, take the right turn into Wigley Bush Lane. It appeared thus on Chapman and Andre's map of Essex in 1777 and was revived in the 1970s, after a period when the name was Vicarage Lane. On the left hand side of the road is Luptons, an early 18th century house which was inhabited by Edward Ind in 1848. He was a partner in the Ind Coope brewery at Romford. His partner, Octavius Coope MP lived at Rochetts, the entrance to which is opposite Queen Mary's chapel. It was largely destroyed by fire in 1975. Opposite Luptons is Wealdcote, a 16th century building, to which was added a 17th century extension. Further down on the right had side is the school, built between 1957 and 1968 to replace the original building which stood opposite the present church car park and is now demolished. On the left hand side are the almshouses. Ten of these, together with a chapel, were designed by S S Teulon and built in 1854. They were originally established in 1567, through benefactions in the will of Sir Antony Browne. Two additional almshouses were added in 1966. Continuing towards Brentwood, the present vicarage, dating from about 1926, is on the right and succeeded on the left by Weald Hall. The name is misleading, as the original Weald Hall was always in Weald Park. The house dates from 1825 and was built as his vicarage by Charles Belli, whose munificence restored the church and built the school in the village.

After crossing the bypass, Brook Street is reached at the junction with the main road. This was probably the route of the Roman road from London to Chelmsford and Maldon. The Nags Head, built in the 18th century, gives it name to the lane opposite. It was so called in 1777.

Turning left towards Brentwood, Stone House is encountered on the left after about 200 yards. An unusual sight, it was built about 100 years ago of random brick, stone and flint. Adjoining the house is a row of early 18th century cottages, succeeded in turn by the Bull, probably another 18th century house. At the traffic lights, Spital Lane commemorates the leper hospital which stood on the corner from the 12th to 16th centuries.

Two of Brook Street's oldest buildings are reached within 200 yards. On the left is the Golden Fleece, a large 15th century building. Almost opposite is the Moat House Hotel. It had been known as 'The Place' in 1514, but was completely rebuilt in the 17th century.

🍁 SOUTHMINSTER

Southminster is situated in the Dengie Peninsula, between the rivers Crouch and Blackwater with the North Sea to the east.

It dates from around AD 640 when the village grew up around the parish church of St Leonard. The sea came up as far as Pandole Wood, an ancient wood with a small earthwork, and wool merchants came from across the North Sea up to Southminster. Two Dutchmen were employed to advise on reclaiming the land, and the remains of two sea walls can be seen. The sea is now four miles away, across peaceful marshes, full of wildlife, with a view over to Foulness Island, and in summer yachts from Burnham-on-Crouch can be seen coming from the Crouch to the North Sea. Access to the sea wall is not now available, but it can be reached by walking the sea wall from Burnham to Bradwell.

St Leonard's church is of Saxon origin and is situated in the centre of the village. The south doorway being of Norman origin, many Roman bricks were used in building this part of the church. In 1450 the church was rebuilt in Perpendicular style. It has historical connections with Nelson, his chaplain being Dr Alexanda Scott, who was with him when he died and was also later a vicar of Southminster. Relics in the shape of a chart table, bookcase, chest commode and a fireplace were brought from the *Victory* and can been seen in the parish church today.

Southminster has changed in that it was once a farming community. In the 1930s pea-picking was the chief way of earning extra money by the majority of the residents, supplemented by gypsies or travellers who came in brightly coloured caravans to stay in Battlesmoor, a small field on the northern outskirts of the village. Some of these people have now settled in the village and bought their own homes. The coming of the nuclear power station to Bradwell-on-Sea in the 1960s made a lot of difference in bringing work to members of the village. A large estate was built to house the workers who came from the North of England. Southminster still has a few farms, but the majority of residents now commute to London or Southend, or work in the light industrial factories.

The old school, a fine big building, was replaced by two new schools: St Leonard's junior school and the county infants school. Southminster has a good variety of shops, something for everyone including restaurants and pubs! Being rural, it has many walks and is noted for its fresh air.

🍁 SPRINGFIELD

It has been said that the history of England is made up of the combined history of all the village churches and churchyards throughout the country. Springfield is proud to have played its part in that history, and hopefully will continue to do so for many years to come. Heroes of the battle of Waterloo lie in our churchyard. For more than 300 years the church bells have spoken of joy, or of sadness, on many great occasions, and have also joined in more local celebrations. On Tuesday 11th September 1990, for 44 minutes the evening air echoed across the village green and surrounding areas as the ringers rang 1,260 changes in a quarter peel of ten methods doubles to celebrate 75 years of the WI!

Although the village has been incorporated into the neighbouring town of Chelmsford, and virtually swamped by modern development, traces of the old village can still be seen. It is to be hoped that old inns like the Endeavour and the Tulip, and the cottages surrounding them, will stay with us for many more years and maintain the village identity. Stage coaches no longer change horses at the Plough Inn, but the car park there serves as assembly point for parties boarding more modern transport going to places far beyond the reach of the old system.

The old village school, founded by the church in 1812, became totally inadequate for the demands placed upon it, and has been replaced by a new interdenominational establishment, which it is hope will carry on the education tradition. Other schools have also been added to cater for the population explosion, and are already developing their own history.

🍁 STAMBOURNE

This rural village, first recorded in the Domesday Book, lies 50 miles to the north-east of London along the Roding road, 13 miles past Great Dunmow. It has retained its sense of isolation by its being distant from any large centre or main route. It never had a railway station and the three now nearest to it are each some 20 miles away. The name, from the Anglo-Saxon roots 'stan' and 'burn' for stony brook, probably derives from the two large flat stepping stones in the rivulet below the church.

It is a street village on the H-plan. Its centre was devoid of substantial dwellings, other that two of the three manor houses and the old rectory, until after the Second World War. There are some 100 houses, of which about 30 are 17th century, though much altered; only eight are still thatched. The Hall and the Red Lion inn have still much Elizabethan oak construction. The inn was Moone Hall and housed the courts. The third manor, Grevill's, is now represented by a cottage, completely rebuilt when its moat was filled in, on the Yeldham road; it still has some massive old beams. The population of about 300 is well down on its Victorian peak of 577 at the 1871 census, but the three dozen horses are the highest number for decades.

The finest monument is the impressive squat Norman tower of the church. It is mainly of local flint with Saxon traces and Roman bricks and was built soon after the Conquest, probably about 1085. The greatest treasure is the medieval stained glass in the east window with its complete heraldic pedigree of the MacWilliams. Sadly only two of their portraits survive in it, that of the donor's father Henry and of his mother, Elizabeth Hartishorn.

This was a Nonconformist area from well before the Civil War. The Rev Henry Havers BA, rector 1651–1662, formally founded the Stambourne Meeting when he was ejected under the Bartholomew Act. He left the village only for short periods and was preaching regularly here until his death in 1707. He was buried by the rector in the Anglican churchyard for the first chapel was not built until 1716/17 on a 'Parcell of the Wast' granted to his son, also Henry, in 1710. A third Henry continued the Presbyterian Ministry making a total family pastorate of 86 years. Clopton Havers MD, son of the first Henry, was the village's most famous resident. His name is known to every medical student from his description of the Haversian canals in bone and he was elected an early Fellow of the Royal Society during the presidency of Samuel Pepys. The present Congregational chapel dates from 1969 and is the third on the site.

There are two memorials to the First World War; a cross in the churchyard and a plaque on the wall of the chapel. Interestingly, the names on them differ since many of the Congregational members came from nearby Birdbrook.

❧ STAMBRIDGE

Stambridge is a very small village situated about seven miles from Southend-on-Sea. There is the modernised Royal Oak public house and village store and post office, surrounded by a collection of cottages and bungalows opposite which there is the Baptist chapel. A long narrow strip of land bounds the river Roach. Along the main road in a south westly direction is the Memorial Hall and on the opposite side of the road stands the old rectory, now a nursing home, as well as the present day rectory. Further along in the same direction is the Stambridge church of St Mary and All Saints. Parts of the original Saxon building can be seen, but it is difficult to say exactly how long a church has stood on this site.

The most famous inhabitant of Stambridge was John Winthrop, 1588–1649. In 1630 he and his family set sail for America in the *Arbella*. Not only was John Winthrop the first Governor of Boston, having been elected in London the previous year as Governor of The Massachusetts Bay Company, he also helped to found the American shipbuilding industry which has made the port of Boston famous throughout the world.

There has always been a mill at Stambridge, dating back to Domesday times. Three hundred years on, the original mill was replaced and a tide mill was working there at the end of the 18th century.

In 1814 Rochford windmill was removed from its site south of Rochford village to Little Stambridge in its entirety. Further improvements were made during the 1840s by William Rankin, and a new wharf was constructed to accommodate vessels up to 120 tons. In 1868 Alfred and Hugh Rankin purchased the mill house, water mill and windmill. The milling and agricultural business continued to flourish and was eventually sold to ABC Foods Ltd.

Originally there was a small settlement near the mill know as Winters Corner, with a row of clapboard cottages (now demolished), and a successful brewery which it is thought later became a factory. Later still this building became a private country dwelling house, passing into the possession of A M & H Rankin in 1936. During the Second World War this house, now know as 'The Old Brewery' was used as a hostel for the Women's Land Army, and after the war, during Mr Donald Tanton's residency, the name was changed to 'Winters'. Mr and Mrs Tanton would hold grand Christmas parties for the children of Stambridge school and church.

There is a still a small beach area near Stambridge mill which can be approached by public footpath from Mill Lane, skirting Rankin's cricket pitch, still widely used, passing in front of Broomhills, then down a lane to the river bank. It is a favourite spot for local people at weekends and school holidays, where families can picnic whilst children play.

🍁 STANFORD RIVERS

Approaching the village from the south-east along the London road, one sees scattered cottages, several farmhouses and a lovely view on the right over the Roding Valley. Waylett's, Mitchell's, Tracey's and Murrells are all 15th to early 18th century farmhouses, of timber and plaster construction, bricked in later. Close to each other on the right, are the Woodman and White Bear inns. On the right again, as one enters Little End is Stanford Rivers House, 17th century with a 15th century core.

The old Union workhouse was for many years Piggott's Tent factory

St Margaret's church, Stanford Rivers

which, until 2000, provided the huge tent at the Chelsea Flower Show. Opposite the factory is the site of the former Congregational church where a single gravestone remains. To mark the Millennium, a black wrought-iron parish sign was erected in the old gateway of the chapel, which was burned down in 1927. It was here the young David Livingstone preached, before becoming the famous missionary and explorer.

The road to Toot Hill is flanked on both sides by farmland, and there are distant views of old farmhouses, and the spire of St Margaret's church stabbing the sky from its nest of mature trees. St Margaret's was built around 1150, and has been in the gift of the Duchy of Lancaster since 1557. It is a Norman-style church with a 15th century bay roof.

'Noel Gay', born Reginald M Armitage and the composer of *The Lambeth Walk* and *Run, Rabbit Run*, popular songs from musical comedies of the 1930s, is buried in the churchyard, and there are still people who can remember the influx of show business personalities attending his funeral in 1954.

Stanford Rivers Hall is an early 19th century building on the site of the baronial hall that in the 11th century had been in the estate of Earl Eustace of Boulogne. Its garden abuts the churchyard.

Stewart's and Blake's Farms are two more of the farmhouses of the parish. Both are 18th century buildings on the site of older houses. An 18 hole golf course has been created here. Bugle Cottage, standing near the small surviving fragment of village green, is an amalgamation of three 17th century cottages with possibly some medieval features.

On the western border or the parish the former Central Line stations of North Weald and Blakehall fringe Ongar Park Wood. An old Roman road to Dunmow has been traced across this area, and legend has it that a ghostly legion can sometimes be seen marching through!

STANSTED MOUNTFITCHET

Stansted Mountfitchet, situated in the pleasantly undulating countryside of North-West Essex, in the District of Uttlesford, is one of the largest parishes in the county. The name is Saxon, compounded of 'stan', a stone, and 'sted', a place. The village appears in the Domesday Book as 'Stansteda'. With the coming of the Normans, William the Conqueror granted the lordship of the Manors of Stansted and Bentfield Bury to the Gernon family, who later changed the family name to Montfitchet (derived from Montfiquet in Normandy) and thus gave the place its additional title.

The family lived in the castle on its artificial mound and a reconstruction on the site has become a popular tourist attraction. The township of Stansted probably grew up in the shadow of the castle in the part now called Lower Street. Until 100 years ago this was known as The Street or Stansted Street and was one of two main roads, the other being Stansted Chapel, now Cambridge Road, named after an ancient medieval chapel or hermitage which stood on the site of the present Fountain. Here stands an iron milestone cover, said to be the largest in Essex.

The drinking fountain erected in 1871 was presented to the village by Henry and Walter Gilbey, who together with their brother Alfred, founded the famous firm of wine merchants. They were local benefactors and Henry Parry Gilbey also paid for the Working Men's Club in Lower Street, now the Mountfitchet Social Club. The Gilbeys were joined in Stansted by their nephew and partner James Blyth who rebuilt Wood House and renamed it 'Blythwood'. James Blyth, who became Lord Blyth of Stansted Mountfitchet in 1907, had a model dairy built at Blythwood. This building aroused much interest and was visited by many notables including the Prince of Wales, later King Edward VII. The dairy is now a private house but the old Blythwood House was destroyed by fire in 1926.

Cambridge Road was the turnpike road and there were at least three coaching inns situated along it. At one time there were 13 inns and alehouses in Stansted, now reduced to nine within the parish.

The many interesting buildings range from half-timbered and thatched, through Georgian, Victorian and modern day, showing a continual occupation and growth of the village over many hundreds of years. Church Road to the east leads to St Mary's church, with remaining Norman features. Although much restored in the 1800s the chancel is 13th century and the brick tower dates from 1692. Behind the church stands Stansted Hall, rebuilt in 1875 following a fire, which is now the Arthur Findlay College for Psychic Research.

St John's church in the centre of Stansted was designed by W D Caroe, a leading architect of his day, and built in 1889, mostly at the expense of the Pulteney family of Hargrave Park. To the south is the brick tower windmill built in 1787, no longer working but containing most of the original machinery, and a listed ancient monument. It was given in trust to the village by the second Lord Blyth and is open to the public on several occasions in the year and attracts a good number of school groups. Not far from the windmill, beside the main road, is a carved wooden village sign erected to commemorate the Silver Jubilee of Queen Elizabeth II. A similar sign stands at the northern approaches to Stansted.

On a site near the crossroads a shop has stood since 1687. The building there now was known as Green's Stores from 1840 when Joshua Green expanded the premises, until it was taken over by other traders in the 1960s. It provided all the necessary commodities for the local population. The wide range included ladies' corsets, hats, household linen, groceries, shoes, candles and children's clothes and menswear. The bacon and cheeses were stored in the large cellars below the shop. At one end there was a small counter with a window at pavement level, where the grocery manager used to grind coffee in an antiquated machine, by turning the very large handle.

A big impact was made to the area with the coming of the railway in 1844. During the Second World War Stansted Airfield had one of the longest runways in Great Britain and was used by heavy bombers. After the war it was brought into use as a commercial airport, at one time largely for cargo. After several public enquiries expansion was approved as London's Third Airport and the new terminal building was opened by Her Majesty Queen Elizabeth in March 1991. The building of the M11 motorway and the present day expansion of Stansted Airport are bringing further changes, but a village centre to Stansted Mountfitchet still remains.

🍁 STANWAY

Stanway is situated three miles west of Colchester and has, as part of its boundary from the town, Grymes Dyke, now the only Iron Age dyke in the United Kingdom. It is a large village covering some four square miles and at one time known as Great Stanway and Little Stanway, forming part of the great forest of Essex.

Stanway, or 'Stoneway', took its name from the old Roman road, Stane Street, running from Bishops Stortford to Colchester through the centre of the village, which is now London Road. At the eastern end of the road is situated the old Union Workhouse erected to house 200 paupers, where many a vagrant could be seen making his way for a night's lodging. At the western end, on Swan Green, the annual sheep fairs used to be held and an oak tree was planted there to commemorate the Coronation of Edward

VII. Nearby, at the farm, was the parish pound, now stabling.

Stane Street was used by many a pilgrim on his way to Walsingham. On the site of the now parish church, St Albright's, stood a small Saxon chapel, which it is thought could have been an oratory chapel and, therefore, a place of pilgrimage itself with Albright, a holy man and hermit, living in a crude hut dwelling next door. The weary travellers could refresh themselves at three nearby inns; the Swan, the White Hart, and the Turkeycock, now converted into houses. The poor folk would camp in the fields opposite the little chapel where Miracle and Mystery plays were performed and stalls set up giving the area the name of 'Playing Stalls'. Almshouses are now on this site.

Gradually, from the 14th century, St Albright's church was built and extended. During 1826 a Queen Anne card table served for an altar beneath which the parish library was kept, the rector's butler dispensing books on Sunday after divine service!

The original parish church, All Saints, was situated by another Roman road in the south of the village about two miles away. It gradually fell into disrepair and it is reputed that half of it was torn down by Parliamentary men to help with materials for the Great Siege of Colchester.

🍁 STEBBING

Stebbing lies roughly mid-way between Great Dunmow and Braintree, north of Felsted. The village is still small enough to merge naturally into the environment, nestling round its one dominant building, the church. Stebbing is said to owe its name to the Saxon tribe of Stybba which had settled in an 'ing' or meadow on one of the well-drained gravel outlyers scattered over the Essex landscape. The great earth mound which they fortified, remains today at Stebbing Park, surrounded by a moat and in spring resplendent with daffodils.

The Domesday Book records the village being divided into two manors shared between two Norman lords, Henry de Ferrers and Ralph Peverell. Although there was no census, it would seem the village had a larger population in 1087 than now.

During the late medieval period to Tudor/Stuart times, Stebbing supported its share of the great Essex woollen cloth industry and the teasels, whose prickly seed heads were used in the felting process, still grown abundantly in the village.

The people of Stebbing did not escape the many religious changes of the 16th century. Within a span of eleven years, that handsome 14th century church of St Mary saw the decorations and ceremonies change from Roman Catholic to Protestant; and back again. Altars, crosses and rood loft were alternately set up then pulled down, culminating in a battle between roundheads and villagers, when the church lost most of its stained glass windows, leaving today's congregation with a bright open place of worship. Happily the rare stone screen survived the turmoil and still remains intact.

Stebbing continued as a typical rural community until well into the 20th century and many local surnames found in 19th century records remain today. There is still a shop cum post office, a pub and the school and these have been joined by more modern businesses; garages, fancy dress hire, IT businesses, builders, a garden centre and many more. In a recent survey over 30 businesses were recorded as having Stebbing addresses.

The village has a happy mixture of inhabitants. It is a place where the newcomer is not regarded as an intruder and most residents become involved in the many social and sporting activities. Currently, there are 28 clubs and societies, supported by the 1,200 population. Most clubs operate from one of the two very fine halls, the Village Hall and the Old Friends Meeting House. Village people recently restored both to extremely high standards.

Stebbing's claim to fame in recent times has been due to the Elizabethan Fayre. Held every fourth year, the village reverts to Tudor times with villagers and visitors dressing in costume to enact a pageant and enjoy a lusty weekend of Elizabethan I & II entertainment against a pantomime scene backdrop of the comfortably leaning buildings along the High Street.

Visually the parish owes much of its charm to a kind balance still maintained between agriculture and eco-friendly aspects of the countryside; the brook's banks where kingfishers dart; marshes and thickets, which remain comparatively undisturbed. The rolling cornfields give an air of spaciousness and crops of blue flax and yellow rape add vibrant colour below the wide expanse of Constable sky. Meadows and hedgerows add an intimacy not always found in country so intensively farmed. The atmosphere remains rural with a quality of comfortable unpretentiousness.

So far, Stebbing has escaped great development but with the expansion of Stansted Airport and its connected growth, some change is inevitable.

Nonetheless, whatever the future, at the start of the 21st century, Stebbing is still a very green and pleasant place.

STEEPLE BUMPSTEAD

Nurse Edith Cavell died in Brussels on 12th October 1915, shot by a German firing squad for helping Allied soldiers to escape. She became, of course, a legend for bravery and sacrifice. But her ties with Steeple Bumpstead occurred long before that and before she became a nurse. During 1886, Edith was appointed governess to the four children of the Reverend Charles Powell, vicar of Steeple Bumpstead.

The vicarage, where a stone plaque commemorates her stay, is no longer the residence of the local vicar, but it is still there, a private residence, on the corner of Chapel Street and Finchingfield Road. There is, in the 11th century village church, a plaque to Edith Cavell and there is also a road named after her.

There has been a long history of non-conformist belief in the village. A Bumpstead man was burnt to death in the parish for his beliefs in the days of the Catholic church. Along the Blois Road, leading from Bumpstead to Birdbrook, is a field that has been called the 'Bloody Pightle', and that is where he is believed to have been martyred.

In 1527 John Tibauld and eight other village residents were seized and taken before the Bishop of London, charged with meeting together in Bower Hall to pray and read a copy of the New Testament. Although the non-conformists in the village were encouraged by the powerful Bendyshe family that lived at Bower Hall, even their influence could not save Tibauld. He was burned at the stake.

Having fallen into ruin after use as a 'concentration camp' in the First World War, Bower Hall was finally demolished in 1926 and the materials sold off. The great staircase found its way to America.

Moot Hall, or 'The Old Schole', symbolises Steeple Bumpstead. Built in 1592 by the inhabitants on land rented from the Crown, in the 1830s when it was 'a school for farmers' sons' the villagers forcibly took possession of it, disputing the claim of George Gent of Moyns to have the right to appoint the headmaster. Eventually an Ecclesiastical Court upheld the villagers' claim.

Colonel J. C. Humphrey, son of the village wheelwright, invented corrugated iron. He built and lived in the Iron House, North Street, which was sadly demolished in the 1960s. At one time Humphreys Ltd of London claimed to be the 'largest works in the world' and held a Royal Warrant as 'supplier to His Majesty King Edward VII.'

🍁 STIFFORD

Anyone going along High Road, North Stifford, must be intrigued by the thatched cottages, St Mary's church, and the very pleasant village green. North Stifford is the old part of the parish of Stifford which nowadays is identified by three areas – North Stiffford, South Stifford and Stifford Clays.

For over 800 years Stifford was a small village with houses along the High Road, the church at the east end and the public house at the west end. Stage coaches on their way from Southend to London called at the Dog and Partridge (the village inn) as a staging post.

From the 16th to the 20th century there were three large houses – Stifford Hall later replaced by Stifford Lodge, Coppid Hall, and Ford Place. The two principal farms were Chalk Pit Farm and Stifford Clays Farm on the south and east borders.

During the 20th century housing and road development radically changed the character of the village. In 1926 the A13 (now A1013) and in the early 1980s a new trunk road (the present A13) have split the village of North Stifford and divided it from Stifford Clays and South Stifford. Of the large houses Stifford Lodge is a Moat House hotel, Coppid Hall has been converted into flats, and of Ford Place only a shell remains. It was destroyed by arson in 1986. Stifford Clays farm was largely swallowed up by housing in the post Second World War period. Chalk Pit farm has been demolished.

In 1980 an interesting find linked the 14th and 20th centuries. Pilgrims on their way to Canterbury used to cross the Thames at South Stifford and would have passed over Stifford Bridge. One of them lost one of his pilgrim's seals near the bridge. The seals were worn in the pilgrim's hats – they seem to have been the 14th century equivalent of 'car stickers'. The pilgrim who lost his seal by Stifford Bridge was obviously on a grand tour. The seal depicts St Peter holding the keys of the Kingdom, and St Paul holding a sword. This seal would have originated from Rome. It was placed in Thurrock's local history museum.

Richard Baker Wingfield was lord of the manor of Orsett and Stifford from 1859–80. He was a good landlord and local benefactor. He provided and endowed the parochial school in the High Road in 1840, well before the advent of compulsory education in 1871.

On his death Stifford, with the Orsett estate, passed to the Whitmore family, and remained under their control until the death of Sir Francis Whitmore in 1962. This marked the start of the development of present day Stifford. The estate and houses were bought by many private individuals. Some of the farmland on the south bank of the Mardyke river was bought by the Thurrock Council and is now a Country Park.

🍁 STISTED

Stisted is situated just outside Braintree in north Essex; a typical village of its type with its church, church school and village shop and a couple of hundred houses representing a wide spectrum of society. Some locals still remain here but there has been an influx of newcomers in recent years which has altered the face of the village to a certain extent.

However, just over 100 years ago in 1881 records show an interesting picture of the village and its structure. There were 174 houses, ten of them unoccupied, containing a population of 381 males and 364 females. It was almost self sufficient and for many there will have been no need to go into Braintree for necessities. It had a miller to grind the corn (no baker, as housewives made their own bread and cakes in those days), a wheelwright, two blacksmiths, a grocer, a butcher, a publican, a post-mistress, a cooper, six boot and shoe makers, a builder, two painters, a bricklayer and two carpenters. The innkeeper was also a blacksmith and a beerhouse keeper. No undertaker, this service was probably provided by the builder as often happens even to this day. No greengrocer either, as much of the fresh produce was grown on the allotments or large vegetable gardens. Travelling salesmen and pedlars would also provide many of the miscellaneous household items which might be needed.

A study of male occupations shows that no less than 84 heads of households were agricultural labourers with 77 of their sons engaged in the same work, a huge figure for what is a small village. Next in numbers came 14 full-time farmers with a few combining farming and another operation. This was then followed by eight gardeners.

Very few of the married women had occupations outside the home and those that did were recorded as laundresses (two), tailoress, charwoman, dressmaker, nurse and one strawplaiter. Most of these tasks could have been carried out at home so probably very few actually worked elsewhere. Apart from these few the large families of the time would have prevented housewives from finding time outside the home to earn something to alleviate their conditions. Five, six and seven children was common enough at this time. Consider the case of Robert, 47, and his wife Hannah Weaver, 41, who already had ten children living at home ranging from 20 years down to eleven months. Returns show that it was not unusual for women to be bearing children into their mid and late forties.

And now, although the village appearance has not changed much, it is no longer self sufficient. Nearly all villagers go to work out of the village, only three farmers are remaining with very few labourers, due to mechanization. The village has a small post office/shop, two public houses, a primary school, a modern village hall and a meeting room and also an 18 hole golf course. Stisted Hall is now a residential home for the elderly run by the Freemasons, the Rectory has been sold and the village share the stipend with Cressing and Bradwell. Sadly, the village no longer has a resident policeman and is part of a rural unit. Two small residential developments have been built but because the village has a conservation order on most of its streets, building is at a minimum. The village playing field is used by the football and rounders teams and there is a children's play area. The population of the village is approximately 800, with many clubs and activities.

❧ STOCK

The full name is really Stock Harvard, but 'Harvard' is little used today except for ecclesiastical purposes.

The village is on a hill, not quite so high as Danbury or Langdon Hills, but high enough to give delightful views in almost every direction over the surrounding typical Essex undulating countryside.

The name goes back to Saxon times, and the Saxon word for 'wood' was 'stok', indicating that at one time, the countryside around here was part of the great forest which covered much of this portion of Essex. 'Harvard' is a derivation of the Saxon word 'hereward', meaning 'steward' and this may indicate a settlement in the forest belonging to 'the steward' – possibly of the Earls of Essex. Wood has always played an important part in local history, as witness the wonderful timber work in the belfry of All Saints church, surviving bombs (in 1940) and the vagaries of weather for some 500 years.

Until recent times, surrounded as it was by rich farmlands, many being ancient manorial farms, agricultural pursuits formed the main occupation of many village inhabitants, while in the village itself the chief 'industries' were pottery, bricklaying and brickmaking. It is thought that one of Stock's claims to fame is the fact that the ancient formula for making bricks with an admixture of ashes in the clay was first used here and given the name 'Stock brick' – now universally used.

The village character is still maintained with the village green with its war memorial and village sign, the ancient windmill and many 18th century dwellings in the streets. For a long time Stock was hardly on the main road to anywhere; the arterial trunk roads (now 'A' roads) passing it by, and that helped to maintain its rural identity as a village. There is also a new village hall, aided by Millennium funds.

There are records of a charter for a fair 'to be holden in Stok' as far back as 1239, and though not many famous personages have lived here, very many have visited, from Royalty downwards. The poet William Cowper wrote of Stock; the famous statesman William Wilberforce loved to visit here, and even today a bishop makes his home in the village. A few families are still here who can trace their residence in Stock from some 300 or 400 years.

STONDON MASSEY

Stondon Massey, two miles south-east of Chipping Ongar, is a very small rural parish. It has a pub, the Bricklayers Arms, a shop and post office. About 700 people live there and the parish consists only of 1,127 acres lying partly in the Roding valley.

Entering the village over Hallsford Bridge from the direction of Chipping Ongar, the road begins its gentle ascent past Little Myles, one of Stondon's 15 listed buildings, to the top of the gravelly Church Hill that gives the village its Saxon name; stone-dun meaning stoney hill. The name 'de Marcy' (Massey) was added after the Conquest by a Norman family who held land in the area. The very hill that gave Stondon its name was recently under threat, for beneath its gravel layer lies London clay which can be made into aggregate.

The lovely view from Church Hill over Green Belt land, which is also designated as a special landscape area, thankfully has been saved for the enjoyment of future generations.

At the top of this hill, overlooking the river Roding valley and Stondon's oldest manor house, Stondon Hall, stands the small church of St Peter and St Paul built around 1100. The Norman builders who erected the church managed to incorporate in their construction some thin Roman tiles. A band of these tiles, in the typical zig-zag pattern of the Normans, can be seen embedded in the mortar at eaves height on the west wall. Other Roman relics have also been found in the area.

In Elizabethan times, Willam Byrd, composer of some of our most beautiful religious music, lived at Stondon Place for over 30 years until his death in 1623. In 1717 Stondon Place was completely rebuilt. Unfortunately this building was destroyed by fire in 1877, after which the present Georgian-style house was built. It was at Stondon Place in 1841 that Stondon's ghost decided to make his presence felt once more.

Jordan's ghost, as it was known locally, had been freely walking in Stondon since the rather difficult burial of Mr Jordon, churchwarden and medical man in 1754. Tradition has it that after Mr Jordon's funeral, at which eleven clergy assisted, the sexton peered into the Jordon vault to make sure that all was well. To his horror, he found it was not! For there, outside the coffin, lay the still and motionless corpse of Mr Jordon. Eventually the unfortunate remains were securely chained down. Such an unusual burial was, perhaps, bound to provide a ghost, although Rev Reeve who recorded this story explains that it was not uncommon practice in those days of body-snatching to chain down coffins.

However, no more has been heard of the ghost since 1845 when he was last seen flitting near Stondon's whipping post on the small grass triangle at the junction of Chivers Road. The whipping post, which attracts many visitors and photographers, was completely refurbished in 2000. There is also now, on the edge of the green, a village sign designed and made by the people of the parish.

❧ TENDRING

The village of Tendring is a scattered one, set in an agricultural area of arable farms to the east of the historic town of Colchester.

The parish church of St Edmund, named after Edmund, king of East

Anglia who was martyred at Framlingham in AD 870, stands in what was the centre of the village. It is an impressive building standing in a prominent position and surrounded by beautiful rural countryside.

The school has always had a close association with the church and quite often the Chairman of Managers has been the rector of the time, the most recent being the late Rev M P McCready MA, who died in October 1945. He was also Platoon Commander in the Home Guard and the training meetings were often held at the rectory, although they usually ended at the Crown where all, including the rector, enjoyed a pint (or two).

The old Crown is now Crown House and a private dwelling. It was built about 1600 as a small coaching inn on the road from Thorpe-le-Soken to Ipswich. It is believed that the inner walls were so built to hide smuggled goods. As one might expect, this is a listed building.

Just across the road from the pub stood the blacksmith's shop and forge, where Charlie Marven shod horses from the surrounding farms, repaired and sharpened harrows and carried out repairs of all kinds. He also had the job of gravedigger across the road in the churchyard and it was said by some that when he saw any newcomers to the village he would make a mental note for future use.

Horses were of course the main source of power on the farms in those days and one well known local character tells of the time when he and the governor were carting muck with two horses and tumbrils and using a trace horse in the field, which was on a steep slope. When he arrived with his load in the field he found the governor's tumbril, load and horse had turned completely upside-down on the hillside, the horse with its feet in the air and unable to move. The trace horse was just standing patiently with the trace chains crossed, and when released simply trotted off home, leaving the two men to disentangle the other horse. Those who used horses for this job in their youth will be well able to picture the scene, but what a pity that no camera was available at the time.

The stone spire of the church was built in 1877 through the generosity of John Cardinall, lord of the manor and owner of a large part of the parish. The Tendring Hall estate was sold by auction on 25th June 1910, in 41 lots situated in the parishes of Tendring, Weeley and Thorpe-le-Soken and four lots at Great Clacton, in all 984 acres.

The present Hall was built on the site of an earlier house that was used as a hunting lodge by King Stephen. The gardens, laid out by the famous landscape gardener Percy Cain in the late 1920s, have as their centrepiece a magnificent Cedar of Lebanon which is about 600 years old, close by two lakes and flanked by a really wonderful display of rhododendrons, azaleas, other shrubs and trees.

🍁 TERLING

Early man wandered up the river Ter, found very good springs here and settled. By 1066 there were two water mills, and slowly the village grew around the river. It is only a little winding river of 13 miles, but the banks are beautiful, especially in summer.

Villages, like human beings, are individuals, no two are alike and Terling is a village of outstanding beauty. It is seven miles from Chelmsford and if approached from Hatfield Peverel along a tree-lined country road where the cows graze on either side in the meadows, you will feel a sense of peace and tranquillity and find it difficult to realise you have come only three miles from the busy A12 road.

This peace and beauty enhances the rustic architecture to perfection. It is rare today to find a village so carefully maintained, particularly the preservation of the original features of the houses and cottages, many of which date from the 16th century.

This was a time of prosperity and progress when the Church Green boasted a brewery and a malting house, which must have added to the gaiety of the annual fair and helped the trade of the thriving market, both of which took place on the green. Today there are houses only on the south side of the green, some very early examples, with small windows and low roofs.

Tudor House standing on the east end of the green is a wonderful example of 16th century domestic architecture, with exposed timbers, two cross-gables and a large west chimney stack decorated with a blank stepped gable. Here, there is the original plaque required when insurance was introduced.

Terling is fortunate in having four pleasant greens, two on the east of the river and two on the west. On Flacks Green a large attractive house called New House was built in 1726. It is surrounded by a beech hedge and a fine old brick wall. Inside the house is a beautiful Jacobean fireplace, thought to be the only relic of the Old Palace which stood in grounds behind the church.

On the site of the Old Palace now stands Terling Place, a fine late Georgian country house built between 1771–1780. The garden is full of lovely trees and shrubs which have been planted through the years and is carpeted with snowdrops, spring bulbs and dwarf cyclamen.

An old man who died recently in his 97th year, had been a gamekeeper all his life as his father before him. He worked side by side with nature, out in the fields and woods and his knowledge of birds, wild life of all sorts, trees and plants was endless. A window in the church which has recently been restored bears his name, together with a pheasant engraved in the glass, in memory of a true countryman.

From the churchyard there is a splendid view across the valley of the river, up to the cricket field and beyond. There are many sporting activities in the village and the cricket club has a delightful setting for its pitch and a thatched roof to its pavilion. The Cricket Club was founded about 1881 as during that year records show that 'As a cricket match was being held in the village, there would be no scripture lesson that afternoon and school dismissed at two pm'.

One of the interesting features of Terling is its smock mill, now restored and turned into a very attractive residence. Up until 1950 the mill ground the corn from the farms and gleanings from the cottagers but this came to a sad end when by a tragic accident the miller's coat became entangled in the machinery and he was killed. In the mid 1930s the mill was used in a film called *Oh! Mr Porter* starring Will Hay. The camera crews spent a fortnight here on location, the people in the village, especially the children, being most amused by their antics.

🍁 THEYDON BOIS

Theydon, once a mere hamlet in a forest clearing, has always had close associations with the neighbouring forest, once the Forest of Waltham, now known as Epping Forest. The name is probably of Saxon origin – 'Thugn Dun' or Thane's Hill, the domain of a Saxon thane. After the Norman Conquest the manor was divided into three – Theydon Bois, Theydon Garnon and Theydon Mount. All three manors appear in the Domesday Book.

The original parish church of Theydon Bois stood about one mile south of the centre of the village, and next to the original manor, Theydon Hall. The Hall was in earlier times know as Gaunts House because John of Gaunt, son of Edward III and father of Henry IV, lived there. The name is also perpetuated in Gaunts Wood and Gaunt Cottage. The present

Hall is early 18th century. Another historic house within the parish is Parsonage Farm, where it is believed clergy from St Bartholomew's in Smithfield in the City of London, to whom the parish church was gifted in the 13th century, would stay overnight when attending the church. The house is now a Country Hotel.

The old 13th century church was demolished in 1843 and replaced by a new church more central to the village, at a cost of £2,231. This church was consecrated in 1844, but because of poor construction and weakened foundations it was pulled down in 1850 and the present church built (at a cost of £1,574!). The church stands in a delightful setting surrounded by forest land.

One of the oldest buildings in the village is the Bull Inn, which has probably been an inn for about 400 years, although a much more ancient building stood on the site, called the 'Tylehouse'. This building was located close to a gate into the forest, known as Theydon Green Gate. Another of the village's four inns is the Sixteen String Jack, named after a notorious highwayman of the early 18th century, called Jack Rann. His title arose from his appearance in the dock at the Old Bailey with 16 coloured ribbons tied at the knees of his breeches.

In the 19th century the lords of the manor were a family called Hall-Dare. They planted the avenue of 62 oak trees across the green, many of which still stand, despite suffering severe damage in the gales of October 1987. The manorial rights were purchased by Mr Gerald Buxton, of Birch Hall, in 1900.

A building which stands in front of the churchyard of St Mary's parish church was the original village school, built in 1840. This building was enlarged and extended over several years, but ceased to function as a school in 1959 when the present primary school in Orchard Drive was opened. The old building is now occupied by the College of Teachers. Another educational establishment in Theydon Bois is Wansfell College, a residential college which holds a wide variety of adult courses in all fields.

There is little doubt that the present situation of Theydon Bois owes much to the preservation of Epping Forest, dedicated in 1882 by Queen Victoria for 'public recreation and enjoyment'. This extremely attractive village, with about 4,500 inhabitants, plays host to many visitors in the summer, driving out to enjoy picnicking on the expansive green, still officially part of the Forest and the responsibility of the Epping Forest Conservators. Modern development has inevitably crept in, but the local Parish Council and the Rural Preservation Society do their best to ensure that the rural aspect of Theydon Bois, less than 20 miles from the centre of London, is jealously guarded, surrounded as it is by the Green Belt and large areas of farmland.

 THORPE LE SOKEN

Thorpe Le Soken is in the Tendring Hundred. The earliest time Thorpe is mentioned is 1119 when a charter of the Abbey of St John the Baptist at Colchester refers to the tithes of Torp. In 1147 there was certainly a church; the sole relic of this building is now the font base.

Thorpe Hall has been in various hands, but the most famous was the Viscount Byng of Vimy, a former Governor General of Canada.

Thorpe has three religious meeting houses, the parish church of St Michael, the Baptist church (1801) and the Methodist church (1867). There are records of a school in Thorpe since 1648 and on 31st October 1870 the James Rolph Church of England school was opened with some 38 pupils.

Thorpe Le Soken is a growing village with modern problems with the volume of traffic through its main street (where parking is unrestricted) heading for the coast of Walton on the Naze and Frinton on Sea.

Who was Pretty Kitty Canham? Kitty was the only daughter of Robert and Judith Canham of Thorpe. Robert was a prosperous man, living in the Tudor manor house of Beaumont Hall. In 1745 a lonely incumbent by the name of Henry Gough arrived in Thorpe. After a year's courtship, he and Kitty were married. It was a stormy marriage of bitter rows and lasted only three years, before Kitty ran off to London. There she caught the eye of a rich young man named John Primrose. The second wedding of Kitty took place in secret to avoid John's father, Lord Rosebery, serving a writ of lunacy on him!

Kitty died in Verona in 1752. On her deathbed she confessed to John that she was a bigamist and begged him to take her body home to Thorpe for burial. John set out on the journey but when the boat was searched at Brightlingsea, the finding of Kitty's embalmed body aroused the suspicions of the authorities and they arrested him. He was locked up with the coffin in the vestry of St Leonard's church on Hythe Hill and the public flocked to see him and his strange companion. Kitty Canham's funeral was said to have been the most elaborate and costly funeral possible. From Colchester to Thorpe's St Michael's church she travelled in a handsome coffin with six large silver plates, carried by a hearse pulled by stately, black-plumed horses.

🍁 THORRINGTON

Thorrington is a small, but sprawling village situated between Colchester and Clacton.

Spread around the village there are five 16th century houses. The most impressive of these is Thorrington Hall which is a large farmhouse standing just north of the church, built probably shortly after St John's College, Cambridge became lords of the manor. That has obtained to the present day and the estate has been let to a series of tenant farmers who have resided in the hall.

Thorrington watermill (Coopers Mill) is, however, the most well known building. The mill, a four-storeyed timber-framed and boarded building, stands at the head of Alresford Creek on the outskirts of the village. It is the last surviving watermill in Essex, though it is many years since the waterwheel was turned to grind corn and when sailing barges came up the creek to the mill wharf.

The church of St Mary Magdalene stands down a lane away from the main village. The building dates from the 14th century, although there has been a small worshipping community in the parish from at least the 12th century. The most prominent feature is the fine East Anglian type knapped flint and embattled west tower, built c1480. A fine ring of six bells are still heard every Sunday – rung by a splendid and talented band of ringers.

In the mid 18th century the parish of Frating was united with that of Thorrington – and although there was a church in Frating, used until being declared redundant during the later 1970s, this had now been sold as a private dwelling.

Robert Bickersteth Mayor became rector of Frating with Thorrington in 1863, a living he held until his death in 1898. On a site in the middle of the parish, presented by St John's College, he built a school and house. The school played a most important part in the life of the parish up to the middle of the 20th century. He then turned his attention to the two churches; in 1866 he commenced the drastic, but necessary, restoration of Thorrington church, largely at his own expense. He also built a parsonage which became a residence for the curate; later it became the rectory, and has in recent times been replaced by a modern house. In 1870/72 he was solely responsible for the restoration and enlargement of Frating church, making it one of the prettiest little parish churches in the district.

❧ TILBURY

Tilbury is of course best known for its docks, which were built in the 1880s. However, Tilbury was first known as Tulla Burgh and the Romans are known to have been in West Tilbury. Roman pottery was found in the Thames mud and an incineration burial was found at Low Street.

The Normans built a church where the present church stands in West Tilbury, but very little of their time is now left. There were five bell in the church, dating from the 17th century. William Laud built the West Tilbury rectory in 1609–1616, which had a spring said to possess healing powers.

Queen Elizabeth I made her famous speech somewhere in the vicinity of Mill House Camp, probably near Tunpike Cottages. Turnpike Cottages were one of the stagecoach stops on its way to Tilbury Fort, others being the Blue Anchor inn and the King's Head.

Henry IV built the fort earthworks at Tilbury in 1402. Henry VIII, fearing the Papal wrath, built the blockhouse. To summon reinforcements, beacons were lit at Fobbing Hill, Beacon Hill and Langdon Hill. The fort fell into disrepair several times and was open to Dutch attacks till it was repaired by Sir Bernard de Gomme in about 1682. It is the same today, with its moat and chapel.

❧ TILLINGHAM

Tillingham is in the Dengie Hundred and lies on the edge of the Essex marshland. It is the oldest manor held by the Dean and Chapter of St Paul's. In early Saxon times King Ethelbert of Kent gave this manor to St Paul's, who have owned land in the village every since, a fact recorded in the Guinness Book of Records. The many white weatherboarded houses are an attractive feature of the village.

Parts of the parish church of St Nicholas are Norman, the chancel and sanctuary 13th century. In 1708 the church was rebuilt through a rate levy on the population. It was again restored in 1807, and the tower partly rebuilt in 1888 after being struck by lightning. There is also a

Congregational church and a Peculiar People's chapel. The former Baptist and Primitive Methodist chapels have been converted into dwelling houses.

The village school was built in 1868. It came to the end as an all age school in 1958 when children over eleven years of age were transferred to St Peter's school in Burnham.

An important feature is the village green, once an acre in size, now divided by diagonal roads and known as The Square. It has been the venue for many events and seen many changes. Here cricket was played, water fetched from the pump and fights took place frequently. A petition from the villagers resulted in the closure of the Cock Inn; later it became the doctor's surgery, where you could also get a tooth pulled out in an emergency.

Once the green was the site for visiting pedlar's fairs, the celebrations of the Silver Jubilee and the Coronation, Nativity plays and village festivals. It was the meeting place of the local Hunt, and during one very severe winter when it was blowing a gale from the east, the Square was full of geese blown in from the North Sea.

🍁 TOLLESBURY

Tollesbury's church of St Mary is well worth visiting. The chancel was rebuilt in 1872. The small octagonal font bears round the margin of the bowl 'Good people all I pray take care, that in ye Church you do not swear, as this man did'. The parish register explains the unusual warning – August 30th 1718 Elizabeth, daughter of Robert and Eliza Wood baptised in new font bought out of £5 paid by John Norman who some months before came drunk into church, cursed and talked loudly during a service.

Carved on either side of the lectern is a plough and sailing ship, symbol of two kinds of work which engaged most of the male population. This has been the symbol to this day for Tollesbury.

Tollesbury achieved fame as a yachting centre, yachts from Tollesbury sailing round the world. Tollesbury mariners sailed in the Royal yacht *Britannia*, one time skippered by Charles Leavett, and a number contended in the America's Cup races.

There were four oyster packing houses on the saltings. In 1876–7 Tollesbury and Mersea (Blackwater) Oyster Fisher Co (Ltd) was formed.

Herons, tern and shelduck at Tollesbury

Its aim was to give protection to men and oysters. This was in the time when men's only way of providing for their families was through their work, no work meant no money.

Other forms of fishing roundabout Tollesbury included 'Five Fingering' ie catching starfish. These starfish would be used on farms for manure or perhaps go to Colchester for distribution. Winkles and eels were also sought after.

On October 1st 1904 the Crab and Winkle Express ran from Kelvedon low level railway station on its nine miles journey to Tollesbury. The Crab and Winkle faithfully served on this same line to 47 years.

The railway was revived during the Second World War when the War Department took over the derelict Tollesbury Pier Extension as part of the defence system against invasions. The Kelvedon and Tollesbury Light Railway fought a valiant war, ferrying troops to the coastal defence batteries and carrying mobile anti-aircraft guns.

Farming was one of the main occupations for the male population. Women obviously worked during picking seasons such as peas, beans and potatoes.

Tollesbury is a village used by boat lovers, boasting a marina and a Sailing Club. Now workers commute to towns although some light industry has flourished. It has remained a popular village, newcomers always finding friendly faces and a welcome.

🍁 TOLLESHUNT D'ARCY

Tolleshunt D'Arcy is an attractive village situated on the Blackwater estuary. The word Tolleshunt comes from the Angle-Saxon 'Tolleshunta' which means 'Toll's spring'. It is thought Toll was an Anglo-Saxon chief who settled large areas of forest, establishing clearings where water was readily available. Neighbouring parishes are Tolleshunt Major and Tolleshunt Knights.

William the Conqueror gave the manor to Ralph Peverell for services rendered during the Conquest. The latter part of the village name altered as female heirs changed the name to that of their husbands. It became in turn, Tolleshunt Tregoz, Tolleshunt Valoines and Tolleshunt de Boys. John D'Arcy married a daughter of the De Boys family. By this match the estate came to the D'Arcy family in the 1400s. It remained in the family until the death of Thomas D'Arcy in 1593.

During that period D'Arcy Hall was built as the family home. A splendid early 16th century building which still remains. Inside is some fine panelling bearing Anthony D'Arcy's initials and the date 1540. A bridge spanning the moat dates from the Elizabethan period as does the dovecote in the grounds. The russet D'Arcy Spice apple originated from these gardens in 1840.

At the heart of the village stands the Maypole. This is a 'listed building' of indeterminate age, but believed locally to be one of less than a handful of genuine Maypoles remaining in the country. The base is now protected by a wooden cage.

In close proximity to the Maypole is D'Arcy House. A well proportioned Queen Anne style dwelling this has been the home at different periods of two of Tolleshunt D'Arcy's most famous residents.

It was the home of Dr John Salter from 1864 to 1932. Born in 1841, the eldest son of a country gentleman, he had a long and varied career. The Doctor was a prized winning horticulturist, Vice-President of the English Kennel Club, and in his 70s he became Provincial Grand Master of the Freemasons. He will probably be best remembered for his diary which he kept from 1849 until 1932.

Later the house became the home of well known author Margaret Allingham, creator of the fictional detective Albert Campion, and her husband Lt Col Philip Youngman Carter. He was a skilled illustrator who followed up a spell as Features Editor for the *Daily Express* with ten years in the Editor's chair at the *Tatler*.

Tolleshunt D'Arcy still retains its village shop and post office, which are important features of village life – as are the church, the village hall, and the three public houses.

The parish church of St Nicholas is in the Perpendicular style with a west tower, and a nave ceiling which was decorated in 1897 by Ernest Geldart. Villagers have contributed to a stained glass window to celebrate the Millennium. The window represents the village, the nearby river Blackwater, and the surrounding industries of agriculture and horticulture. The village's unique apple variety is also depicted. A local artist, Michael Smee, designed the Millennium window.

TOLLESHUNT KNIGHTS

There are many stories and legends connected with the history of Tolleshunt Knights. Barnhall appears to be the subject of the best known legend, though there are very many variations. The tale has been recorded both in prose and verse.

It is the tale of the celebrated 'Virley Devil' who objected to the start of building in the Devils Wood when he challenged the workman who had been left to guard the site that night. In answer to Satan's cry of 'Who is there?' the workman replied 'God, myself and my three spey bitches' and the Devil went away. This was repeated on the second night. However, when the Devil made his challenge on the third night the man answered 'Myself, my three spey bitches and God'. He had put it the wrong way round, so the Devil reached out his claws and tore the heart out of the man's body. He took a beam from the house and threw it up the hill saying:

'Where this beam shall fall
There shall ye build Barnhall'

The watchman's heart was reputed to have been buried in the wall of the old Bushes church at Tolleshunt Knights and the beam with Satan's claw marks is still visible in the cellar of Barnhall.

Of greater interest to lovers of local history is the effigy of a knight in the old Bushes church. This knight was probably Sir John Atte Lee, he is shown in armour of about 1380. He wears a helmet called a bascinet and in his hands he holds a heart. The lower part of the tomb on which the figure lay came to light in 1953.

The present day life of the village is very varied with a great mixture of residents who have spent most of their lives in the area and are fully versed with all its history, and newcomers who have settled in Tolleshunt Knights and are just as interested in its past.

The well known and very active St John the Baptist Monastery is situated in Rectory Road.

🍁 TOOT HILL

Toot Hill is one of the small hamlets that make up the parish of Stanford Rivers. In common with many small Essex hamlets, it has seen much change in recent years; and yet, despite is proximity to London it still retains much of rurality. The Toot Hill Horticultural Show whose origins go back to the last decade of the 19th century is as popular as ever after its revival some 40 years ago. The nearby village hall, recently refurbished, offers a venue for various functions, and a brand-new village sign stands on the village green. The old Green Man Inn attracts many outside visitors, as does the newly opened golf course.

Toot Hill is said to be one of the highest points in West Essex, and legend has it that in pagan times there was a temple here where ancient Britons gathered to worship the Sun. According to this legend the name Toot Hill derived from the 'Temple on the Hill'.

🍁 TOPPESFIELD & GAINSFORD END

Toppesfield is a quiet, attractive village lying two miles away from a very busy main road, boasting some splendid panoramic views of open country, enhanced by the rising nature of the land that leads to the village. It is blessed with a plentiful supply of trees, some a legacy of bygone days, like the beautiful pink chestnuts lining one side of The Causeway which is the main approach to the village. On the other side of The Causeway there is a row of council built houses, as well as individual ones, with a wide grass verge to the road and where the council, in their wisdom, have planted pink blossomed almond trees.

In 1990, the village history was well researched and documented in a book written by the late Mr Sidney Read. He relates one crime that was committed in 1835 which resulted in a grim ending at Chelmsford Assizes. A certain James Passfield confessed to firing some stacks belonging to Mr Daire of Toppesfield. For this he was condemned to death. A petition for his reprieve was turned down by the then Home Secretary, and it was calculated that there were well over a thousand people present at Chelmsford to witness the public execution.

Nowadays, Toppesfield moves placidly along about its everyday business. Farming has long since ceased to be its main employer and many of its residents travel way out of the village to work, in some cases many miles daily. There is still a good sprinkling of amenities to help the village along. There is also one pub left, the Green Man. Alas, the Village Stores is no more. It is sadly missed. The post office is the only retail business left. It stocks a few dry goods but suffers lack of space.

Unfortunately, there is no 'incumbent' of either church or chapel residing in the village. Although there is still the old rectory, plus a new one, built by the Church just a few years ago, the Rector of St Margaret's resides in Great Yeldham and the church has to take its turn as one of the five parishes incorporated in the living. There is still a thriving school in the village, catering for children from five to eleven years of age. Numbers are kept up by pupils who come in each day from surrounding villages.

Talking of surrounding villages, Gainsford End is just on the outskirts and is incorporated with Toppesfield, sharing the amenities, having none of its own. A dedicated group of people worked extremely hard to provide a community programme to herald the new Millennium and residents responded with spirit. On the actual day there was entertainment for all ages and lasting mementoes will be the erection of especially designed village signs at both Toppesfield and Gainsford End. A photograph of each resident, with a short potted history, has been lodged at the Record Office. Also, a time capsule has been buried in the village.

The number of residents has changed greatly over the years. When the Domesday survey was made, about 70 people were recorded as living in the parish. According to the 1841 census, the number had risen to just over 1,000. Now, the number at the start of the new Millennium is very nearly 500, incorporating both villages.

🍁 TWINSTEAD

Twinstead is an attractive little village which can be found four and a half miles north of Halstead on the Essex–Suffolk border. The main part of the village and hamlet lies just off the A131 Halstead–Sudbury road.

The church of St John the Evangelist is a small red brick building dating back to 1859. On the west wall is fixed a large board describing the 17th century charity which required the owner of Twinstead Hall, 'every year for ever, Cause to be killed upon the premises at Christmas time in every year, one good bull in good plight and case to be killed upon the premises, and give out all thereof Except the hide, with assistance and derection of the Church wardens and overseers of the poor for the time being of Twinstead aforesaid and the poor people of the sverall parishes of Great Henny, Pebmarsh, Lamarsh and Alphamston, in the Said County of Essex.' This Isaac Wyncoll Charity (or Bull Money) is now administered by the Charity Commission. Instead of a bull being killed, a small sum of money is distributed to the needy at Christmas.

There has never been a shop in the village and with little transport, people in the past were very grateful to old 'Niddles Howard' and his donkey cart. He could neither read nor write, but with various notes and shopping lists tucked into his many pockets, he would shop in Halstead, Sudbury or Earls Colne – always returning with the correct goods and change.

The post came by way of Sudbury, the postman either walked or cycled, starting his delivery in Ballingdon, then on to Henny Street and across the fields to Twinstead; he also brought the newspapers with him. He stayed in the village all day, cooking himself a meal in his small hut on the village green and repairing people's shoes, returning to Sudbury with the afternoon post.

The homes are of many, varied styles ranging from small cottages to the large Manor House and Hall. The erstwhile pub, now a private house, not only brewed and sold beer but also supplied the village with pork. In 1830 Roses, a charming old house, was moved on logs pulled by horses, to a better position near the road, where it still stands.

At one time long shallow pits were cut out of the village green. These were then filled with broken chalk brought in from Sudbury and mixed with water, and when dried out, the chalk was cut up and sold for he whitening of houses and other buildings. If cow dung was added preparing this for use it would enable the mixture to stick and also last much longer, without, strangely enough, discolouring it.

The village hall today, found near the Church, used to be the school from 1860–1907. On its closure, the children had to walk to Wickham St Paul's, Pebmarsh or Great Henny, sometimes bowling their hoops to help them on their way and in the summer, stopping to pick the wild fruits in the hedgerows. Unfortunately on wet days, they had to sit in their extremely damp clothes all day.

Wildlife has changed. No longer do we hear partridges; there used to be two or three coveys in every stubble field, with six to ten pairs of hares racing after each other in the Spring. The colonies of rooks in many hundreds would fly in black clouds across the sky; they were nicknamed 'The Doctors'. A well known recipe was breast of rook soaked in milk, also rook pie. It could be said that no house garden was without its trees, apple, greengage, plum, sloe, walnut, cob and hazelnut. Most families kept a pig and it was quite an event in the village when the animal was to be slaughtered by a well known character, Mr Russia Binks, who lived locally.

🍁 UGLEY

Ugley – a name to conjure with! and surely the magic of the place must have cast a spell on the Norseman, Ugga as he made his little clearing or ley in this part of the great East Anglian forest.

Bluebell woods still surround the 'ley' and here and there the huge puddingstones, glacial deposits of some 150–180 million years ago, bob up as markers, some say, for the route of medieval pilgrims.

St Peter's church stands well to the north-east, isolated except for the Hall and a farmhouse. Part of the church is 13th century but an early church at Bollington, now a hamlet, and belonging to King Harold was re-erected when in ruins as a chapel on the south side of St Peter's. The church was enlarged with a west tower in the 16th century and re-built with additions in the 19th century.

Of the ancient charitable trusts, the Buck family of Bollington Hall who were haberdashers and drapers left bequests in 1558 for providing suits or materials for three poor men and women, but Robert Buck in 1620 specified that the gifts were to be 'sheepskins and an ell of roan canvas' and for the women 'fustian for bodices and sack-cloth for petty-coats'. With a legacy from Edward Sandford in 1863 (for coal or clothing) these two trusts now bring in £48 annually, distributed as money.

Sarah Camberlayne, born at Orford House, left in 1858 a sum to be paid yearly to several villages and for land to be bought for almshouses for 5 poor persons in Ugley. But no land became available, so trustees were appointed to enable eight people to receive £7 quarterly.

Halfway from London to Newmarket, on the old Epping road, Orford House at Ugley was said to be a convenient overnight stop for Charles II on his way to the races. Now in the hands of the Home Farm Trust, 'Orford' gives a home, work and a settled future to some 20 young handicapped men and women.

In 1997 village residents assisted the Woodland Trust to plant an extension of seven acres to the established wood planted by the late Linnet Latham. The woods are open at all times to the general public for all to enjoy.

🍁 UPSHIRE

Upshire lies on the outskirts of Epping Forest between Waltham Abbey and Epping. It comprises two hamlets, Upshire or Upstra – which means 'hilly road' – and Copt Hall Green (Copt means 'top of a hill'). Its traceable history goes back to the Iron Age, when the earthworks known as Ambresbury Banks were constructed. Legend has it that Boadicea mustered her army there for her last battle against the Romans at nearby Nazeing. Two 18th century obelisks, standing about a mile apart, are supposed to mark the spots where she took poison and died.

The oldest building is probably Upshire Hall, which is believed to be medieval. It is a listed building and it contains a window pane which is ornamented by the signature of the Prince Regent. Most other houses date from the 18th century onwards.

For over a hundred years, Upshire was home to the Buxton family (of Truman, Hanbury and Buxton, the brewers). They lived first at Warlies Park and then at Woodredon House. Warlies once belong to Samuel Foxe, son of John Foxe of *Foxe's Book of Martyrs* fame. Latterly, it became a Dr Barnardo's Home and is now owned by the Conservators of Epping Forest. They also own Woodredon. The Buxtons were active in many areas of social reform and education.

Sir Winston Churchill was often seen in Upshire when he was a guest of Sir Herbert and Lady Llewellyn Smith, who lived nearby. Perhaps his artists's eye was caught by the 'Blue Row', a row of white weatherboarded cottages with blue front doors.

Present day Upshire is struggling to come to terms with the effect of having the M25 driven straight through it. Despite the constant noise,

Upshire has become a more desirable place to live because of its proximity to two motorways.

Many Upshire people, like their forbears, work on the land. Some are farmers, some work for the Conservators of Epping Forest and others at local riding establishments. The remainder follow a multiplicity of trades and professions. Living in Epping Forest gives them the rights to gather fallen wood and graze cattle in the forest.

🍁 VANGE

Since Saxon times Vange has had many different spellings of its name. The Domesday Book records it as having two manors, that later became united into one. In 1953 a Bronze Age hoard was found in the grounds of Swan Mead School, and a coin of Emperor Gratian, AD 375–378 was found at Merricks Farm.

Clement Dawes is stated to have farmed the land at Vange Hall in 1581. The hall was extended in the 19th century and had a large cellar, dairy and 20 rooms. In 1886 the owner, Mr R. Curtis, discovered two hidden rooms in the roof with boarded floors, nails and hooks for clothes. It is thought they were probably used as hiding places for Catholic priests in Elizabethan times.

In the early 1920s an advert appeared for 'Vange Water – cure all ills'. This natural spring water came from Cash's Farm and was bottled and then sold for medicinal purposes, one wine glassful being the stated dosage. This did not last for long, but for a while people came from near and far to taste this spring water in the hope of a miraculous cure.

All Saints church has parts dating back to the 11th and 12th centuries; the nave is reputed to be late 11th century. Customs of Vange are few and far between, but it is noted that in 1503, the body of John Sawnder was carried to Vange churchyard for burial and before it was driven a sheep. Apparently, this medieval custom was known as the foredrove, an offering at death of an animal or animals to the church, which were driven before the funeral procession, and was peculiar to this part of England.

At the beginning of the 20th century land plots were sold off to Londoners, who commuted down by train at weekends to build small weekend bungalows to live in for their holidays. Plots at Vange 20 feet × 100 feet were advertised and sold for approximately £5 each, a lot cheaper than todays prices!

In the 1970s one of Vange's country houses built in 1420 was sacrificed to provide a gypsy camp in Burnt Mills Vange. The majority of the Old Vange Village has now been swallowed up by the development of Basildon New Town, but memories still linger.

🍁 WEELEY

Weeley is on the railway line from Colchester to Walton. It has its own railway station, which was built when the line first opened in 1866.

The village is known to many people because of Weeley Hall Wood. This is one of the largest ancient woodlands in the county. It belongs to the Essex Wildlife Trust and is normally open only to members of the Trust. There is no public right of way across the farmland to the wood. However, during the first weekend of May each year, the Trust opens it to the public, so that they may enjoy the sight of the carpet of bluebells which covers almost half the area of the wood. Deer, foxes, badgers and many small mammals are known to be present. It is not known how old the wood is, but it is at least possible that part of the present wood could have survived from the virgin forest which once covered much of the Tendring peninsula.

The church stands in open farmland near to Weeley Hall Wood, dedicated to St Andrew. Although the main part of the church building is comparatively recent, having been rebuilt in 1881, the tower is thought to have been built in about 1512. For a building nearly 500 years old, it is in remarkably good condition. Its builders obviously intended it to last and the walls of the tower, at ground level, are five feet thick.

The village is proud to have its own church school. The oldest part of the school dates from 1867, but many additions have been made to the original building. The village also has its own village hall. This was built in 1987 and replaced the old hall which had been in use since 1921. The old hall consisted mainly of two old ex-army huts from the First World War.

🍁 WENDENS AMBO

Wendens Ambo is one of many little villages surrounding the market town of Saffron Walden in the north-west corner of Essex. Despite its small size, with a population of only about 360 people, it has a very long history.

Originally there were two villages, Wenden Magna and Wenden Parva. They were both mentioned in the Domesday Book of 1086, when the population of Great Wenden was given as some 95 people and that of Little Wenden approximately 45 people.

Little Wenden church disappeared before the end of the 17th century. Great Wenden church was extended in the 13th century, when the south aisle was added and the chancel completely rebuilt, no doubt to accommodate the increasing population. A further extension was made early in the 14th century by adding a north aisle, and columns were inserted to support the roof. Further alterations were made in later centuries, but a harmony was kept by using only local materials, polled flints and chalk stone. One interesting feature, however, is the Norman door in the tower which has a rounded-headed arch of Roman bricks that

were taken from the remains of a Roman villa about half a mile to the south-west.

The name, Wenden, came from Saxon times and meant a 'winding valley'. The Saxon settlers must have been attracted to the fertile valley, with a clear stream of water, and protected by the surrounding chalk hills. This was when the two Wenden villages originated.

In 1662 the two parishes of Little and Great Wenden were formally united and became Wendens Ambo, 'Ambo' being Latin for 'both'. The vicarage of Little Wenden was retained, together with the church of Great Wenden. The other church and vicarage have since disappeared.

In the early 18th century the prosperity of the Earls of Suffolk declined, and in 1721 it was decided to demolish the greater part of nearby Audley End House, as the cost of upkeep was so enormous. The back of the central court is all that remains of the house today. The Audley End estate was divided in 1753, and the smaller part that included Wendens Ambo went to the Earl of Bristol. He remained until 1810 when his estates in Wenden and elsewhere were sold to the second Lord Braybrooke who, by this time, had already succeeded to the rest of the estate which had been partitioned in 1753. The Audley

Audley End House near Wendens Ambo

End estates thus controlled the most important part of Wenden, but not all, as the rest of the parish south of the stream was privately owned.

In 1844/45 a railway line was built from Bishop's Stortford to Cambridge, passing through the east side of Wendens Ambo and the Audley End estates. The local station, built on land purchased from Lord Braybrooke, was appropriately named 'Wenden', but only for three years, as on 1st November 1848 it was changed to 'Audley End'.

🍁 WEST BERGHOLT

West Bergholt is reputed to mean 'a wood on a hill' and an investigation carried out by the local Workers' Educational Association in 1985 established certain wooded areas as being 3,000 years old. Various 'finds' over the years of coins and traces of Roman roads indicate that there were Roman settlements in the vicinity.

Records recall that the village has always been an industrial area as there were mills before the Norman Conquest. From the 14th century they were used as 'fulling mills' in connection with the cloth making process, and as this trade declined they were converted into corn and oil mills. Properties stand on those same sites today bearing the original names of Cooks Mill and Newbridge Mill. There was also a working windmill.

Agriculture and farming were the main source of employment until the founding of a family brewing business by Thomas Daniell in 1820. This greatly altered the environment of the village because, as the business grew and prospered, houses were built for the workers, which increased the population and created a general expansion. The brewery remained the hub of village life until its closure in the early 1980s.

St Mary's Old Church, which is now redundant, dates from before the Norman Conquest and a wall painting that was uncovered in 1986 depicts the Royal Coat of Arms of James I and is dated 1605.

A philanthropist by the name of Thomas Love who died in 1565 left a legacy of £120 to buy land, the rent from which was to go to the poor of several parishes. West Bergholt was one such beneficiary and is still in receipt of money today. In 1836 three to eight yards of calico was given to the poor depending on the size of their families. Oral tradition states that Mr Love visited neighbouring parishes disguised as a beggar and those who treated him well were included in the bequest, others were sent a whip.

During the 1850s a body of agricultural workers became known as 'the fire raisers' for starting nine fires as a protest against low wages and the introduction of farm machinery. West Bergholt was called 'the most ignorant village in the county' and it was suggested that the only way to stop the fires and riots was to get the people back to church and to provide schools to educate the young to 'better ways'. The present school was built in 1858 on the heathland by the Church of England.

At the beginning of the 20th century West Bergholt was a truly rural community with a population of little more than 1,000. The school, church and chapel were the focal points. A resident doctor, district nurse and a policeman, a few small shops and public houses supplied all the other needs. This 'closed in' environment continued until after the Second World War, when technical advances meant that people could travel further distances to work. Residents and properties old and new blend together to make up the present population of approximately 3,000. Green areas of open spaces still remain thanks to the earlier philanthropists who left them in trust. There is the modern facility of a medical centre and the village is fortunate to have retained a selection of shops. Three public houses also remain.

WEST & EAST HORNDON

The easiest way to approach West and East Horndon is along the Southend Road from London. After the junction of the M25 the countryside takes on a rural look, with hills rising as high as 100 metres on one's left, covered in trees and here and there arable fields, while on one's right is fenland of London clay.

Originally there were three manors in the area of West Horndon, Tillingham Hall being the one which had most of the land in its borders. In 1066 Alwin, a free woman held it, but by 1086 it had passed to Swain of Essex in the Hundred of Barstable. Following this the Tillingham family held the Hall for several hundred years. It was eventually sold to Sir William Bawd, who conveyed it to Cogglesham Abbey, where it remained until the Dissolution of the Monasteries.

One cannot miss the church of All Saints standing on rising ground above East Horndon at the junction of the London/Southend road and the Brentwood/Tilbury road. The church is built almost entirely of brick, the present one being the third on the site. The village of Torinduna

(Thornhill) referred to in the Domesday survey was around this hill. The Saxon church was built around AD 807, then rebuilt in the Norman style by the Neville family about 1200.

There were two manors in East Horndon, Heron on the north of the church, and Abbots on the south. By the 14th century the Tyrells of Herongate had been gaining influence, and became the patrons of the church. This family demolished most of the Norman church, rebuilding it in the present style. The chancel and south transept are late 15th century. There is a splendid limestone figure of Alice, wife of Sir John Tyrell, flanked by her children, all named.

Two legends persist about the church. One tells of Sir James Tyrell who went to slay a dragon and died. It appears that he had been asked to kill a serpent-type animal, which escaped from a ship in the Thames and roamed the woods round the manor of Herongate and the church, terrifying the people. He managed to slay it, chopping off its head, but he died from his exertions. His son, looking for him, trod on a bone of the animal and, gangrene setting in, he lost his leg. There is a glass window at Heron depicting a one-legged man. The second legend is that Queen Anne Boleyn's head or heart is buried there.

Below, on the south of the church, East Horndon is reduced to the original old road to Herongate, winding up the hill, two restaurants and two houses. Crossing the road bridge to the other side and turning back the way we have come, we find the old road running off towards the Thames, and in its angle is East Horndon Hall, the old manor of Abbots. There is reputed to have been a tunnel from the Hall to the church across the present Southend road.

Thorndon Avenue is a long straight road leading to the heart of the modern village of West Horndon with the station, built in 1886 on the London to Southend line. A definitive history of the village has recently been written by one of the villagers of long standing.

🍁 WEST MERSEA

West Mersea is on the island of Mersea and is sometimes cut off from the mainland by the only road when the tide is high. The origin of the name Mersea was Meres-ig, the Island of Mere and the West is merely to differentiate it from East Mersea.

The heart of the village is centred around the lovely old church of St

Oysters at West Mersea

Peter and St Paul. It is believed that the first church was built on Roman foundations in the late 7th or 8th century. It was rebuilt in the mid 10th century and the base of the present tower probably dates from this building. It is here in the centre that we find most of the shops, etc, but there are also shops dotted about the village, often rubbing shoulders with houses, just as the old cottages do with the new houses. Perhaps it is this hodgepodge which gives the village its charm, for charm it most certainly has.

It is not surprising, since it is so near to Colchester, to learn that there are Roman mosaics to be found but the most famous Roman relic is undoubtedly the Barrow, a Roman burial mound believed to have been erected in the 1st century AD, which is situated beside the East Mersea Road.

In the past farming and fishing (not to mention the famous oyster beds) were the main occupations and there is more than a suspicion that in days gone by some of the inhabitants of Mersea, like those of many of the villages round the estuary, were engaged in smuggling. There is still a small fishing fleet and of course there are still farms. It is a haven for yachtsmen and there is a flourishing Yacht Club. Wind-surfing and water-skiing are popular sports.

The village appears to have had more than its share of hauntings. By Barrow Hill the sound of heavy wheels and horses have been heard for generations and a retired schoolmaster recalls the time when, with a car full of children, the apparition of a Roman chariot and horses appeared across the bonnet. In the Lane, the oldest part of Mersea, ghostly footsteps are heard in the bedroom of the cottage where the rector, hundreds of years ago, murdered his ne'er-do-well son and then hanged himself in remorse. The happy laughter of a Roman lady friend of Claudius with whom she spent weekends, but who was drowned during a midnight swim, is still heard at West Mersea Hall, which is built on the site of a Roman villa!

🍁 WETHERSFIELD

In 1806 a young man arrived in Wethersfield to take up the position of curate. That man was none other than Patrick Bronte who was later to move to Yorkshire and father a son, Branwell and three famous daughters, Emily, Anne and Charlotte. During his three year stay in the village, however, love blossomed. He expereinced a romantic courtship with his first love, a local girl, Mary Burden. But this was not to last and he moved away taking an alternative curacy in Shropshire.

The register of the parish church of St Mary Magdelene records his stay. This building, standing proudly on the hill dates in part from Norman times with its massive 28 foot square tower erected in about the year 1200. The visit of another famous figure is remembered in a small stained glass lozenge in a south side window. It depicts a symbol of Anne Boleyn, famous wife of Henry VIII. The bells of this historic building ring out loud and clear across the village.

The village, situated only nine miles from Braintree, has its own post office, as well as a primary school and smart new fire station, built to replace the wooden shed used until 1983 which remains on the road out of the village towards Finchingfield, the village's famous neighbour.

The USAF air base which was such a feature locally has now closed, and the site is the headquarters of the MOD police.

Of its name, it is believed that Wethersfield stems from Wutha, the name of a Viking-Scandinavian sea raider who, some time in the 8th to 10th centuries, tramped from Mersea, up the valley of the river Pant and made a clearing in an ancient forest thus creating 'Wuths' feld' (Saxon clearing or field).

🍁 WICKEN BONHUNT

Wicken Bonhunt comprises two small Domesday hamlets – Wica and Banhunta. The latter, at a bend of the B1038 about a mile from the main village towards Newport, where the M11 crosses the road, now consists of two houses and a farm (converted to a private house) together with a tiny Saxon or very early Norman chapel, which was for many years used as a barn. This was the church of St Helen, once attached to the manor of Bonhunt, and is by far the oldest building in the district.

Wicken, the main part of the village, sprawls along the road, which here follows the stream known as Wicken Water. Now dry for most of the year, with its bed becoming overgrown with grass and weeds, 30 years ago it ran with a foot or two of water all year round.

While a church has stood on this site since the 11th century all that remains of this structure is the massive Norman font. Most of the church you see today dates effectively from Victorian times, when the ruinous state of the building necessitated such extensive repairs that it amounted to a virtual rebuilding. Fortunately the village had at that time a wealthy vicar who footed most of the bill, and at the same time built himself the massive vicarage, in the Victorian Gothic taste.

It was probably at the time of this renovation that the ancient custom of the curfew was reintroduced – the nightly ringing of the 8.00 bell to remind villagers that bedtime was drawing near. This continued, with a break during the Second World War, down to the mid 1960s, and was only abandoned then because no one could be found to replace the retiring verger, George Goodwin MM, whose job it had been for many years. George was one of those chosen to receive the Royal Maundy money when the Queen distributed this annual charity at Chelmsford Cathedral.

Behind the church is Wicken Hall, the main manor of the village to which the largest farm was at one time attached. The most interesting house in the village is Brick House built in about 1602 for the Bradbury family. Though in those days a brick house was a bit of a novelty – the usual in these parts being lath and plaster on a timber frame – the bricks used were second-hand. It has recently been found that most of the bricks had been 'turned' with their weathered faces inward to preserve the outward appearance of the house. The ancient tithe barn attached has also been converted into a private house of unusual design.

🍁 Wickham Bishops

Wickham Bishops village is situated about four miles equidistant from Maldon and Witham. Its population is about 2,000. Amenities include a well-preserved early 19th century church, which has recently added a new function hall, a village hall with playing field, two public houses, a garage, a village store containing a sub-post office, the East Essex Scout Headquarters, a library, and a twice weekly doctor's surgery. Primary school children attend the Great Totham primary school, which is just outside the Wickham Bishops boundary.

There can be hardly a field in Wickham Bishops without its own special name. It is not easy to learn much about these names. Some, like Matthew's Etch, Turner's and Collins are derived from the name of some owner or copyholder. Some are descriptive, such as Humpy Meadow, Thorney-hedgepiece, and Heathpiece.

Those who use Handley's Lane will take pleasure in the thought that their ancestors also experienced its peculiar delights for Mr. Grimes' Orchard bore the apt title of Plain Slough.

But who was Loblolly, and who named the Rainbow Field?

🍁 Wickham St Paul

The small attractive rural village of Wickham St Paul is situated on the north Essex/Suffolk border, between the two nearby market towns of Halstead (Essex) and Sudbury (Suffolk). It is often misspelled as Wickham St Paul's, and has been described as a 'blink and you'll miss it' kind of place due to its size – in fact it has been known for visitors to bypass it completely!

The village name was derived from its connection with the Dean and

Chapter of St Paul's, dating back to the 11th century. The main and obvious attraction, and pride, is the large village green. This is well cared for and well loved by residents and visitors alike, though the sheep, horses and cows which once grazed it are long gone.

Until a few years ago the village schoolchildren would also have been seen on the green. The children from Wickham and the adjoining village of Twinstead were taught at the village school, which through small in size had great character. Unfortunately character and charm were not enough and now the school is a private house.

Situated just outside the main part of the village is the small but attractive church of All Saints. The earliest part was built in the 12th century, with additions in the 14th and 16th centuries, and it was restored in the 19th century.

There used to be a shop, which was a boon to villagers. Unfortunately, probably due to the size of the village, it had to close. The shop is much missed, especially during winter months, as it was a general store selling everything from eggs to bootlaces. Anything you needed that was not stocked was 'got in specially'. The shop was also renowned for being the place to go for any gossip – a true village pastime!

Wickham St Paul is a farming community, though only a few are now proper, working farms. There are still many small cottages and even the modern houses do not look out of place. The broad country accent still remains, as does the image of distinctive country characters. Community spirit is one of the main aspects of village life, and it is certainly alive in Wickham St Paul.

🍁 WIDDINGTON

The village of Widdington has been described as 'the biggest cul de sac in Essex'. Situated between Saffron Walden and Stansted, the road into Widdington really only serves the village. The river Cam flows between Widdington and the main road, the B1383.

It was thought the Romans passed it by, but during a survey on Priors Hall by English Heritage some Roman tiles were found. This find does not prove Priors Hall to be a Roman site as the tiles may have been brought from another area, but English Heritage did establish Priors Hall as Saxon, not Norman as previously thought. Priors Hall is a private house. Priors Hall Barn is definitely Norman, and can be viewed by the public, as the barn is managed by English Heritage.

Mole Hall is very old and still has a moat around it. The grounds are a Wild Life Park, where hundreds of visitors come each summer. Many are children from London who delight in the animals and butterflies.

The village is surrounded by many footpaths with lovely names: Moon Lane, Jock Lane, Green Croft Lane, Samsons Lane, Beetle Lane, America Brook. The large open fields also have fascinating names: Jingling Baulk, Little Hartley, Big Hartley, Small Pieces, March Field, Four Acres. Two fields are called the Americas as they are supposed to look like America in shape. Many of these field names are mentioned in the court rolls and rentals of Queen Elizabeth I.

Within living memory there were some ten working farms, each farm employing an average of ten workers. Today many of the old farm houses are private homes. The workers today commute to London or to the towns nearby.

The church of St Mary was reopened in 1873 after much restoration. It is on the original site of the first church built in the 12th century. Although there is only a small congregation it is a much loved church and well cared for, with many items of interest for church historians.

🍁 WIDFORD

Widford was originally called Wedeford. The Clovil family cleared the forests and built a house at Highlands, the village growing up in this area. One hundred years ago the village had a life of its own. Under the patronage of Arthur Pryor, who lived at 'Hylands' from 1858 to 1904, it received a new church building at St Mary's in 1862, its own school building in 1867 and even a railway station in 1882, although this took the form of a siding for railway coaches reserved especially for visitors and guests at Hylands.

Today Widford is incorporated in the Borough of Chelmsford and has lost some of its character and old buildings, such as the post office and shop, and the only Silent Woman in Essex. The latter was a public house on the old main road opposite the White Horse. The original pub sign showing a picture of a woman with her head cut off is now in the Chelmsford and Essex Museum in Oaklands Park.

The Sir Evelyn Wood, another unique pub sign, paid tribute to the Essex celebrity of that name who was born in the vicarage in Cressing in 1838 and became a great military hero in Victorian times. Large crowds gathered at the Shire Hall, Chelmsford, when he was presented with a Sword of Honour on the 14th October 1879, and again in 1903 when he received the Freedom of the Borough in recognition of his promotion to Field Marshal. He died at Harlow in 1919 at the age of 71 years.

The new Princes Road (until recently the A12) was opened by the Duke of Kent in 1930 near the Chelmsford Wood Street roundabout; this was later joined by another road constructed to bypass the village. This in effect destroyed the rural atmosphere of the village; many of the cottages were pulled down to make way for modern houses.

🍁 WILLINGALE

Within ten miles due west of the county town of Chelmsford can be found the villages of Willingale Spain and Willingale Doe. Set in the heart of fine Essex farmland, the 500 or so members of Willingale's population enjoy more than their fair share of the tranquility of rural life.

The rare historical feature to be discovered in Willingale is the sight of two well preserved churches standing side by side in the same churchyard. Legend has it that two sisters, quarrelling about their own individual rights, settled the dispute, simply, by building a church each. Since the churches were built 200 years apart, this can hardly be true but, like all good village legends, there are many who prefer it to the truth.

The village names are taken from the post-Norman Conquest landowners, Hervey d'Espana and William D'Ou. The older church of St Andrew has a spire and dates back to the 12th century. It is now only used on Palm Sunday when the palms are blessed before a procession is made to the newer church of St Christopher. Its tower stands majestically as the focal point of the village and can be seen from all the approaches to Willingale. From the rear of the churchyard, one can savour splendidly picturesque views of the Roding valley and beyond.

Willingale has not, however, always been a picture of peace and tranquillity. A Class A airfield was built here between 1942 and 1943 by the 831st Engineer Battalion (Aviation) of the US Army. It became the home of the 387th Bomb Group of the US Eighth Air Force's 4th (subsequently 3rd) Bomb Wing. Operations began on 15th August, 1943 with B-26 Marauders. On one of the early missions, 55 B-26s took off virtually blind in early morning mist. One aircraft crashed at the end of the runway killing all but the tail gunner. The 387th remained at Willingale until July, 1944. Evidence of this brief but significant moment in Willingale's history can still be found in remnants of the perimeter track and a number of buildings.

Things may not be quite what they were in the days of thriving shops and a busy blacksmith. But you can still hear the gentle sound of leather on willow as 22 men in white compete on the village cricket green on a summer afternooon and then you feel that, perhaps, things have not changed so much after all.

✦ WIVENHOE

Until recently Wivenhoe always lived by the river; fishing, boat building and smuggling, though not necessarily in that order! Boat building, and its attendant trades of carpentry, sail and rope making, were thriving industries. One famous shipbuilder, Philip Sainty, combined his talent with an equal talent for smuggling. He used his knowledge of fast yachts for the well-to-do to build fast get-away boats for smugglers.

The Ropery was situated at The Cross and prospered until the First World War. The 'rope walk' is remembered by some older residents as a deep ditch running from the works down The Avenue as far as Harvey Road. The large yachts, which were crewed and skippered by Wivenhoe men, were laid up in the river for the winter then recommissioned, painted and provisioned in the spring. They, or their owners, did not survive the war, so with diminished trade, the Ropery closed.

Fishing for sprats, shrimps and oysters provided a living for residents and also for the crews of the large yachts. These were paid off when their ships were laid up for the winter, and they had to sustain themselves and their families until spring when, hopefully, they were re-employed. There was a fish canning business on The Quay until recently but now closed with the decline in fishing.

The Cook's Shipyard closed in the 1980s, and 300 dwellings are now being built on the site of Wivenhoe Port, which has accelerated the trend for Wivenhoe to become a dormitory town for London and Colchester.

The church of St Mary the Virgin dates back to the 12th century, but has been much repaired and modified over the years. A notable building in East Street is the Garrison House, which is the finest example of pargetting in Europe. It derives its name from the Roundhead troops stationed there during the siege of Colchester during the Civil War in 1648.

Wivenhoe Park which features in the Constable painting of that name, is still extant, though somewhat overwhelmed by the modern buildings of Essex University close by.

WIX

Wix is a small village on the old road from Colchester to Harwich. It now has about 200 houses and 680 residents. The houses range in age from those of the 16th or 17th centuries to those built within the last few years.

The centre of Wix is fairly compact. It has two public houses, the Waggon at Wix at the crossroads and the White Hart by the War Memorial. There are also two shops, one of which houses the post office, two garages, a school, a Methodist chapel and the parish church of St Mary. The present school was opened in 1931, taking over the education of the children that was previously provided by Church schools. In 1975 the village school at neighbouring Wrabness closed and the children from there are now bussed to Wix.

The main business in the village is Anglian Timber. This wood-yard was started in 1837 by Edward Paskell and the ownership passed from father to son until it came under the control of Roger Paskell who was a well-known authority on timber and who travelled far and wide to find suitable trees. He was also known to be a helpful source of specialist needs such as the special shovels required for the maltings at Mistley. One noted employee of the firm was a venerable character called William Wilberforce Wake – a highly skilled wheelwright who could saw up a complete trunk of a tree by hand over a sawpit.

Across the road from the wood-yard was the village forge which supplied the iron bands for the wheels and other iron fitments to complete the carts. Another off-shoot from the wood-yard was an undertaking business as, of course, there was a ready source of wood for the coffins. On the death of Roger in 1980 the wood-yard was sold to Anglian Timber and the nature of the business has changed. The firm now mostly deals in soft wood for the construction industry. The undertaking business has moved to Manningtree, but still trades under the name of Paskell and Son.

The history of Wix goes back a long way as it was mentioned in the Domesday Book. At that time the land was owned by Edith, queen of Edward the Confessor, and she gave it to Walter the Deacon whose children in turn gave it for the foundation of Priory for Benedictine Nuns. It was suppressed in the time of Henry VIII when he ordered the Dissolution of the Monasteries. From then on the church was allowed to deteriorate. It is probable that materials from the Abbey were used to build the Abbey Farmhouse. The church itself was renovated about 1740 and again in 1888. Of the two bells, one hangs in a little turret on the church itself, and this is used to call the faithful to services, while the other, known as the Danyell Bell, is thought to have been made about 1460 by the bell-founder John Danyell and is contained in a bell-cage in the churchyard. Up to about 30 years ago this bell was always tolled for funerals, but now it remains silent.

🍁 WOODHAM FERRERS

Woodham Ferrers, situated some nine miles south-east of Chelmsford, is a linear village along a highway, running from north to south.

The southern end is the bottom of Town Hill, where the village sign is located. This is the junction of Workhouse Lane (or Moss's Lane or Ilgars Lane, so called as it leads to one of the ancient manors of the parish called Ilgars) on the left and Edwins Hall Lane on the right. At the moment the area is known as Happy Valley, which is a bit incongruous as the cottages on the left stand on the site of the old workhouse. Behind is Mill Hill, another misnomer as a mill has never stood upon it, nor is it the burial ground of plague victims as some people think. It would indeed take an incredible amount of bodies to make a hill that big!

Edwins Hall Lane leads, naturally, to Edwins Hall. Originally it was Edwards Manor but was renamed after Edwin Sandys, Archbishop of York 1576–1588, who lived there for a time with his wife Cicelie whose fine memorial is in St Mary's church in the village. Edwins Hall is a fine moated Tudor House, said to be haunted, and today only about a third of the original dwelling is standing.

St Mary's church is built on an old Saxon site in the most elevated position in the village. It was built by Robert de Ferrers in the reign of Henry II, using local materials, mainly pebble, ragstone, flint and fragments of brick. In 1703 the tower collapsed and was rebuilt on a smaller scale in 1715, but again by 1774 this was unsafe and so in 1793 a small wooden belfry was built to house the one remaining bell.

At the entrance to the churchyard is the war memorial. This used to be situated near the Bell car park on the opposite side of the road but was moved between the wars to its present site. It has the distinction of listing all those villagers who served in the First World War and not just those who died.

If you walk up the hill you pass some old 16th century cottages and on the right is the Bell pub, the only one in the village nowadays. Next door to that is the old post office which closed only a few years ago. Nearby is Forge House, obviously the site of the village smithy, and next to that is the old rectory. This is reputedly haunted by an old lady both in the house and walking towards the church.

The road divides just here, with the older original road to the right, called The Street. Here used to be sited the Eagle pub (where Eagle House now stands) and opposite was the wheelwright's shop. Woodham Ferrers used to be a small town with a market, and there were probably many shops in this area around The Street.

On the corner of Crows Lane used to stand Wantz Farm, an older clapperboard farmhouse which was demolished in 1965. This whole area is called Woodham Wantz – 'wantz' is an old word meaning crossroads.

The last building of note in the village is Woodham Hall, a farmhouse. This is one of the old manors of Woodham Ferrers and the present house, dated about 1800, replaced a much earlier timber moated dwelling to the east of the present farmhouse. The moat still remains and the foundations of a bridge over the water have also been found.

🍁 WORMINGFORD

The village was part of the land owned by Earl Godwin (King Harold's father) and after the conquest it was divided into four manors, Garnons (mentioned in Domesday), Woodhall, Church Hall and Wormingford Hall. These, together with the Grove, the Grange and Rotchfords, still lie within the parish. The manor houses, built mostly in Tudor and Stuart times, have great character and are still inhabited. Some families have lived there for many generations, particularly the Tufnells and the Boggis-Rolfes who are an embodiment of the tradition of patronage of church and school.

The main feature of the village is St Andrew's church which dates from the 12th century. It commands a magnificent view of the Stour valley and this part of the parish is in the Dedham Vale Conservation Area. There are tombs of some of the Constable family in the churchyard and there is also the grave of John Nash, the painter who lived in the village over 50 years until his death in 1977.

Although dedicated to St Andrew the church has a stained glass window depicting St George slaying the dragon. It is a modern window given in gratitude for those returning from the Second World War but it also commemorates the Wormingford dragon. It may be significant that the name of the village changed to Wormingford in the Middle Ages and Worm was the name for a dragon!

There is another glass window of historical interest in Church Hall, a 16th century Tudor rose roundall which commemorates the visit to the house of Queen Elizabeth I in 1561.

During the Second World War Wormingford was host to the USAF. American veterans still return to the village to remember those who died and as well as a commemorative plaque in the Crown public house, a War Memorial stands on the Fordham road, next to the airfield. The airfield is now home to the Essex-Suffolk Gliding Club.

Wormingford has a population of about 450. Many old dwellings remain, mainly near the church, but there have been new houses built in the village centre and on the main road. Of the several farms, only one is dairy, but there is one poultry and one pig farm. The village still has a shop with post office, a public house and a regular bus service to both Sudbury and Colchester.

The Crown is one of the ancient inns of Essex as its name appears as a landmark on deeds in 1691. In 1982 whilst extensive repairs were being carried out two mummified cats were found, one each side of the chimney. It was customary among cottage and inn builders in the Middle Ages to mummify a cat by burial alive in the walls to provide psychic protection. The cats date the inn to about 1600 when Elizabeth Newman, the Witch of Wormingford, was accused and tried for practising witchcraft.

🍁 WRABNESS

Wrabness is a small village on high ground on the south bank of the river Stour. Its extent is about 1,100 acres.

All Saints' church overlooks the river and has several traces of its Norman origin, with two remarkable features in the porch. One is the arch over the inner doorway, which supports above it traces of another arch of Norman origin, the second is the 13th century stone coffin top, with a consecration cross, that has been inserted in the west wall.

The tower fell many years ago and a wooden belfry containing a single bell is now in the south-west corner of the churchyard. It was probably built in the 17th or 18th century and is now a listed building, recently restored using as much of the original oak as possible. The bell is rung every Sunday calling people to church.

On the north side of the churchyard there was once a schoolroom. There are no records of any burials on a piece of ground measuring 25 by 30 feet, where, it is said, the schoolroom stood, until it was pulled down and the rubble used to build the new school in 1872. Today the school has been converted into a house and both old and new rectories sold to private residents.

On an 18th century map there is a spot off the Ness named Cunningford Loading. Within living memory posts were still visible in the river where barges could be moored. Cargoes of baled hay and straw would be sent to London.

🍁 WRITTLE

Writtle is an ancient village with many interesting old buildings – and strangely it was from here that a part of the modern age began when the first wireless telephone broadcasts were made by Marconi.

One local resident is descended from the King family, who carried on a coal merchant's business in the village last century. She remembers: 'My grandfather and his family first lived at the Gas House, on St John's Green, which at that time had a tar pit, and a Chelmsford doctor would send his patients to walk around it as a cold cure.

'The family later moved to Maltese House in Bridge Street. The horses were shod at either Pamplin's or Wallace's, blacksmiths in the village. Maltese House was originally part of the maltings. The family made the first floor into living quarters and the open spaces on ground level which had served as drying areas for the hops, were used as stables and coal storage.

'From the windows of Maltese House could be seen the famous hut belonging to Marconi, where broadcasting first started in February 1922. One of the engineers working there married a local publican's daughter.

Another had taken a fancy to a maid in one of the big houses, and the story goes that he would climb into the roof of the hut with flags and send her a semaphore message. At a pre-arranged time, no doubt, she would be conveniently dusting her lady's bedroom and would answer with the wave of her duster from the open window.'

🍁 INDEX